C000046074

SCOTTISH RELIGIOUS POETRY

from the sixth century to the present

AN ANTHOLOGY

edited by
Meg Bateman, Robert Crawford and James McGonigal

First published in 2000 by
Saint Andrew Press
121 George Street, Edinburgh EH2 4YN

Copyright © Meg Bateman, Robert Crawford and James McGonigal 2000

ISBN 0 7152 0775 X

All rights reserved. No part of this publication may be reproduced or transmitted in any form or by any means, electronic or mechanical, including photocopy, recording, or information storage and retrieval system, without permission in writing from the publisher. This book is sold, subject to the condition that it shall not by way of trade or otherwise, be lent, re-sold, hired out or otherwise circulated without the publisher's prior consent.

British Library Cataloguing in Publication Data
A Catalogue record for this book is available from the British Library.

ISBN 07152 0775 X

Printed and bound by Bell and Bain Limited, Glasgow

Contents

Introduction

The Scottish Museum of Religion is to be found in a square between the Cathedral of St Mungo and the Glasgow Royal Infirmary, overlooked on one side by a motorway flyover and on the other by an imposing Necropolis with its ornate tombs. It is a modern building, although modelled on the Bishop's Palace which occupied the site until the Reformation, and it is in some ways an unsettling place. It raises questions about whether religions should ever be exhibited in glass cases, whether they can ever be defined simply by their artefacts, whether they can be rebuilt.

Yet the museum also manages somehow to create a vibrant sense of Scottish religion at the start of the third millennium. Christian symbols from various denominations sit side by side not merely with each other but with Tibetan Buddhist paintings from a monastery in Eskdalemuir and Sikh, Islamic, Jewish and Hindu sacred objects, many of them presented to the museum by local communities of believers. All of this is to be seen in the midst of the life of a busy city, with its motorway traffic and hospital, its universities and schools and shops.

One of the most intriguing exhibits is just outside the building, in a walled triangle where a Japanese garden has been created from pebbles, boulders and heather. Designed to evoke the mindfulness of Buddhist meditation, it is entitled 'Where we are now', and seems to show an estuary or bay with a thin grey boat (of rock) making its way across the raked white waves of pebbles. The builders of this garden may have come from the East, but its boulders came from the West, selected and brought out of Ireland. It may remind us that Scottish Christianity too came from there, in the persons of those other great spiritual builders, Columba and his brother monks in their boat. 'Where we are now' in the religious life of Scotland is closely interlinked with 'where we were then'. The garden can often create in those who contemplate it a quiet confidence, as stones, light and stillness combine with the little boat's steady beating across a quartz-white bay to reach its oriental Inner Hebrides in this corner of Glasgow.

Where *are* we now, in religious terms? This anthology presents a variety of answers to that question but raises as many more, as it reflects upon where we have been, and the journey from there to here. Such questions, perhaps, are simply signalling that we are dealing with mystery, and the halting attempts of humankind to comprehend it.

In the case of Scottish religious poetry, however, we are dealing with three mysteries, or rather, mystery to the power three. Each of those terms, 'Scottish', 'religious' and 'poetry', offers its own problematic associations; but in combination their complexity is truly daunting. That may be one reason why no representative anthology of Scottish religious poetry through the centuries and across all of our linguistic and cultural traditions has ever been published before. In itself that is an intriguing fact, for Scotland is a country where religion still matters enough to be argued over in the media, or occasionally fought over in the streets. Is this, then, an anthology of poetry that is looking for trouble?

The categories are indeed troublesome. 'Scottish' (setting aside its Irish provenance) signals Scotland, obviously, but this nation within a state has seemed to some commentators to be a triumph of sheer imagination over political fact – and yet it is believed in overwhelmingly by Scots as a source of identity and pride. Is it Scotland, however, or more particular Scotlands that we really believe in, when differing experiences of Lowland, Highland, rural, urban, industrial, post-industrial or even virtual Scottish realities increasingly mesh and clash at this start of the millennium? Too easy polarities are unhelpful in articulating or celebrating the differences between Edinburgh and Glasgow, Lewis and Barra, Kirkwall and Kilmarnock. Even our language diversity provides no easy mapping of Highland Gaelic to Lowland Scots to the more or less Scottish English of governance, trade and education, since most Scots are 'bilingual' to a greater or lesser extent in any two of these, shifting their codes in context with remarkable subtlety. Poets do this too, and it is one reason why this anthology speaks in most of the historical languages of Scotland: Gaelic, Latin, Old English, Old Norse, Scots and English. Thinking historically, we ought to acknowledge that the earliest poems in this volume are linked to a territory we now call 'Scotland' but were composed before this country was.

Our religious history has further entangled that already complex reality. Continuities with Catholic European culture were broken at the Reformation of 1560, although some parts of the Western Highlands and Islands were reconverted by seventeenth-century Franciscan and Dominican friars. Preparing this anthology, it has come to seem increasingly important for us to recognise the Gaelic experience in all its subtlety and harshness as a symbol of the whole truth of the construction of Scotland's national identity, and of what was destroyed in order to build or shore that up. Gaelic verse and translations from it figure strongly, partly for such reasons of continuity and redress. The twentieth-century repair of Iona Abbey under the direction of the Reverend George MacLeod and the refounding of a community there to welcome pilgrims to the island were important actions of similar redress. More recently, anthologies such as *Iona: The Earliest Poetry of a Celtic Monastery* (1995), edited by Thomas Owen Clancy and Gilbert Márkus, and Clancy's *The Triumph Tree: Scotland's Earliest Poetry AD 550–1350* (1998) have extended that process of refamiliarisation.

An earlier and troubled re-engagement with immigrant Irish people and their spirituality had taken place in the darkest conditions of the nineteenth-century industrial revolution. Here Scottish entrepreneurial inventiveness was creating not only exciting technological advance but also profound social disarray among the families of factory and foundry workers and miners of the ironstone and coal which fuelled that revolution. Native Calvinism too seemed, in obscure ways, to fuel that drive, or at any rate to have designed a particularly powerful engine for it: Rudyard Kipling's famous portrayal of the Scottish engineer McAndrew catches the terrible fascination we feel for a man who is so confidently at one with remorselessness:

> From coupler-flange to spindle-guide I see Thy Hand, O God –
> Predestination in the stride o' yon connectin'-rod.
> John Calvin might ha' forged the same – enorrmous, certain, slow –
> Ay, wrought it in the furnace-flame – *my* 'Institutio'.[1]

'Scottish' and 'religious', then, are loaded terms which seem historically to have multiplied diversity and tension in our social life. Perhaps it is only the third element, 'poetry', which at its best can find the necessary words to explore fully, subtly, with irony or celebration or conviction, the mysterious and unpredictable relationship of God and human beings. That relationship may be perplexing to us because the meaning of God is essentially beyond our language. In the twentieth century, silence has seemed to Wittgenstein and others to be the best response; for even Christ can become a sort of rough dialect in which we argue endlessly about that meaning.

Poems at least have the merit of usually refusing to offer simple answers. We have seen in recent European history as well as in Scotland's past how fatal reductive definitions can be, both to the 'enemy' or Other, so defined, and to ourselves. This anthology of Scottish religious poetry is an attempt at interlacing these three mysteries. The collection should not be read as a knot to be unravelled or

---

[1] The reference is to Calvin's *Christianae Religionis Institutio* (1536). 'McAndrew's Hymn' is included in Edwin Morgan's *Albatross Book of Longer Poems* (1963) with full annotation.

cut clean through, but rather as if modelled on the illumination of Celtic art, where intricacy is part of the picture, and patience a virtue in the writing and in the understanding of it.

Poems seem designed to handle and maintain complexity (of rhythm, sound, words and meanings) within their overall resolution of pattern and a harmony of elements. But which Scottish poems were we to choose, and is 'religious poetry' in any case a lesser subdivision of the broader field of secular poetry? Some have thought so – even poets. Doctor Johnson considered devotional religious poetry as an impertinence, inserting its artifice between the direct honesty of prayer and its recipient, God. T. S. Eliot thought that in writing religious verse and in exploring their own religious lives, poets such as George Herbert and Gerard Manley Hopkins consigned or confined themselves to minority status (unless, like Dante, the religious view of life itself could have become their epic subject). Donald Davie, in his introduction to the *Oxford Book of Christian Verse*, makes a spirited claim for all the poetry of certain ages to be read as Christian poetry, refusing to bracket religion off from all our moral and physical life in this created world. He does, however, restrict himself to poems which evoke, or work from, Christian doctrine. And he includes many hymns in his selection, as part of the great Nonconformist history of English poetry.

We do not include many hymns here, nor even Psalms. Our chief editorial concern was to select poems for their power rather than their piety, and most hymn lyrics alone lack the music and congregation which together give them life and communal meaning. But to ignore them totally would have been wrong, for the Psalms have rung through Scottish religious life for centuries, sung in the monasteries in Latin, sung in translation in kirks and on hillsides in the post-Reformation and Covenanting years; and the evangelical energies and tensions of the nineteenth century are well nigh impossible to comprehend without the hymns which expressed their aspirations. This linking of religious texts or ideas in continuity through far-reaching social and political change seems vital in any proper evaluation of religious poetry; individual poems can then serve as local maps which let us read the different landscapes and check what really mattered when, where and to whom. In such poems and lyrics, we may find our contemporary values rocked back by the simplicity or beauty or ferocity of their expressions of faith.

However, as the critic and anthologist Helen Gardner reminds us, religion is 'more than attitudes, aspirations, emotions, speculations and intentions'.[2] While including these things, it expresses all of them within a framework of ritual and

---

[2] 'Religious Poetry: a Definition', in her *Religion and Literature* (1971), pp.134ff.

obligation. Unlike much other poetry, religious poetry does not present itself as newly invented but rather as working within something already given or handed on. There is an implied commitment in religious poems to values which are not simply the poet's own, but to a revelation of the power and mystery of the divine, to which the poem is a response and seems, in turn, to invite the reader's response.

Two things follow which apply to this anthology. The human response to revelation does not confine religious poetry to Christian poetry. And, since the response can be 'no' as well as 'yes', religious poems here include some in which rejection of the Christian revelation, or doubt about its truth, or satire on the different systems of revelation, can validly take their place.

Any anthology of Scottish religious poetry must aim for a balance between rival and (in many ways) irreconcilable theologies, attempting to appreciate the context in which each poem is spoken. We have tried to do this through an editorial team comprising one Catholic of Irish-Scots parentage, one Presbyterian, and one about whose beliefs the others (in typically guarded Scottish fashion) have not enquired too deeply. All three are poets, as well as academics; all share a long-standing interest in religious poetry and a commitment to the enlargement of Scotland's contemporary culture. We have grown up in a time when most of the younger generation have become notably more relaxed about religion than their parents, but in which, nevertheless, religion in the Scottish context still makes news: whether as political debate about the future of denominational schools, or in reporting of any sufficiently violent manifestations of a poisonous conjunction of football rivalry and religious bigotry.

Compiling this anthology has itself been a salutary ecumenical exercise, as the editors offered each other poems for inclusion which seemed, to each individual, to express 'the truth' – but as often found another truth already in its place. Yet we listened to each other's choices patiently, trying to hear those other intonations and intimations.

Our shared aim was to focus upon the spiritual impact of the poems selected. Yet we also sensed a historical duty to inform about the role and place of religion in national as well as personal life. To that extent, we decided to include as many poets as possible across the centuries, even if this meant representing most of them only by one or two poems. In the context of Scottish history, religious poetry includes remembering a diaspora of exiles who carried their faith and their Bibles with them to North America or the Antipodes and, like any migrants, used their religion to strengthen a lost sense of identity, finding comfort in the Biblical archetypes of exile and a new Jerusalem, but being changed in the process, as Iain Crichton Smith's poem 'When They Reached the New Land' movingly suggests.

The history must also include a whole set of transitions: from Celtic to Roman Christianity; from medieval Church to Renaissance reformations; from a covenanted faith to Enlightenment rationalism; from utilitarian religion in the service of the imperial enterprise to late twentieth-century recovery of religious mystery, as well as doubt. This story has never been fully documented.

One wonders why it has not been told before. Possibly there has been some suppressed unease since the Reformation about the erasure of a wholly different way of talking to or about God. The destruction here of almost all traces of Catholic theology, and of the many monasteries whose broken forms still ghost our landscape, may actually have made it impossible to talk about the values which had caused such swiftly sacrificial action to be undertaken.

Differences between the Catholic and Protestant faiths were and are profound. It is well-nigh impossible to enter into the experience of another's faith. We might usefully study its import or respect its integrity, yet all the while be recognising our distance from whole-hearted assent. To consider such a complex matter with any accuracy, a multi-dimensional matrix seems called for, in which the varied Scottish religious experience might be seen to range, along one axis, from the immanent to the transcendent; along another, from faith as community experience to faith as individual or private experience; and along yet another, from a literal reading of Scripture to a metaphorical or analogical or even an aesthetic one. Individuals or faith communities might plot their own positions at different points on those criss-crossing roads.

Yet such fundamental differences are almost brought together by a need to respond to a 'post-Christian' or relativistic world. Such a shared need has more recently brought about an ecumenical discovery of what these different Christian visions actually might share. The role of women and women's spirituality has been important here, in the recovery of a perspective closely involved with the beauty and energies of creation. Poetic evidence of this may be traced here from the nineteenth century to the present through the poems of Jessie Anne Anderson, Naomi Mitchison, Kathleen Raine, and Kathleen Jamie, each in her own way reclaiming a spiritual territory through confident engagement with the mysterious forces which emerge at moments of transition in life and in death.

These thematic patterns are rewarding to explore. Another might be imaginative visions of Mary, where we may find Dunbar's aureate and tender 'Hale, Sterne Superne' prefigured by the Gaelic celebration of Mary's regal beauty in 'Éistidh riomsa, a Mhuire mhór'; and then fast-forward through the collection to the quirkily honest modern realism of 'The Virgin Punishing the Infant' by Carol Ann Duffy. Such explorations should always be set, however, against the cultural contexts which our chronological ordering reflects.

We begin with Columba's great poem of praise to 'The Maker on High', which is remarkable not only for its metrical subtlety (wonderfully caught in the translation by Edwin Morgan) but also for the sweep of its theological vision and its driving sense of mission. Its 'abecedarian' form (the first stanza beginning with a, the next with b, and so on) complements in its correct ordering of letters the essential rightness of the whole message. Here is important news to be carried throughout the pagan islands of Britain, and on to Europe, cutting across dynastic and territorial boundaries.

The visionary and heroic Anglo-Saxon poem, 'The Dream of the Rood', newly translated by Robert Crawford, is more often seen as one of the earliest English poems. We present it here as at least partly Scottish. Lines from the poem, carved in runic characters on the eighteen-foot-high cross which now stands inside the kirk at Ruthwell by Dumfries, were translated before a manuscript version of the whole text was discovered in a north Italian monastery on the pilgrim route to Rome. The presence of its Northumbrian dialect in what is now Scottish territory also reminds us that the Anglian, British, Scottish and Pictish kingdoms of Scotland all lacked firm boundaries, and that the impact of the Christian message had a powerfully overarching effect. The energetic missionary journeys of Columba's monks meant that Scotland itself became a source of holiness, crossed and recrossed in the service of the heroic presence of Christ, and conveying the paradoxes of His life and death to pagan societies in terms which chimed with but also challenged their warrior codes.

Not all such societies would listen, of course, as the Old Norse 'Mockery of Irish Monks on a Windswept Island' reminds us, but gradually the blending of pre-Christian and Christian religious sensibilities developed what is, to modern ears, an oddly satisfying harmony. Such notes are still to be heard in the *Carmina Gadelica*, old prayers, charms and invocations collected in the Western Isles by Alexander Carmichael in the nineteenth century and reprinted today in various anthologies of 'Celtic Spirituality': despite the literary polish and Victorian circumspection of Carmichael's versions, it is the making holy of every single detail of life which still appeals, and an airy continuity of the temporal and the eternal. Gaelic poetry and the Hebridean landscape can still catch that note, as in Derick Thomson's sparkling 'Leòdhas as t-Samhradh/Lewis in Summer' or Kenneth White's 'A High Blue Day on Scalpay'. Yet it appears difficult for Scots to appreciate such perceptions consistently: see Alastair Reid's wary 'Scotland', where beauty quickly fades into a sourer judgmental vision. And it is possible, of course, to read Thomson's poem in a similar light, as a sarcastic comment on the self-righteousness of those guardians of the faith who can keep an eye on the less godly members of their community with their binoculars, the clear skies giving them a clear knowledge of God's mind!

Scottish literature in Scots begins in the late Middle Ages, effectively with such poets as Robert Henryson (?1424–?1506), William Dunbar (?1456–?1513) and Gavin Douglas (c.1474–1522). This was an ecclesiastical age and one in which metaphorical and metaphysical correspondences pertained between the world above and the world below: an ancestral Catholic world which for most readers now can only be reconstructed imaginatively.[3]

Of the greatest three poets then writing, Douglas was a bishop, Dunbar had possibly studied to be a Franciscan friar and later became a priest, and Henryson spent much of his life as a schoolmaster in the Abbey school of Dunfermline. In many ways they would have taken their religion for granted, and its blending of homely moral teaching through fables (as in Henryson's 'The Preiching of the Swallow') with the elevated and rhythmical 'aureate' diction of Dunbar's 'Hale, Sterne Superne', or with the rough humour and self-mockery of 'The Dregy of Dunbar'. Here we find a carnivalesque ability to subvert, for a while, that which is recognised as vital to existence, the better to sense its value afresh. The hierarchical late medieval world had many ways of ensuring its own continuity through the to-and-fro of knockabout humour and ribaldry. 'The Dregy' is a great example of this, with its easy incorporation of mock-Latin prayers.

One wonders what caused so many of the Scots immediately after the Reformation to lose their sense of humour, and with it, apparently, their sense of proportion – and which loss came first. The change is clear in the Latin poetry of the sixteenth-century humanist George Buchanan, a scholar with a European reputation but also a particularly Scottish line in anti-papal invective, which quite hijacks his poised and formal elegy for John Calvin. Buchanan's personal experience of the authoritarianism of the Church when he was teaching on the Continent would not have endeared the papacy to him. In becoming tutor to the future James VI of Scotland, his teaching may have had some longer term influence on the King's commitment to reform in Scotland.

Anyone reading about the development of the Reformation across Europe, or even seeing it solely in terms of the British Isles, soon recognises that the path and pace of reformation varied hugely in different countries.[4] Political power and greed, however, everywhere played vital roles in a drama of destabilisation. The Church in pre-Reformation Scotland had proved willing to begin to make

---

[3] Peter Ackroyd's biography *The Life of Thomas More* (1999) provides detailed reflection on religious experience just prior to the Reformation: see, for example, Chapters X–XI, pp.93–113.

[4] Michael Lynch's *Scotland: A New History* (1992) gives a clear account of this troubled period, pp.186ff. On the varied impact of reformation in practice, see Michael Mullett's *Catholics in Britain and Ireland, 1558–1829* (1998).

reforms, until political rivalries among leading churchmen from competing noble families subverted all initiatives towards improvement. Radical change followed quickly. From an artistic point of view, the iconoclasm of a reformist vision which stripped out almost all mediation of religious experience through music, sculpture and verse changed the course of the cultural life of Scotland. In terms of the matrix model which was described above, there had occurred a sudden foreshortening of the metaphorical and aesthetic end of the spiritual continuum, in which writers and artists, of course, work most confidently. The deeper poetry of the Bible itself, the mystery of revelation and the encounter of God and humankind, must suffice.

In terms of ordinary or 'well-doing' people, however, it can be said that the Reformation released democratic energies which sing out, for example, in 'The Gude and Godlie Ballates' of 1567. Here translations of Lutheran hymns, adaptations of popular songs to religious ends, satirical verse on Catholic Church abuses and vernacular versions of the Psalms convey a lively sense of the freedoms and possibilities which often immediately follow the dismantling of an ideological system that has drastically lost touch with its original truth and its contemporary society. (The same point could be made about the ministers of the newly formed Free Church in the mid-nineteenth century who supported the tenantry during the Highland Clearances, while ministers of the Church of Scotland often aided and abetted the landlords.)

Unfortunately, the ploughed-up field of one tyranny is often reseeded with elements of another. The thoroughgoing revolution in spirituality at the Reformation seemed posited on a version of human faith and failings which was bound to cause difficulty, not least to poets. In their refocussing on a Pauline justification by faith rather than through pious works of prayer and liturgy (which had become particularly corrupted by the practice of paying for Masses to ensure the speedy passage of the dead through purgatory and into heaven), Calvinist reformers seemed to downplay the spiritual worth of all such traditions, replacing them with a positivist system of social care. An example of this is their focus on widespread school education, at least for males. These reforms, nevertheless, placed great power to control community life and curriculum in the hands of small groups of citizens closely associated with the Kirk and its government. The potential for disruptive rivalries, moral policing and tight-lipped condemnation begins to open up social fissures which poets register as material for satire: Robert Burns's 'Holy Willie's Prayer' is the great exemplar here.[5]

---

[5]It is, then, with a start of recognition at the freshness, if not at the doctrine, that we read the Evangelical outpourings that came with the late-eighteenth-century revivals.

Political differences came to mirror doctrinal ones. The relative roles of Church and Monarchy; the vexed prerogative of re-imposing bishops on a society which had already rejected them; ancient external antipathies between Scottish and English polity, and internal ones between Presbyterian Lowland burghs and the still largely Catholic and Episcopalian Highland straths and glens – all of this combined to set up centuries of conflict that prevented advancement of the Scottish artistic climate of the earlier Renaissance, which in music and poetry had once seemed poised to grow in scope and sophistication. Through the seventeenth century, a growing Protestant martyrology replaced the discredited Catholic litanies of saints, and religious sensibilities seemed driven back upon the private and domestic: however, Alexander Hume's tranquil 'Of the Day Estivall' and William Drummond of Hawthornden's sonnets from 'Flowres of Sion' exemplify the real artistic and personal satisfactions to be derived from this interiorisation of spirituality.

In another, more hierarchical society, this private and personal focus might have led to the more rapid growth of the novel; in Scotland it leads, perhaps, to the stress on individual will and perception in the work of our greatest philosopher, David Hume, and to the intense private scrutiny of James Boswell. Eighteenth-century Edinburgh of the Enlightenment offered a focus on the mind's perceptions, developing a very Scottish and reformist 'common-sense' approach both to the practical sciences and to mathematics and philosophy, a realistic or even sceptical sense of grappling with the physical world and its problems. Thus Robert Fergusson's poem 'To the Tron-kirk Bell' hears it only as a jangling nuisance, and both Burns and Byron satirise conventional (mis-) understandings of religion and the afterlife. Yet these poets also seem wary of religion's residual power. For Burns, that strength of family religion is celebrated in 'The Cotter's Saturday Night' with awkward yet evident sincerity.

There is also evidence of that tendency of the Scottish supernatural to burst forth into the normalities of social life, destroying any confident sense of the defeat of the powers of darkness by right religion.[6] This is a theme which runs through much Scottish literature: in Burns's poem to him, the Devil is suddenly open to familiar address: 'O Thou!' Such sudden intrusions of evil might be said to signal some psychological disruption brought about by the loss, in the reformed religion, of the earlier sacramental mechanisms for dealing with forgiveness and atonement (beyond such social means as exhortation, disapproval and the stool of repentance). Whether or not this is so, the ancient power of the underworld

---

[6]See Colin Manlove's *Scottish Fantasy: A Critical Survey* (1994) and *An Anthology of Scottish Fantasy Literature* (1996).

remains part of Scottish folklore and literature into our own time: Jackie Kay's haunting 'Baby Lazarus' is a recent manifestation. Occasionally, the sudden apparition can be a positive force for good, as in the comforting Lady of Hogg's 'Cameronian Ballad', a rescuer in circumstances of extreme suffering, possessing an almost archetypal power. Hogg's deep knowledge of the oral tradition of the Border ballads may be echoing significantly here.

What role, then, did the Church of Scotland now play in Scottish literary life? There was the quite far-reaching influence of the energies invested by churchmen in the Belles Lettres tradition of late-eighteenth- and early-nineteenth-century university studies of rhetoric. This helped to open up a new subject of English Literature, with literary texts often being used as teaching exemplars of appropriate style or discourse. Emigration of Scottish graduates throughout the British Empire, as well as sales of Scottish textbooks, then significantly shaped the curriculum of schools and universities in America, India, Australia and New Zealand.[7] There was, too, the rhetorical and poetic energy which went into the construction of sermons: those in Gaelic often preserved and enlarged a vocabulary fit to deal with a range of intellectual and spiritual experience; while those in Scots English reinforced through their rhetoric the potential of poetic imagery which was darkly or brightly archetypal. Poets in congregations could not avoid being shaped by such resonance, even while possibly rejecting its doctrinal content. There was, however, no Bible translated into Scots.

In the Highlands, many ministers became caught up in the Ossianic controversy and used their skills in literacy in the collection of oral literature. Murdo MacDonald, minister of Durness, Sutherland, recognised the moral value of Rob Donn's work and introduced the poet to the work of that great English social commentator, Alexander Pope, albeit in Gaelic translation. For Rob Donn and his contemporary Dùgall Bochanan, an evangelist, there was no conflict between Enlightenment thought and religion, for they envisaged a better society where the individual was dignified through working rationally for the commonwealth.

The nineteenth century benefited materially from the practical scientific advances of the Enlightenment and suffered metaphysically from the murkiness of the moral problems which the expansion of Industry and Empire entailed: immigration and urban slums; involvement or investment by Scots in African slave economies, as well as in more positive missionary activities; the shadow side of the decent values of hard work and enterprise becoming evident in unjust factory systems and mistreatment of workers, women and children. In an age of

---

[7]See Robert Crawford, ed., *The Scottish Invention of English Literature* (1998).

evangelism, powerfully exemplified in Thomas Chalmers' work for the poor in the slums of Glasgow, renewed schisms in the Church of Scotland over the autonomy of congregations to appoint their own ministers would take decades even to partially resolve. Meanwhile the fiery challenge of new systems of thought – materialist, scientific and anthropological – cast as lurid a light across the later decades of the century as the flames of iron foundries famously did at midnight in industrial Lanarkshire. 'Let us all be unhappy on Sunday' sings Lord Neaves, and who does not feel willing to join in the chorus?

Darkness even inhabits the powerful evangelical hymns of the time which we reprint here; and the dark continent of Africa accepts and destroys David Livingstone, the self-taught missionary from the industrial mills of Blantyre. James Thomson creates a powerful correlative for all of this in 'The City of Dreadful Night'. In the closing years of the century, John Davidson, by turns optimistic and despairing, begins to exploit the potential of this new urban scene for poetic ends, a precursor of modern poetry in his imagery and attitudes, 'knocking at the door' of the twentieth century.

The twentieth century was one in which historical events, profound social change, and advances in science and technology combined to push against traditional or unexamined versions of religious practice. Religion has become at once more nuanced and more radical in response. In artistic terms, the century was one in which exploration of religious imagery and themes in Scottish poetry continued to defy any premature or simplistic pronouncements on the death of religion. In the Highlands, even the most anti-clerical poetry (by, for example, Am Puilean, Iain Crichton Smith, Derick Thomson and Donald MacAulay) denies the pertinence not of the questions posed by religion, but of the answers! The sheer variety and scope of their poetic response is one reason why we have included so many twentieth-century poets in this anthology; the relevance of their experience and spiritual questioning to contemporary life is another.

Edwin Muir (1887–1959) and Hugh MacDiarmid (1892–1978) were writers who differed radically and publicly on matters of language and form in modern poetry, Muir preferring English with traditional stanzas and imagery, and MacDiarmid Scots, within a restlessly ranging modernity. What both shared, however, was an almost mystical awareness, bound up with landscape and symbolic forms of journey, of renewal, of earth, time and the cosmos, which can create in their poems dizzying shifts of perspective from eternity to the present Scottish moment and back again within the vibrant space of a single work. Both were rendered politically aware, and left psychologically scarred, by their encounters with metropolitan Glasgow and London; they were critical of what the Scots had made of religion and what religion had made of them, as Muir's 'Scotland 1941' and MacDiarmid's poetry *passim* make clear.[8] Yet both are acutely sensitive to religious perspectives on human suffering and despair and the best of their poems manage to link the sublime and the mundane, as it were hand-in-hand.

That this might be, in fact, quite an ordinary Scottish religious perception is also suggested by Kirkpatrick Dobie's remarkable child's-eye view of World War I and the impact of its slaughter on local Christian faith. What we often find in Scottish religious verse is just such a principled refusal to accept desperate dichotomies: the sharply physical, ordinary detail of this world is not to be abandoned for a promised better one; there is a refusal, in George Campbell Hay's words, to stay 'locked in the human cage' of a reading of creation which stresses flaws, joylessness and judgment – instead of that mysterious shimmering of significance to be sensed just on the edge or below the natural surface of the land we live on.

Norman MacCaig and Sorley Maclean are examples of poets who stay true to that vision. Their poems here reveal how Scottish religious poetry often seems to work by plucking two dissonant strings of emotion or thought, which then resonate paradox and make a strange new sound comprising oscillations of opposites so swift that they become one new thing. Edwin Morgan's 'Message Clear' is another example, which is magnificently unclear and questioning before it suddenly resolves itself – but only into a deeper silence in which the reader is left to ponder what Christ's statement meant, and means.

What is exciting about contemporary Scottish poetry is the way in which younger poets are willing to work out experimentally the full significance of their early religious experiences in a range of tones. The descendants of Irish immigrants, such as Tom Leonard, John Burnside and Carol Ann Duffy, reveal a combination of familiarity (which can be irreverently easy about serious issues precisely because they matter) with a devotional or 'sacramental' perception of the natural or social world. In Tom Leonard's 'The Good Thief', the coincidence of three o'clock crucifixion and three o'clock football match kick-off is made significant, and the gospel story once again surges forward into the present. These poets, often the great-grand children of immigrant people, have managed to survive and grow through education into autonomy. They are now bringing back to the Scottish tradition echoes of an almost lost spirituality, a sense of the sacredness and continuities of existence.

Modern Scotland is a country of many faiths. The present generation of Asian Scots have so far begun to publish in prose rather than verse, but we may expect their religious insights to appear in the poetry of this new millennium. Buddhism

---

[8]See, for example, his excoriating 'After 2000 Years'. *Complete Poems* (1993) Vol. 1. p.559.

has influenced the poetic practice of Kenneth White and others. A.C. Jacobs writes out of the 'Scots-Yiddish' experience of his upbringing in Glasgow. Meanwhile contemporary poets brought up in different Scottish Protestant traditions present us with other images, symbols, discoveries, or songs gathered on their own life journeys through the world. They are willing to travel far in space (hence the Tibetan funeral practices encountered on Himalayan journeys in Kathleen Jamie's 'Sky Burial') or in time: Columba's monks make a mysterious reappearance in W.N. Herbert's 'The Manuscript of Feathers', their missionary journeys ending, or opening afresh, in the riddling messages of meditation.

'The World's End' by Roddy Lumsden brings our anthology to a close with its ambiguous sense of boundaries still to be crossed:

> a place some call a border, some an edge
> as if the many missing or a saviour
> will rise in welcome when we step over.

This seems a very Scottish moment, as well as a religious one, in the uncertainty of its interpretation, the sceptical 'as if', the Celtic tradition of hospitality and welcome to strangers, and our ancient understanding of the dead as standing quite close by. It seems right to end this anthology of Scottish religious poems with just such a strange yet familiar beginning.

What, finally, might we look for in Scottish religious poetry? Not just the empathic natural imagery linking earth and heaven that is everywhere to be found in Irish religious verse, nor yet the mystical quests of the best of English religious poets, although we possess good examples of both sorts of writing. Something more difficult than these, seeming more surprised or vulnerable or hurt (at times) by the force of its own logic, or by God's. There's dissonance which suggests a willingness to stay close to the paradoxes of suffering; to that extent it edges towards the life of Christ as we have it in the Gospels. There's boldness in the swooping cosmic movements between worlds; there's the living stillness of meditation; there's anger and tenderness by turns, as we find in the Psalms. We see the rich biblical inheritance of imagery and symbol being turned back by poets on those who preach it less than worthily; we hear speech tones and rhythms discovering words where no words can rightly reach. What Hugh MacDiarmid pointed out in another context seems true in this regard: the poetic language of Scotland does indeed provide us with 'names for nameless things'.

JMcG, RC, MB

Editors' Note

In this anthology aimed at the general reader we have tried to use reliable texts throughout, but have made no attempt to standardise Scots or Gaelic orthography. Where they seemed helpful, line-by-line glosses of Scots words have been supplied, sometimes by the editors and sometimes by Dr Nicola Royan, whose glossing we acknowledge with gratitude. Acknowledgement is also due to Ms Jill Gamble for indexing, and to the School of English, University of St Andrews, for institutional assistance in the making of this book; to Professor Derick Thomson, whose work has been of great help to the editors; to Dr Thomas Clancy and Mr Hamish Whyte for advice, encouragement, and assistance.

We have decided to use poetic translations throughout, since we wanted the reader's experience to be one of poetry rather than prose. Though the editors are all poets with an interest in religion, it seemed inappropriate to include our own original work; however, we have supplied some translations of poems where this seemed fitting. We owe a debt to Edwin Morgan in particular for his spirited translations of poems by St Columba and George Buchanan, which he made specially for this anthology.

In order to allow readers to meet the poems with as little as possible prose interference, we have supplied almost all biographical and other notes at the back of the book, where they are arranged chronologically according to the dates of the poet's birth (or, in the case of a few anonymous poems, the date of composition).

ST COLUMBA

ALTUS PROSATOR

Altus prosator vetustus dierum et ingenitus
erat absque origine primordii et crepidine
est et erit in saecula saeculorum infinita
cui est unigenitus Christus et sanctus spiritus
coaeternus in gloria deitatis perpetua
non tres deos depromimus sed unum Deum dicimus
salva fidei in personis tribus gloriosissimis.

Bonos creavit angelos ordines et archangelos
principatum ac sedium potestatum virtutium
uti non esset bonitas otiosa ac majestas
trinitatis in omnibus largitatis muneribus
sed haberet caelestia in quibus privilegia
ostenderet magnopere possibili fatimine.

Caeli de regni apice stationis angelicae
claritate praefulgoris venustate speciminis
superbiendo ruerat Lucifer quem formaverat
apostataeque angeli eodem lapsu lugubri
auctoris cenodoxiae pervicacis invidiae
ceteris remanentibus in suis principatibus.

Draco magnus taeterrimus terribilis et antiquus
qui fuit serpens lubricus sapientior omnibus
bestiis et animantibus terrae ferocioribus
tertiam partem siderum traxit secum in barathrum
locorum infernalium diversorumque carcerum
refugas veri luminis parasito praecipites.

Excelsus mundi machinam praevidens et harmoniam
caelum et terram fecerat mare aquas condiderat
herbarum quoque germina virgultorum arbuscula
solem lunam ac sidera ignem ac necessaria

THE MAKER ON HIGH

Ancient exalted seed-scatterer whom time gave no progenitor:
he knew no moment of creation in his primordial foundation
he is and will be all places in all time and all ages
with Christ his first-born only-born and the holy spirit co-borne
throughout the high eternity of glorious divinity:
three gods we do not promulgate one God we state and intimate
salvific faith victorious: three persons very glorious.

Benevolence created angels and all the orders of archangels
thrones and principalities powers virtues qualities
denying otiosity to the excellence and majesty
of the not-inactive trinity in all labours of bounty
when it mustered heavenly creatures whose well devised natures
received its lavish proffer through power-word for ever.

Came down from heaven summit down from angelic limit
dazzling in his brilliance beauty's very likeness
Lucifer downfalling (once woke at heaven's calling)
apostate angels sharing the deadly downfaring
of the author of high arrogance and indurated enviousness
the rest still continuing safe in their dominions.

Dauntingly huge and horrible the dragon ancient and terrible
known as the lubric serpent subtler in his element
than all the beasts and every fierce thing living earthly
dragged a third – so many – stars to his gehenna
down to infernal regions not devoid of dungeons
benighted ones hell's own parasite hurled headlong.

Excellent promethean armoury structuring world harmony
had created earth and heaven and wet acres of ocean
also sprouting vegetation shrubs groves plantations
sun moon stars to ferry fire and all things necessary

3

aves pisces et pecora bestias animalia
hominem demum regere protoplaustum praesagmine.

Factis simul sideribus aetheris luminaribus
conlaudaverunt angeli factura pro mirabili
immensae molis Dominum opificem caelestium
praeconio laudabili debito et immobili
concentuque egregio grates egerunt Domino
amore et arbitrio non naturae donario.

Grassatis primis duobus seductisque parentibus
secundo ruit diabolus cum suis satellitibus
quorum horrore vultuum sonoque volitantium
consternarentur homines metu territi fragiles
non valentes carnalibus haec intueri visibus
qui nunc ligantur fascibus ergastulorum nexibus.

Hic sublatus e medio deiectus est a Domino
cuius aeris spatium constipatur satellitum
globo invisibilium turbido perduellium
ne malis exemplaribus imbuti ac sceleribus
nullis unquam tegentibus saeptis ac parietibus
fornicarentur homines palam omnium oculis

Invehunt nubes pontias ex fontibus brumalias
tribus profundioribus oceani dodrantibus
maris caeli climatibus caeruleis turbinibus
profuturas segitibus vineis et germinibus
agitatae flaminibus thesauris emergentibus
quique paludes marinas evacuant reciprocas.

Kaduca ac tyrannica mundique momentanea
regum praesentis gloria nutu Dei deposita
ecce gigantes gemere sub aquis magno ulcere
comprobantur incendio aduri ac supplicio
Cocytique Charybdibus strangulati turgentibus
Scyllis obtecti fluctibus eliduntur et scrupibus.

birds fish and cattle and every animal imaginable
but lastly the second promethean the protoplast human being.

Fast upon the starry finishing the lights high shimmering
the angels convened and celebrated for the wonders just created
the Lord the only artificer of that enormous vault of matter
with loud and well judged voices unwavering in their praises
an unexampled symphony of gratitude and sympathy
sung not by force of nature but freely lovingly grateful.

Guilty of assault and seduction of our parents in the garden
the devil has a second falling together with his followers
whose faces set in horror and wingbeats whistling hollow
would petrify frail creatures into stricken fearers
but what men perceive bodily must preclude luckily
those now bound and bundled in dungeons of the underworld.

He Zabulus was driven by the Lord from mid heaven
and with him the airy spaces were choked like drains with faeces
as the turgid rump of rebels fell but fell invisible
in case the grossest villains become willy-nilly
with neither walls nor fences preventing curious glances
tempters to sin greatly openly emulatingly.

Irrigating clouds showering wet winter from sea-fountains
from floods of the abysses three-fourths down through fishes
up to the skyey purlieus in deep blue whirlpools
good rain then for cornfields vineyard-bloom and grain-yields
driven by blasts emerging from their airy treasuring
desiccating not the land-marches but the facing sea-marshes.

Kings of the world we live in: their glories are uneven
brittle tyrannies disembodied by a frown from God's forehead:
giants too underwater groaning in great horror
forced to burn like torches cut by painful tortures
pounded in the millstones of underworld maelstroms
roughed rubbed out buried in a frenzy of flints and billows.

Ligatas aquas nubibus frequenter cribrat Dominus
ut ne erumpant protinus simul ruptis obicibus
quarum uberioribus venis velut uberibus
pedetentim natantibus telli per tractus istius
gelidis ac ferventibus diversis in temporibus
usquam influunt flumina nunquam deficientia.

Magni Dei virtutibus appenditur dialibus
globus terrae et circulus abyssi magnae inditus
suffultu Dei iduma omnipotentis valida
columnis velut vectibus eundem sustenantibus
promontoriis et rupibus solidis fundaminibus
velut quibusdam basibus firmatus immobilibus.

Nulli videtur dubium in imis esse infernum
ubi habentur tenebrae vermes et dirae bestiae
ubi ignis sulphureus ardens flammis edacibus
ubi rugitus hominum fletus et stridor dentium
ubi Gehennae gemitus terribilis et antiquus
ubi ardor flammaticus sitis famisque horridus.

Orbem infra ut legimus incolas esse novimus
quorum genu precario frequenter flectit Domino
quibusque impossibile librum scriptum revolvere
obsignatum signaculis septem de Christi monitis
quem idem resignaverat postquam victor exstiterat
explens sui praesagmina adventus prophetalia.

Plantatum a prooemio paradisum a Domino
legimus in primordio Genesis nobilissimo
cuius ex fonte flumina quattuor sunt manantia
cuius etiam florido lignum vitae in medio
cuius non cadunt folia gentibus salutifera
cuius inenarrabiles deliciae ac fertiles.

Quis ad condictum Domini montem ascendit Sinai?
quis audivit tonitrua ultra modum sonantia
quis clangorem perstrepere inormitatis buccinae?
quis quoque vidit fulgura in gyro coruscantia

Letting the waters be sifted from where the clouds are lifted
the Lord often prevented the flood he once attempted
leaving the conduits utterly full and rich as udders
slowly trickling and panning through the tracts of this planet
freezing if cold was called for warm in the cells of summer
keeping our rivers everywhere running forward for ever.

Magisterial are his powers as the great God poises
the earth ball encircled by the great deep so firmly
supported by an almighty robust nieve so tightly
that you would think pillar and column held it strong and solemn
the capes and cliffs stationed on solidest foundations
fixed uniquely in their place as if on immovable bases.

No one needs to shows us: a hell lies deep below us
where there is said to be darkness worms beasts carnage
where there are fires of sulphur burning to make us suffer
where men are gnashing roaring weeping wailing deploring
where groans mount from gehennas terrible never-ending
where parched and fiery horror feeds thirst and hunger.

Often on their knees at prayer are many said to be there
under the earth books tell us they do not repel us
though they found it unavailling the scroll not unrolling
whose fixed seals were seven when Christ warning from heaven
unsealed it with the gesture of a resurrected victor
fulfilling the prophets' foreseeing of his coming and his decreeing.

Paradise was planted primally as God wanted
we read in sublime verses entering into Genesis
its fountain's rich waters feed four flowing rivers
its heart abounds with flowers where the tree of life towers
with foliage never fading for the healing of the nations
and delights indescribable abundantly fruitful.

Quiz sacred Sinai: who is it has climbed so high?
Who has heard the thunder cracks vast in the sky-tracts?
Who has heard the enormous bullroaring of the war-horns?
Who has seen the lightning flashing round the night-ring?

quis lampades et iacula saxaque collidentia
praeter Israhelitici Moysen iudicem populi?

Regis regum rectissimi prope est dies Domini
dies irae et vindictae tenebrarum et nebulae
diesque mirabilium tonitruorum fortium
dies quoque angustiae maeroris ac tristitiae
in quo cessabit mulierum amor ac desiderium
hominumque contentio mundi huius et cupido.

Stantes erimus pavidi ante tribunal Domini
reddemusque de omnibus rationem affectibus
videntes quoque posita ante obtutus crimina
librosque conscientiae patefactos in facie
in fletus amarissimos ac singultus erumpemus
subtracta necessaria operandi materia.

Tuba primi archangeli strepente admirabili
erumpent munitissima claustra ac poliandria
mundi praesentis frigora hominum liquescentia
undique conglobantibus ad compagines ossibus
animabus aethralibus eisdem obviantibus
rursumque redeuntibus debitis mansionibus.

Vagatur ex climactere Orion cadeli cardine
derelicto Virgilio astrorum splendidissimo
per metas Thetis ignoti orientalis circuli
girans certis ambagibus redit priscis reditibus
oriens post biennium Vesperugo in vesperum
sumpta in proplesmatibus tropicis intellectibus.

Xristo de caelis Domino descendente celsissimo
praefulgebit clarissimum signum crucis et vexillum
tectisque luminaribus duobus principalibus
cadent in terram sidera ut fructus de ficulnea
eritque mundi spatium ut fornacis incendium
tunc in montium specubus abscondent se exercitus.

Who has seen javelins flambeaus a rock-face in shambles?
Only to Moses is this real only to the judge of Israel.

Rue God's day arriving righteous high king's assizing
dies irae day of the vindex day of cloud and day of cinders
day of the dumbfoundering day of great thundering
day of lamentation of anguish of confusion
with all the love and yearning of women unreturning
as all men's striving and lust for worldly living.

Standing in fear and trembling with divine judgement assembling
we shall stammer what we expended before our life was ended
faced by rolling videos of our crimes however hideous
forced to read the pages of the conscience book of ages
we shall burst out into weeping sobbing bitter and unceasing
now that all means of action have tholed the last retraction.

The archangelic trumpet-blast is loud and great at every fastness
the hardest vaults spring open the catacombs are broken
the dead of the world are thawing their cold rigor withdrawing
the bones are running and flying to the joints of the undying
their souls hurry to meet them and celestially to greet them
returning both together to be one not one another.

Vagrant Orion driven from the crucial hinge of heaven
leaves the Pleiades receding most splendidly beneath him
tests the ocean boundaries the oriental quandaries
as Vesper circling steadily returns home readily
the rising Lucifer of the morning after two years mourning:
these things are to be taken as type and trope and token.

X spikes and flashes like the Lord's cross marching
down with him from heaven as the last sign is given
moonlight and sunlight are finally murdered
stars fall from dignity like fruits from a fig-tree
the world's whole surface burns like a furnace
armies are crouching in caves in the mountains.

Ymnorum cantionibus sedulo tinnientibus
tripudiis sanctis milibus angelorum vernantibus
quattuorque plenissimis animalibus oculis
cum viginti felicibus quattuor senioribus
coronas admittentibus agni Dei sub pedibus
laudatur tribus vicibus Trinitas aeternalibus.

Zelus ignis furibundus consumet adversarios
nolentes Christum credere Deo a Patre venisse
nos vero evolabimus obviam ei protinus
et sic cum ipso erimus in diversis ordinibus
dignitatum pro meritis praemiorum perpetuis
permansuri in gloria a saeculis in saecula.

You know then the singing of hymns finely ringing
thousands of angels advancing spring up in sacred dances
quartet of beasts gaze from numberless eyes in praise
two dozen elders as happiness compels them
throw all their crowns down to the Lamb who surmounts them
'Holy holy holy' binds the eternal trinity.

Zabulus burns to ashes all those adversaries
who deny that the Saviour was Son to the Father
but we shall fly to meet him and immediately greet him
and be with him in the dignity of all such diversity
as our deeds make deserved and we without swerve
shall live beyond history in the state of glory.

translated from the Latin by Edwin Morgan

DALLAN FORGAILL
fl.600

from AMRA CHOLUIMB CILLE

I

Ní díscéoil duë Néill.
Ní uchtat óenmaige,
mór mairg, mór n-deilm.
Dífulaing riss ré as-indet:
Columb cen beith, cen chill.
Co india duí dó, sceo Nere:
in faith Dé de dess Sion suidiath.
Is nú nad mair, ní marthar lenn,
    ní less anma ar suí.
Ar-don– cond íath con-róeter bïu –bath,
ar-don-bath ba ar n-airchend adlicen,
ar-don-bath ba ar fíadat foídiam;
ar ní-n fissid fris-bered omnu húain,
ar nín-tathrith to-sluinned foccul fír,
ar ní-n forcetlaid for-canad túatha
    Toí.
hUile bith, ba háe hé:
Is crot cen chéis,
is cell cen abbaid.

II

At-ruic ro-ard rath Dé do Cholumb cuitechta;
find-fethal frestal, figlis fut baí.
Boí saegul snéid,
boí séim sáth.
Boí sab suíthe cech dind,
boí dind oc libur léig-docht.
Lassais tír túath,
Lais túath *occidens,*
cot-ro-lass *oriens*
ó chlérchib crí-dochtaib
Fó díbath Dé aingeil
i rré as-id-rocaib.

from ELEGY OF COLUMBA

I

Not newsless is Níall's land.
No slight sigh from one plain,
but great woe, great outcry.
Unbearable the tale this verse tells:
Colum, lifeless, churchless.
How will a fool tell him – even Neire –
the prophet has settled at God's right hand in Sion.
Now he is not, nothing is left to us,
    no relief for a soul, our sage.
For he has died to us, the leader of nations who guarded the living,
he has died to us, who was our chief of the needy,
he has died to us, who was our messenger of the Lord;
for we do not have the seer who used to keep fears from us,
for he does not return to us, he who would explain the true Word,
for we do not have the teacher who would teach the tribes of the
    Tay.
The whole world, it was his:
It is a harp without a key,
it is a church without an abbot.

II

By the grace of God Colum rose to exalted companionship;
awaiting bright signs, he kept watch while he lived.
His lifetime was short,
scant portions filled him.
He was learning's pillar in every stronghold,
he was foremost at the book of complex Law.
The northern land shone,
the western people blazed,
he lit up the east
with chaste clerics.
Good the legacy of God's angel
when he glorified him.

V

Raith rith rethes dar cais caín-denum.
Faig feirb fithir.
Gáis gluassa glé.
Glinnsius salmu,
sluinnsius léig libru,
libuir ut car Cassion.
Catha gulae gaelais.
Libru Solman sexus.
Sína sceo imm– ríma –raith.
Rannais raind co figuir eter libru
    léig.
Legais rúna, ro-ch –uaid eter scolaib
    screptra,
sceo ellacht imm-uaim n-ésci im
    rith,
raith rith la gréin ngescaig,
sceo réin rith.
Rímfed rind nime, nech in-choí cech
    ndiruais
ro– Columb ó Chille –cúalammar.

X

Amrad inso ind ríg ro-dom-rig.
For-don-snáidfe Sïone.
Ro-dom-sibsea sech riaga.
Rop réid menda duba dím.
Dom-chich cen anmne
húa huí Choirp Cathrach con húasle.
Oll rodiall, oll natha nime nemgrían,
nímda húain.

V

He ran the course which runs past hatred to right action.
The teacher wove the word.
By his wisdom he made glosses clear.
He fixed the Psalms,
he made known the books of Law,
those books Cassian loved.
He won battles with gluttony.
The books of Solomon, he followed them.
Seasons and calculations he set in motion.
He separated the elements according to figures among the books
    of the Law.
He read mysteries and distributed the Scriptures among the
    schools,
and he put together the harmony concerning the course of the
    moon,
the course which it ran with the rayed sun,
and the course of the sea.
He could number the stars of heaven, the one who could tell all
    the rest
which we have heard from Colum Cille.

X

This is the elegy of the king who rules me.
He will protect us in Sion.
He will urge me past torments.
May it be easily dark defects go from me.
He will come to me without delay,
the descendant of Cathair's offspring, Coirpre, with dignity.
Vast the variations of the poem, vast the splendid sun of heaven,
I have no time.

translated from the Old Gaelic by Thomas Owen Clancy

ANONYMOUS

c.700

THE DREAM OF THE ROOD

Hwæt! ic swefna cyst secʒan wylle,
hwæt me ʒemætte to midre nihte,
syðþan reordberend reste wunedon.
Þuhte me, þæt ic ʒesawe syllicre treow
on lyft lædan leohte bewunden,
beama beorhtost: eall þæt beacen wæs
beʒoten mid ʒolde: ʒimmas stodon
faeʒere æt foldan sceatum, swylce þær fife wæron
uppe on þam eaxleʒespanne. Beheoldon þær enʒel dryhtnes ealle
faeʒere þurh forðʒesceaft: ne wæs ðær huru fracodes ʒealga,
ac hine þær beheoldon haliʒe gastas,
men ofer moldan ond eall þeos mære ʒesceaft.
Syllic wæs se siʒebeam ond ic synnum fah,
forwunded mid wommum. Ʒeseah ic wuldres treow
wædum ʒeweorðode wynnum scinan,
ʒeʒyred mid golde, ʒimmas hæfdon
bewriʒene weorðlice wealdes treow:
hwæðre ic þurh þæt gold onʒytan meahte
earmra ærʒewin, þæt hit ærest ongan
swætan on þa swiðran healfe. Eall ic wæs mid sorʒun ʒedrefed.
Forht ic wæs for þære fæʒran ʒesyhðe; ʒeseah ic þæt fuse beacen
wendan wædum ond bleom: hwilum hit wæs mid wætan bestemed,
beswyled mid swates ganʒe, hwilum mid since ʒegyrwed.
Hwæðre ic þær licgende lanʒe hwile
beheold hreowceariʒ Hælendes treow,
oð ðæt ic ʒehyrde, þæt hit hleoðrode;
ongan ða word sprecan wudu selesta:
Þæt wæs ʒeara iu (ic þæt ʒyta ʒeman),
þæt ic wæs aheawen holtes on ende,
astyred of stefne minum. Ʒenaman me ðær stranʒe feondas,
ʒeworhton him þær to wæfersyne, heton me heora wergas hebban;
bæron me ðær beornas on eaxlum, oð ðæt hie me on beorg asetton,

THE VISION OF THE CROSS

Listen! Hear how I dreamed a great dream
After midnight while most men slept.
It seemed I saw the tree of glory
Held high in heaven, haloed with light,
Blazing as a beacon. Every bough was
Brilliantly golden; gleaming jewels
Girdled earth's surface – five shone also
Ranged at right-angles – and crowds of angels
All through the universe viewed it with awe,
No gangsters' gallows. High, holy spirits
Marvelled with men and all of mighty creation.
   That symbol was sacred, and I was stained
With sinful scars. I saw glory's tree
Shawled with light, joyfully shining;
Gems had clothed those forest branches,
Yet through gold's glint I still could glimpse
Tokens of torture, of that first time
Blood ran from its right side. Writhing,
I dreaded my dream. The shifting symbol
Changed colours and coating; once, wet with blood,
It stood in gore; once, again, it glittered with treasure.
   I lay a long time, anxiously looking
At the Saviour's tree, till that best of branches
Suddenly started to speak:
   'Years, years ago, I remember it yet,
They cut me down at the edge of a copse,
Wrenched, uprooted me. Devils removed me,
Put me on show as their jailbirds' gibbet.
Men shouldered me, shifted me, set me up
Fixed on a hill where foes enough fastened me.

ᵹefæstnodon me þær feondas ᵹenoᵹe. Ᵹeseah ic þa Frean mancynnes
efstan elne mycle þæt he me wolde on ᵹestiᵹan.
Þær ic þa ne dorste ofer Dryhtnes word
buᵹan oððe berstan, þa ic bifian ᵹeseah
eorðan sceatas: ealle ic mihte
feondas ᵹefyllan, hwæðre ic fæste stod.
Onᵹyrede hine þa ᵹeonᵹ hæleð (þæt wæs God ælmihtiᵹ)
stranᵹ ond stiðmod: ᵹestah he on ᵹealᵹan heanne
modiᵹ on maniᵹra ᵹesyhðe, þa he wolde mancyn lysan.
Bifode ic, þa me se beorn ymbclypte: ne dorste ic hwæðre buᵹan to eorᵹan,
feallan to foldan sceatum: ac ic sceolde fæste standan.
Rod wæs ic aræred: ahof ic ricne cyning,
heofona hlaford; hyldan me ne dorste.
Þurhdrifan hi me mid deorcan næᵹlum, on me syndon þa dolᵹ ᵹesiene,
opene inwidhlemmas: ne dorste ic hira næniᵹum sceððan.
Bysmeredon hie unc butu ætgædere. Eall ic wæs mid blode bestemed,
beᵹoten of þæs guman sidan, siððan he hæfde his ᵹast onsended.
Feala ic on þam beorge ᵹebiden hæbbe
wraðra wyrda: ᵹeseah ic weruda God
þearle þenian: þystro hæfdon
bewriᵹen mid wolcnum Wealdendes hræw,
scirne sciman; sceadu forðeode,
wann under wolcnum. Weop eal ᵹesceaft,
cwiðdon cyninᵹes fyll: Crist wæs on rode.
Hwæðere þær fuse feorran cwoman
to þam æðelinge: ic þæt eall beheold.
Sare ic wæs mid sorgum ᵹedrefed, hnaᵹ ic hwæðre þam secᵹum to handa
eaðmod elne mycle. Genamon hie þær ælmihtiᵹne God,
ahofon hine of ðam hefian wite; forleton me þa hilderincas
standan steame bedrifenne: eall ic wæs mid strælum forwundod.
Aledon hie ðær limweriᵹne, ᵹestodon him æt his lices heafdum,
beheoldon hie ðær heofenes dryhten ond he hine ðær hwile reste
meðe æfter ðam miclan ᵹewinne. Onᵹunnon him þa moldern wyrcan
beornas on banan ᵹesyhðe, curfon hie ðæt of beorhtan stane,
ᵹesetton hie ðæron siᵹora wealdend. Onᵹunnon him þa sorhleoð ᵹalan
earme on þa æfentide, þa hie woldon eft siðian
meðe fram þam mæran þeodne: reste he ðær mæte weorode.
Hwæðere we ðær reotende gode hwile
stodon on staðole; siððan . . . up ᵹewat

18

I looked on the Lord then, Man of mankind,
In his hero's hurry to climb high upon me.
I dared not go against God's word,
Bow down or break, although I saw
Earth's surface shaking. I could have flattened
All of those fiends; instead, I stood still.
Then the young hero who was King of Heaven,
Strong and steadfast, stripped for battle,
Climbed the high gallows, his constant courage
Clear in his mission to redeem mankind.
I flinched when he touched me, but dared not fall
Or stoop to the soil. I had to stand.
Created a cross, I carried the King,
The stars' strong Lord. I dared not bow.
They drove in dark nails, deep, cruel wounds
Are in me still, I could not stop them.
They cursed us both. I was black with blood
Sprung from His side once he sent His Soul on its way.
On that hill I held out in horror,
Saw Heaven's Ruler ceaselessly racked;
Low clouds lessened the Light of Lights,
God's corpse; darkness cut in
Black under cumulus, creation wept,
Crying for the King's death, Christ on his wooden cross.
Yet keen men came from far up-country,
Walking to the King. I kept watch.
    Though scarred with sorrow, I stooped to their hands,
Totally humble. There they held God,
Hefted him from his hard trials, left me
Shot through with arrows, standing streaming with blood.
They laid him down, weary, stood at his head
Just looking at God; tired out after his torments,
He took time to rest. They started to hew
Out of bright stone in sight of his slayers
The strong Saviour's tomb. They sang,
Sobbed, and sang in that sorry gloaming,
Saddened to go again, leaving behind
The lonely Lord laid there. Then we three crosses
Witnessed and wept; a wail went up

hilderinca: hræw colode,

fæʒer feorgbold. Þa us man fyllan ongan

ealle to eorðan: þæt wæs egeslic wyrd!

Bedealf us man on deopan seaþe: hwæðre me ðær dryhtnes þegnas,

freondas ʒefrunon; . . . . . .

gyredon me golde ond seolfre.

Nu ðu miht ʒehyran, hæleð min se leofa,

þæt ic bealuwara weorc ʒebiden hæbbe,

sarra sorʒa. Is nu sæl cumen,

þæt me weorðiað wide ond side

menn ofer moldan ond eall þeos mære ʒesceaft

ʒebiddaþ him to þyssum beacne. On me bearn Godes

þrowode hwile; forþan ic þrymfæst nu

hlifiʒe under heofenum ond ic hælan mæʒ

æʒhwylcne anra, þara þe him bið eʒesa to me:

iu ic wæs ʒeworden wita heardost,

leodum laðost, ær þan ic him lifes weʒ

rihtne ʒerymde reordberendum.

Hwæt! me þa ʒeweorðode wuldres ealdor

ofer holmwudu, heofonrices weard,

swylce swa he his modor eac Marian sylfe

ælmihtiʒ God for ealle menn

ʒeweorðode ofer eall wifa cynn.

Nu ic þe hate, hæleð min se leofa,

þæt ðu þas ʒesyhðe secʒe mannum:

onwreoh wordum, þæt hit is wuldres beam,

se ðe ælmihtiʒ God on þrowode

for mancynnes maneʒum synnum

ond Adomes ealdʒewyrhtum.

Deað he þær byriʒde: hwæðere eft dryhten aras

mid his miclan mihte mannum to helpe.

He ða on heofenas astaʒ: hider eft fundaþ

on þysne middanʒeard mancynn secan

on domdæʒe Dryhten sylfa,

ælmihitʒ God ond his englas mid,

þæt he þonne wile deman, se ah domes ʒeweald,

anra ʒehwylcum, swa he him ærur her

on þyssum lænum life ʒeearnaþ:

ne mæʒ þær æniʒ unforht wesan

From warrior comrades; the corpse,
Seat of the soul, grew cold.
Suddenly someone started to axe us
Flat to the field. The three crosses crashed.
God's friends, His servants, found me buried,
Dumped in a deep pit. They decorated me
With silver and gold.
                              Hear now, friend,
How I tholed the work of the wicked,
Tearings and torments. The time has come
When worshippers honour me far and wide
Across all countries, throughout creation
Men pray to this sign. On me God's Son
Suffered; for that I am set up high
Shining in heaven, and I can heal
Any person who fears me in faith.
Once I was taken for toughest torture,
Monstrous to men, before I opened
The right road for people on earth.
God in His glory, the sky's Guard, gave me
To tower above trees, as He made in grace
His mother also, Mary herself,
Much more marvellous in all men's minds
Than the rest of the race of women.

      My friend, you must obey your vision.
Work out in words, tell people this dream
Of the tree of glory against which God
Suffered for mankind's many sins
And the ancient evil of Adam.
He dined on death there, but rose up Lord,
Hero and helper, he climbed into heaven
From where He'll descend on the Day of Judgement,
Almighty God, the Lord with good angels,
The mighty Maker, to search out mankind,
Judging each as each on earth
Deserved in this life unlasting.
None on that day can hear without dread

for þam worde, þe se Wealdend cwyð!
Frineð he for þære mæniʒe, hwær se man sie,
se ðe for Dryhtnes naman deaðes wolde
biteres onbyriʒan, swa he ær on ðam beame dyde:
ac hie þonne forhtiað ond fea þencaþ,
hwæt hie to Criste cweðan onʒinnen.
Ne þearf ðær þonne æniʒ unforht wesan,
þe him ær in breostum bereð beacna selest;
ac ðurh ða rode sceal rice ʒesecan
of eorðweʒe æʒhwylc sawl,
seo þe mid Wealdende wunian þenceð.'
Gebæd ic me þa to þan beame bliðe mode
elne mycle, þær ic ana wæs
mæte werede: wæs modsefa
afysed on forðweʒe; feala ealra ʒebad
langunghwila. Is me nu lifes hyht,
þæt ic þone siʒebeam secan mote
ana oftor þonne ealle men
well weorþian: me is willa to ðam
mycel on mode ond min mundbyrd is
ʒeriht to þære rode. Nah ic ricra feala
freonda on foldan, ac hie forð heonon
ʒewiton of worulde dreamum, sohton him wuldres cyning,
lifiaþ nu on heofenum mid heahfædere,
wuniaþ on wuldre ond ic wene me
daʒa ʒehwylce, hwænne me dryhtnes rod,
þe ic her on eorðan ær sceawode,
on þysson lænan life ʒefetiʒe
ond me þonne ʒebrinʒe, þær is blis mycel,
dream on heofonum, þær is Dryhtnes folc
ʒeseted to symle, þær is singal blis;
ond he þonne asette, þær ic syþþan mot
wunian on wuldre, well mid þam halʒum
dreames brucan. Si me Dryhten freond,
se ðe her on eorþan ær þrowode
on þam ʒealʒtreowe for guman synnum.
He us onlysde ond us lif forgeaf,
heofonlicne ham. Hiht wæs ʒeniwad
mid bledum ond mid blisse, þam þe þær bryne þolodan.

God's voice. In front of great crowds
He will ask for the man who might be willing
To brave bitter death as Christ did on those beams.
People will fear Him, few have considered
What to begin to say to the Saviour.
He who on earth has carried the crucifix
Bright in his breast, the best of symbols,
Need not cower then; God shall greet
All who come through the cross to their homes in heaven,
Every soul from the earth.'
    My heart grew happy when I heard that cross.
I lay alone, my spirit longing,
Urging my soul on its journey.
Now, more than all, I live my life
Hoping to see that tree of glory
And worship it well. My will
Spurs my spirit; yon cross protects me.
My strong friends are few. They have gone away
From the wealth of this world in search of God,
Living now with the high Lord of heaven.
Every day I expect that moment
When the cross of the King I caught sight of on earth
Will fetch me far from this fleeting state
To bring me where true glory blossoms
Joyfully in heaven, where the host of God
Banquets in bliss forever;
Then he shall set me to stay in splendour,
Housed with the holy in the hall of my Lord.
Hero, who here in the past knew horror
On earth on the criminal's cross,
Be my friend, God, who gave us our lives,
Redeemer who gave us homes in heaven.
New hope came with bountiful blessings
For those who before knew nothing but burning.

Se Sunu wæs sigorfæst on þam siðfate,
mihtiȝ ond spedig, þa he mid maniȝeo com,
gasta weorode on Godes rice
anwealda ælmihtiȝ enȝlum to blisse
ond eallum ðam halȝum, þam þe on heofonum ær
wundeon on wuldre, þa heora wealdend cwom,
ælmihtiȝ God, þær his eðel wæs.

Mighty and masterful, coming with massed
Hosts of the holy to the house of God,
The one almighty Son was sure
Of victory then, elating with angels
And all of those who had in heaven
Places in glory when their Prince was coming,
The Lord God almighty, home.

translated from the Old English by Robert Crawford

SCHOOL OF COLUMBA

?8TH CENTURY

NOLI PATER

Noli Pater indulgere tonitrua cum fulgore
ne frangamur formidine huius atque uridine.

Te timemus terribilem nullum credentes similem
te cuncta canunt carmina angelorum per agmina.

Teque exaltent culmina caeli vaga per fulmina
O Iesu amantissime, O rex regum rectissime.

Benedictus in saecula recta regens regimina
Iohannes coram Domino adhuc matris in utero
repletus Dei gratia pro vino atque sicera.

Elizabeth Zachariae virum magnum genuit
Iohannem baptistam precursorem Domini.

Manet in meo corde Dei amoris flamma
ut in argenti vase auri ponitur gemma.

Father, do not allow thunder and lightning,
lest we be shattered by its fear and its fire.

We fear you, the terrible one, believing there is none like you.
All songs praise you throughout the host of angels.

Let the summits of heaven, too, praise you with roaming lightning.
O most loving Jesus, O righteous King of Kings.

Blessed for ever, ruling in right government,
is John before the Lord, till now in his mother's womb,
filled with the grace of God in place of wine or strong drink.

Elizabeth of Zechariah begot a great man:
John the Baptist, the forerunner of the Lord.

The flame of God's love dwells in my heart
as a jewel of gold is placed in a silver dish.

translated from the Latin by Gilbert Márkus

MUGRON, ABBOT OF IONA

D. 981

CROS CHRÍST

Cros Chríst tarsin ngnúisse,
  tarsin gclúais fon cóirse.
Cros Chríst tarsin súilse.
  Cros Chríst tarsin sróinse.

Cros Chríst tarsin mbélsa.
  Cros Chríst tarsin cráessa.
Cros Chríst tarsin cúlsa.
  Cros Chríst tarsin táebsa.

Cros Chríst tarsin mbroinnse
  (is amlaid as chuimse).
Cros Chríst tarsin tairrse.
  Cros Chríst tarsin ndruimse.

Cros Chríst tar mo láma
  óm gúaillib com basa.
Cros Chríst tar mo lesa.
  Cros Chríst tar mo chasa.

Cros Chríst lem ar m'agaid.
  Cros Chríst lem im degaid.
Cros Chríst fri cach ndoraid
  eitir fán is telaig.

Cros Chríst sair frim einech
  Cros Chríst síar fri fuined.
Tes, túaid cen nach n-anad,
  cros Chríst cen nach fuirech.

CHRIST'S CROSS

Christ's cross across this face,
across the ear like this,
Christ's cross across this eye,
Christ's cross across this nose.

Christ's cross across this mouth.
Christ's cross across this throat.
Christ's cross across this back.
Christ's cross across this side.

Christ's cross cross this stomach,
(like this it is just fine).
Christ's cross across this gut,
Christ's cross across this spine.

Christ's cross across my arms
from my shoulders to my hands.
Christ's cross across my thighs.
Christ's cross across my legs.

Christ's cross with me before.
Christ's cross with me behind.
Christ's cross against each trouble
both on hillock and in glen.

Christ's cross east towards my face,
Christ's cross west towards sunset.
South and north, ceaselessly,
Christ's cross without delay.

Cros Chríst tar mo déta
   nám-tháir bét ná bine.
Cros Chríst tar mo gaile.
    Cros Chríst tar mo chride.

Cros Chríst súas fri fithnim.
    Cros Chríst sís fri talmain.
Ní thí olc ná urbaid
   dom chorp ná dom anmain.

Cros Chríst tar mo suide.
    Cros Chríst tar mo lige.
Cros Chríst mo bríg uile
   co roisem Ríg nime.

Cros Chríst tar mo muintir.
    Cros Chríst tar mo thempai.
Cros Chríst isin altar.
    Cros Chríst isin chentar.

O mullach mo baitse
   co ingin mo choise,
a Chríst, ar cach ngábad
   for snádad do chroise.

Co laithe mo báisse,
   ría ndol isin n-úirse,
cen ainis do-bérsa
   crois Críst tarsin ngnúisse.

Christ's cross across my teeth
lest to me come harm or hurt.
Christ's cross cross my stomach.
Christ's cross across my heart.

Christ's cross up to heaven's span.
Christ's cross down to earth.
Let no evil or harm
come to my body or soul.

Christ's cross cross my sitting,
Christ's cross cross my lying.
Christ's cross, my whole power
till we reach heaven's King.

Christ's cross across my church,
across my community.
Christ's cross in the next world.
Christ's cross in the present-day.

From the tip of my head
to the nail of my foot,
Christ, against each peril
the shelter of your cross.

Till the day of my death,
before going in this clay,
joyfully I will make
Christ's cross across my face.

translated from the Gaelic by Thomas Owen Clancy

EARL ROGNVALD KALI
(ST RONALD OF ORKNEY)

D. 1158

Sextán hef'k sénar
senn, ok topp í enni,
jarðar ellie firrðar
ormvangs, saman ganga.
Þat bórum vér vitni,
vestr, at hér sé flestar,
sjá liggr út við élum
ey, kollóttar meyjar.

MOCKERY OF IRISH MONKS
ON A WINDSWEPT ISLAND

I've seen sixteen women
at once with forelock on forehead,
stripped of the old age of the earth
of the serpent-field, walk together.
We bear that witness
that most girls here—
this isle lies against the storms
out west—are bald.

women with forelock on forehead: monks with Celtic tonsure, wearing habits which
seem feminine in Norse dress; *old age of the earth of the serpent-field*: *serpent-field*
'gold, on which dragons lie'; its *earth* 'gold-adorned woman'; her *old age* 'facial
hair' (i.e. the monks are clean-shaven); *bald* 'tonsured'.

translated from the Old Norse by Paul Bibire

MUIREADHACH ALBANACH

*fl.*1220

from *EISTIDH RIOMSA, A MUIRE MHOR*

Éistidh riomsa, a Mhuire mhór,
   do ghuidhe is liomsa badh lúdh;
do dhruim réd bhráthair ná bíodh,
   a Mháthair Ríogh duinn na ndúl.

*

Tusa Muire Máthair Dé,
   duine níor ghnáthaigh do ghnaoi,
ríghbhile arna roinn ar thrí,
   Rí fírnimhe id bhroinn do bhaoi.

Mise ar bhar n-aithnibh ar-aon,
   id dhaighthigh agus id dhún,
a anam, a Mhuire mhór,
   a ór buidhe, a abhall úr.

A bhiadh, a édach ar h'iocht,
   a chiabh ghégach mar an ngort.
A Mháthair, a Shiúr, a Shearc,
   stiúr go ceart an bráthair bocht.

*

A Mháthair Dé, dénam síodh,
   ósa ghlédhonn gné do chiabh,
ciúnaigh h'fhearg, a Mhoire mhór,
   a ór dearg i gcoire chriadh.

*

A Thríonóid, a Mhuire mhín,
   tuile gach glóir acht bhar nglóir;
a Cheathrair, caistidh rém dhuain,
   ní geabhthair uaibh aisgidh óir.

from O GREAT MARY, LISTEN TO ME

O great Mary, listen to me,
   praying to you should be my zeal;
on your brother turn not your back,
   Mother of the King of all.

        *

You, Mary, Mother of God,
   no-one ever knew your joy,
a royal tree divided in three,
   heaven's King was in your womb.

May I be guided by you both
   into your good house and your fort,
O great Mary, O my soul,
   O golden apple, apple-tree new-grown.

O food, O clothing to dispose,
   O tresses rippling as in a field,
O Mother, O Sister, O Love,
   your poor brother rightly steer.

        *

Mother of God, let's make peace,
   O great Mary, calm your rage,
whose tresses are most rich in hue,
   red gold ingot in a vessel of clay.

        *

O Trinity, O Mary mild,
   base is every glory but yours,
O Four in One, hear my lay,
   not from you a gift of gold.

A ÓghMhuire, a abhra dubh,
   a mhórmhuine, a ghardha geal,
tug, a cheann báidhe na mban,
   damh tar ceann mo náire neamh.

                    *

Dalta iongnadh dot ucht bhán,
   agus dot fhult fhionnghlan úr,
do Mhac agus t'Fhear ar-aon,
   a shlat shaor gheal ar do ghlún.

Do bhrú aníos ba lomlán leat,
   mar bhíos a bhronnlár 'san bhrioc,
an Coimdhe 's gan loighe lat,
   Mac Moire do-roighne riot.

                    *

Ná rabh bean acht tusa im thigh,
   gomadh tusa bhus fhear air,
na mná fallsa ad-chiú 's na cruidh,
   a bhfuil damhsa riú ná raibh.

Gan sbéis i gconaibh ná i gcrodh,
   ná i sgoraibh, a ghéis ghlan,
easbhaidh chorn cáich is a gcon,
   orm is a sgor mbláith 's a mban.

Tógaibh an malaigh nduibh dhúin,
   is an aghaidh mar fhuil laoigh,
tógaibh, go ros faicinn féin,
   an gcéibh ródaigh slaitfhinn saoir.

Tógaibh dhún an bonn 's an mbois,
   agus an cúl donn go ndeis,
'gus an súil n-ógcruinn ngéir nglais,
   réd chéibh dtais go bhfóbrainn feis.

O Virgin Mary, O dark brow,
    O great nurse, O garden gay,
of all women the most beloved,
    give me heaven despite my shame.

*

A miraculous child for your breast,
    for your pure fair fresh hair,
your Son and Father both
    on your knee, O noble bright branch.

Your belly rises up full
    like the belly of the trout;
without ever lying with you
    the Lord made Mary's Son.

*

No woman but you in my house –
    over it may you be host;
to false women may I not cleave,
    nor to what is mine to own.

With no regard for hounds or herds
    or studs of horses, O white swan,
or others' drinking-horns and stock,
    without their women and their dogs.

Raise to me your dark brow
    and your face like calf's blood,
raise, so that I might see
    the noble bright combed locks.

Raise to me your foot and palm
    and the rich heavy glossy head
and the young round sharp blue eye
    so with your soft tresses I may feast.

translated from the Classical Gaelic by Meg Bateman

ANONYMOUS

14TH CENTURY

from THE INCHCOLM ANTIPHONER

Os mutorum,
lux cecorum,
pes clausorum,
porrige
lapsis manum.
Firma vanum
et insanum
corrige.
O Columba, spes Scotorum,
nos tuorum meritorum,
interventu beatorum
fac consortes angelorum.
Alleluia.

MEMORIAL OF ST COLUMBA

Mouth of the dumb,
light of the blind,
foot of the lame,
to the fallen stretch out your hand.
Strengthen the senseless,
restore the mad.
O Columba, hope of Scots,
by your merits' mediation
make us companions
of the blessed angels.
Alleluia.

translated from the Latin by Gilbert Márkus

ROBERT HENRYSON

?1424–?1506

THE PREICHING OF THE SWALLOW

The hie prudence and wirking mervelous,	
The profound wit off God omnipotent,	
Is sa perfyte and sa ingenious,	so
Excellent far all mannis jugement:	
Forquhy to Him all thing is ay present,	Because
Rycht as it is or ony tyme sall be,	
Befoir the sicht off His Divinite.	

Thairfoir our saull with sensualitie	
So fetterit is in presoun corporall,	prison
We may not cleirlie understand nor se	
God as He is nor thingis celestiall;	
Our mirk and deidlie corps naturall	
Blindis the spirituall operatioun –	
Lyke as ane man wer bundin in presoun.	

In Metaphisik Aristotell sayis	
That mannis saull is lyke ane bakkis ee	soul; bat's eye
Quhilk lurkis still als lang as licht off day is,	which; as
And in the gloming cummis furth to fle;	fly
Hir ene ar waik, the sone scho may not se:	eyes; weak; sun; she; see
Sa is our saull with fantasie opprest	illusion
To knaw the thingis in nature manifest.	

For God is in His power infinite,	
And mannis saull is febill and over-small,	
Off understanding waik and unperfite,	imperfect
To comprehend Him That contenis all:	
Nane suld presume be ressoun naturall	
To seirche the secreitis off the Trinitie,	
Bot trow fermelie and lat all ressoun be.	believe; leave; by

Yit nevertheless we may haif knawlegeing
Off God Almychtie be His creatouris
That he is gude, fair, wyis and bening: *benign*
Exempill tak be thir jolie flouris
Rycht sweit off smell and plesant off colouris,
Sum grene, sum blew, sum purpour, quhyte and reid, *purple*
Thus distribute be gift off His Godheid.

The firmament payntit with sternis cleir, *stars*
From eist to west rolland in cirkill round, *rolling*
And everilk planet in his proper spheir,
In moving makand harmonie and sound;
The fyre, the air, the watter and the ground –
Till understand it is aneuch, iwis, *enough, indeed*
That God in all His werkis wittie is. *wise*

Luke weill the fische that swimmis in the se;
Luke weill in eirth all kynd off bestiall; *of beasts*
The foulis fair sa forcelie thay fle, *so strongly*
Scheddand the air with pennis grit and small; *sweeping through; wings*
Syne luke to man, that He maid last off all,
Lyke to His image and His similitude:
Be thir we knaw that God is fair and gude.

All creature He maid for the behufe *needs*
Off man and to his supportatioun
Into this eirth, baith under and abufe,
In number, wecht and dew proportioun;
The difference off tyme and ilk seasoun
Concorddand till our opurtunitie,
As daylie be experience we may se. *by*

The somer with his jolie mantill off grene,
With flouris fair furrit on everilk fent, *trimmed on every garment*
Quhilk Flora Goddes, off the flouris quene,
Hes to that lord as for his seasoun lent,
And Phebus with his goldin bemis gent *beautiful*
Hes purfellit and payntit plesandly *adorned*
With heit and moysture stilland from the sky. *falling*

Syne harvest hait, quhen Ceres that goddes
Hir barnis benit hes with abundance; *filled*
And Bachus, god off wyne, renewit hes
The tume pyipis in Italie and France *empty casks*
With wynis wicht and liquour off plesance; *strong; delight*
And Copia Temporis to fill hir horne, *the Season of Plenty*
That never wes full of quheit nor uther corne. *pale*

Syne wynter wan, quhen austerne Eolus, *stern Aeolus*
God off the wynd, with blastis boreall *northern*
The grene garment off somer glorious
Hes all to-rent and revin in pecis small;
Than flouris fair faidit with froist man fall, *Then, must*
And birdis blyith changit thair noitis sweit
In styll murning, neir slane with snaw and sleit. *nearly*

Thir dalis deip with dubbis drounit is, *pools*
Baith hill and holt heillit with frostis hair; *forest hidden*
And bewis bene laifit bair off blis *boughs are left bare*
Be wicket windis off the winter wair; *wild*
All wyld beistis than from the bentis bair *heaths*
Drawis for dreid unto thair dennis deip, *fear*
Coucheand for cauld in coifis thame to keip. *Cowering; hollows*

Syne cummis ver, quhen winter is away, *Then; spring*
The secretar off somer with his sell, *seal of office*
Quhen columbie up-keikis throw the clay, *columbine peeks out*
Quhilk fleit wes befoir with froistes fell; *frightened; cruel frosts*
The mavis and the merle beginnis to mell; *blackbird; mate*
The lark onloft with uther birdis haill *aloft*
Than drawis furth fra derne over doun and daill. *concealment*

That samin seasoun, into ane soft morning,
Rycht blyth that bitter blastis wer ago,
Unto the wod, to se the flouris spring
And heir the mavis sing and birdis mo, *other birds*
I passit furth, syne lukit to and fro
To se the soill that wes richt sessonabill,
Sappie and to resave all seidis abill. *receive*

Moving thus-gait grit myrth I tuke in mynd *this way*
Off lauboraris to se the besines – *labourers*
Sum makand dyke and sum the pleuch can wynd,
Sum sawand seidis fast frome place to place, *sowing seeds*
The harrowis hoppand in the saweris trace: *jerking; sower's track*
It wes grit joy to him that luifit corne *loved*
To se thame laubour baith at evin and morne.

And as I baid under ane bank full bene, *lingered, fair*
In hart gritlie rejosit off that sicht,
Unto ane hedge, under ane hawthorne grene,
Off small birdis thair come ane ferlie flicht, *remarkable flock*
And doun belyif can on the leifis licht *straightaway; did*
On everilk syde about me quhair I stude –
Rycht mervellous – ane mekill multitude.

Amang the quhilks ane swallow loud couth cry, *did*
On that hawthorne hie in the croip sittand:
'O ye birdis on bewis heir me by,
Ye sall weill knaw and wyislie understand
Quhair danger is or perrell appeirand;
It is grit wisedome to provyde befoir,
It to devoyd – for dreid it hurt yow moir.' *avoid; fear*

'Schir Swallow,' quod the lark agane and leuch, *said; laughed*
'Quhat have ye sene that causis yow to dreid?'
'Se ye yone churll,' quod scho, 'beyond yone pleuch *labourer*
Fast sawand hemp and gude linget seid? *sowing; linseed*
Yone lint will grow in lytill tyme indeid, *flax*
And thairoff will yone churll his nettis mak, *nets*
Under the quhilk he thinkis us to tak.

'Thairfoir I reid we pas quhen he is gone *advise*
At evin, and with our naillis scharp and small
Out off the eirth scraip we yone seid anone
And eit it up; for giff it growis, we sall
Have cause to weip heirefter ane and all:
Se we remeid thairfoir furth with instante –
Name leuius laedit quicquid praeuidimus ante. *Forewarned is forearmed*

43

'For clerkis sayis it is nocht sufficient   scholars
To considder that is befoir thyne ee;   eye
Bot prudence is ane inwart argument
That garris ane man provyde and foirse   causes; foresee
Quhat gude, quhat evill is liklie for to be,
Off everilk thing behald the fynall end
And swa fra perrell the better him defend.'

The lark lauchand the swallow thus couth scorne,   laughing; did
And said scho fischit lang befoir the net –
The barne is eith to busk that is unborne –   child; easy; dress
All growis nocht that in the ground is set –
The nek to stoup quhen it the straik sall get   blow
Is sone aneuch – deith on the fayest fall: those utterly fated
Thus scornit thay the swallow ane and all.

Despysing thus hir helthsum document,   warning
The foulis ferlie tuke thair flicht anone;   suddenly
Sum with ane bir thay braidit over the bent   a whirr; darted; heath
And sum agane ar to the grene wod gone:
Upon the land quhair I wes left allone
I tuke my club and hamewart couth I carie,
Swa ferliand as I had sene ane farie.   As amazed

Thus passit furth quhill June, that jolie tyde,   season
And seidis that wer sawin off beforne
Wer growin hie, that hairis mycht thame hyde,   hares
And als the quailye craikand in the corne;   croaking
I movit furth, betuix midday and morne,
Unto the hedge under the hawthorne grene
Quhair I befoir the said birdis had sene.

And as I stude, be aventure and cace,   by chance
The samin biridis as I haif said yow air –   same; earlier
I hoip because it wes thair hanting-place,   suppose; habitat
Mair off succour or yit mair solitair –   offering safety and seclusion
Thay lychtit doun: and quhen thay lychtit wair,   alighted
The swallow swyth put furth ane pietuous pyme,   immediately; cry
Said:'Wo is him can not bewar in tyme!

'O blind birdis and full off negligence,
Unmyndfull of your awin prosperitie,
Lift up your sicht and tak gude advertence!   *heed*
Luke to the lint that growis on yone le!   *flax; lea*
Yone is the thing I bad forsuith that we,   *indeed*
Quhill it wes seid, suld rute furth off the eird: *earth*
Now is it lint; now is it hie on breird.   *sprung up high*

'Go yit quhill it is tender and small
And pull it up – let it na mair incres:
My flesche growis, my bodie quaikis all;   *wrinkles in terror*
Thinkand on it I may not sleip in peis.'
Thay cryit all and bad the swallow ceis,
And said: 'Yone lint heirefter will do gude,
For linget is to lytill birdis fude.   *linseed*

'We think, quhen that yone lint-bollis ar ryip,   *flax-pods*
To mak us feist and fill us off the seid
Magre yone churll, and on it sing and pyip.'   *In spite of; twitter*
'Weill,' quod the swallow, 'freindes, hardilie beid: *so be it*
Do as ye will, bot certane sair I dreid;
Heirefter ye sall find als sour as sweit
Quhen ye ar speldit on yone carlis speit.   *spreadeagled; man's spit*

'The awner off yone lint ane fouler is,   *owner*
Richt cautelous and full off subteltie;   *sly*
His pray full sendill-tymis will he mis   *seldom*
Bot giff we birdis all the warrer be;   *if; more careful*
Full mony off our kin he hes gart de,   *caused to die*
And thocht it bot ane sport to spill thair blude:
God keip me fra him, and the Halie Rude!'

Thir small birdis haveand bot lytill thocht   *These*
Off perrell that mycht fall be aventure,
The counsell off the swallow set at nocht,
Bot tuke thair flicht and furth togidder fure;   *went*
Sum to the wode, sum markit to the mure.   *went*
I tuke my staff quhen this wes said and done,
And walkit hame, for it drew neir the none.

The lynt ryipit, the carll pullit the lyne,   *ripersed, flax-stalks*
Rippillit the bollis and in beitis set,   *removed; seeds; small bundles*
It steipit in the burne and dryit syne,
And with ane bittill knokkit it and bet,   *bettle (tool); beat*
Syne swingillit it weill and hekkillit in the flet;   *scutched; dressed it indoors*
His wyfe it span and twynit it into threid,
Off quhilk the fowlar nettis maid indeid.

The wynter come, the wickit wind can blaw;
The woddis grene wer wallowit with the weit;
Baith firth and fell with froistys wer maid faw,   *uneven*
Slonkis and slaik maid slidderie with the sleit: *Hollows and dells*
The foulis fair for falt thay fell off feit;   *went in fear of falling*
On bewis bair it wes nar bute to byde,   *no help*
Bot hyit unto housis thame to hyde.   *hurried*

Sum in the barn, sum in the stak off corne
Thair lugeing tuke and maid thair residence;   *lodging*
The fowlar saw, and grit aithis hes sworne   *oaths*
Thay suld be tane trewlie for thair expence:
His nettis hes he set with diligence,
And in the snaw he schulit hes ane plane,   *cleared; space*
And heillit it all over with calf agane.   *covered; chaff*

Thir small birdis seand the calff wes glaid;   *seeing*
Trowand it had bene corne they lychtit doun;   *Believing*
Bot of the nettis na presume they had,   *suspicion*
Nor of the fowlaris fals intentioun;
To scraip and seik thair meit thay maide thame boun: *got ready*
The swallow on ane lytill branche neir by,
Dreiddand for gyle, thus loud on thame couth cry: *Fearing a trick*

'Into that calf scraip quhill your naillis bleid;
Thair is na corne – ye laubour all in vane;
Trow ye yone churll for pietie will yow feid?
Na, na! He hes it heir layit for ane trane;
Remove I reid, or ellis ye will be slane;   *Get out*
His nettis he hes set full prively,
Reddie to draw; in tyme be war forthy.'   *beware therefore*

Grit fule is he that puttis in dangeir
His lyfe, his honour, for ane thing off nocht;
Grit fule is he that will not glaidle heir
Counsall in tyme, quhill it availl him nocht;
Grit fule is he that hes na thing in thocht
Bot thing present – and efter quhat may fall
Nor off the end hes na memoriall.

Thir small birdis for hunger famischit neir,
Full besie scraipand for to seik thair fude,   *busy scraping*
The counsall off the swallow wald not heir –
Suppois thair laubour dyd thame lytill gude.
Quhen scho thair fulische hartis understude
Sa indurate, up in ane tre scho flew;   *obdurate*
With that this churll over thame his nettis drew.

Allace, it wes grit hartsair for to se   *heartache*
That bludie bowcheour beit thay birdis doun,   *butcher*
And for till heir, quhen thay wist weill to de,   *realised they would die*
Thair cairfull sang and lamentatioun!   *pained*
Sum with ane staf he straik to eirth on swoun,
Off sum the heid he straik, off sum he brak the crag, *neck*
Sum half on lyfe he stoppit in his bag.   *half alive*

And quhen the swallow saw that thay wer deid,
'Lo,' quod scho, 'thus it happinnis mony syis   *many a time*
On thame that will not tak counsall nor reid   *advice*
Off prudent men or clerkis that ar wyis;
This grit perrell I tauld thame mair than thryis;
Now ar thay deid and wo is me thairfoir!'
Scho tuke hir flicht, bot I hir saw no moir.

Moralitas
Lo, worthie folk, Esope that nobill clerk,   *Aesop*
Ane poet worthie to be lawreate,
Quhen that he waikit from mair autentik werk,   *was free from; important*
With uther ma this foirsaid fabill wrate,   *others too*
Quhilk at this tyme may well be applicate   *applicable*
To gude morall edificatioun,

47

Haifand ane sentence according to ressoun. — Having a valid signification
This carll and bond of gentrice spoliate, — husbandman bereft of kindness
Sawand this calf thir small birdis to sla,
It is the feind, quhilk fra the angelike state
Exylit is as fals apostata; — apostate
Quhilk day and nycht weryis not for to ga
Sawand poysoun in mony wickit thocht
In mannis saull, quhilk Christ full deir hes bocht.

And quhen the saull as seid into the eird
Gevis consent unto delectioun, — to indulging
The wickit thocht beginnis for to breird — sprout
In deidlie sin – quhilk is dampnatioun;
Ressoun is blindit with affectioun,
And carnall lust gouis full grene and gay,
Throw conseutude hantit from day to day. — custom practised

Proceding furth be use and consuetude, — by custom
The sin ryipis, and schame is set onsyde; — ripens
The feynd plettis his nettis scharp and rude, — weaves
And under plesance previlie dois hyde; — secretly
Syne on the feild he sawis calf full wyde –
Quhilk is bot tume and verray vanitie — empty; actual
Of fleschlie lust and vaine prosperitie.

Thir hungrie birdis wretchis we may call, — These
Ay scraipand in this warldis vane plesance,
Greddie to gadder gudis temporall, — Greedy
Quhilk as the calf ar tume without substance,
Lytill of availl and full of variance,
Lyke to the mow befoir the face of wind — dust
Quhiskis away and makis wretchis blind.

This swallow quhilk eschaipit is the snair
The halie preichour weill may signifie,
Exhortand folk to walk and ay be wair
Fra nettis of our wickit enemie –
Quha sleipis not, bot ever is reddie,
Quhen wretchis in this warld calf dois scraip,

To draw his net than thay may not eschaip.
Allace, quhat cair, quhat weiping is and wo
Quhen saull and bodie departit ar in twane!
The bodie to the wormis keitching go,   abode
The saull to fyre, to everlestand pane.
Quhat helpis than this calf, thir gudis vane,   these possessions
Quhen thow art put in Luceferis bag
And brocht to hell and hangit be the crag?   neck

Thir hid nettis for to persave and se,   perceive
This sarie calf wyislie to undestand,
Best is bewar in maist propseritie;
For in this warld thair is na thing lestand;   lasting
Is na man wait how lang his stait will stand,   No man knows
His lyfe will lest, nor how that he sall end
Efter his deith, nor quhidder he sall wend.   go

Pray we thairfoir quhill we ar in this lyfe
For four thingis: the first, fra sin remufe;
The secund is fra all weir and stryfe;   war
The third is perfite cheritie and lufe;
The feird thing is – and maist for oure behufe –   fourth; needs
That is in blis with angellis to be fallow.   companion
And thus endis the preiching of the swallow.

49

WILLIAM DUNBAR
?1456–?1513

RORATE CELI DESUPER

Rorate, celi desuper!	Pour down, heavens, dew from above
Hevins, distill your balmy schouris,	
For now is rissin the brycht day ster	
Fro the ros, Mary, flour of flouris.	rose
The cleir sone quhome no clud devouris,	
Surminting Phebus in the est,	
Is cumin of his hevinly touris	Has come from; towers
Et nobis puer natus est.	And unto us a child is born
Archangellis, angellis and dompnationis,	dominations
Tronis, potestatis and marteiris seir,	Thrones; powers; many
And all ye hevinly operationis,	
Ster, planeit, firmament and speir,	sphere
Fyre, erd, air and watter cleir,	
To him gife loving, most and lest,	
That come into so meik maneir	in so humble a
Et nobis puer natus est.	
Synarris, be glaid and pennance do	
And thank your makar hairtfully,	
For he that ye mycht nocht cum to	
To yow is cumin full humly,	in full humility
Your saulis with his blud to by	
And lous yow of the feindis arrest,	free you from
And only of his awin mercy,	own
Pro nobis puer natus est.	For us
All clergy, do to him inclyne	
And bow unto that barne benyng,	child of grace
And do your observance devyne	
To him that is of kingis king.	
Ensence his altar, reid and sing	Burn incense at
In haly kirk with mynd degest,	solemn

Him honouring attour all thing, *beyond*
Qui nobis puer natus est. *who*

Celestiall fowlis in the are,
Sing with your nottis upoun hicht, *notes on high*
In firthis and in forrestis fair
By myrthfull now at all your mycht,
For passit is your dully nycht;
Aurora hes the cluddis perst, *Dawn; pierced*
The son is rissin with glaidsum lycht
Et nobis puer natus est. *And*

Now spring up, flouris, fra the rute,
Revert yow upwart naturaly, *spring up once more*
In honour of the blissit frute
That rais up fro the rose, Mary:
Lay out your levis lustely,
Fro deid tak lyfe now at the lest,
In wirschip of that prince wirthy,
Qui nobis puer natus est.

Syng, hevin imperiall, most of hicht, *highest*
Regions of air mak armony.
All fishe in flud and foull of flicht
Be myrthfull and mak melody.
All *Gloria in excelsis* cry, *Glory in the highest*
Hevin, erd, se, man, bird and best:
He that is crownit abone the sky *above*
Pro nobis puer natus est!

DONE IS A BATTELL ON THE DRAGON BLAK

Done is a battell on the dragon blak;	against
Our campioun Chryst confoundit hes his force;	champion; has overthrown his power
The yettis of hell ar brokin with a crak,	gates
The signe triumphall rasit of the croce.	standard; raised; cross
The divillis trymmillis with hiddous voce,	devils tremble; voice
The saulis ar borrowit and to the bliss can go,	souls; redeemed
Chryst with his blud our ransonis dois indoce:	ransoms; endorse
Surrexit Dominus de sepulchro.	The Lord is risen from the tomb
Dungin is the deidly dragon Lucifer,	beaten
The crewall serpent with the mortall stang,	cruel; sting
The auld kene tegir with his teith on char	fierce tiger; teeth bared
Quhilk in a wait hes lyne for us so lang,	which; ambush; lain
Thinking to grip us in his clowis strang.	claws
The mercifuil lord waid nocht that it wer so;	did not wish
He maid him for to felye of that fang:	lose that prey
Surrexit Dominus de sepulchro.	
He for our saik that sufferit to be slane	
And lyk a lamb in sacrifice wes dicht	made ready
Is lyk a lyone rissin up agane	
And as gyane raxit him on hicht.	giant stretched himself on high
Sprungin is Aurora radius and bricht;	risen is Dawn, radiant
On loft is gone the glorious Appollo;	into the heavens; the sun
The blisfull day depairtit fro the nycht:	separated from
Surrexit Dominus de sepulchro.	
The grit victour agane is rissin on hicht	great
That for our querrell to the deth wes woundit.	cause
The sone that wox all paill now schynis bricht,	sun, grew
And, dirknes clerit, our fayth is now refoundit.	
The knell of mercy fra the hevin is soundit,	
The Cristin ar deliverit of thair wo;	Christians

The Jowis and thair errour ar confoundit: Jews
Surrexit Dominus de sepulchro.

The fo is chasit, the batteil is done ceis;   ended
The presone brokin, the jevellouris fleit and flemit;   gaolers frightened away
The weir is gon, confermit is the peis,   war; ended
The fetteris lowsit and the dungeoun temit;   fetters unbound; emptied
The ransoun maid, the presoneris redemit;   prisoners redeemed
The feild is win, ourcumin is the fo,   field is won
Dispulit of the tresur that he yemit: guarded
Surrexit Dominus de sepulchro.

HALE, STERNE SUPERNE

Hale, sterne superne, hale, in eterne,
star on high; eternity
   In Godis sicht to schyne:
Lucerne in derne for to discerne,
lantern; darkness by which to see
   Be glory and grace devyne!
By
Hodiern, modern, sempitern,
for this day and this age and forever
   Angelicall regyne,
queen of angels
Our tern inferne for to dispern,
darkness; hellish; disperse
   Helpe, rialest roysne
most royal rose
     Ave Maria, gracia plena:
Hail Mary, full of grace
   Haile, fresche floure femynyne;
fresh flower womanly
Yerne us guberne, virgin matern,
diligently; govern; mother
   Of reuth baith rute and ryne.
pity; root and bush

Haile, yhyng benyng fresche flurising,
young; gentle; blossoming
   Haile, Alphais habitakle!
of Alpha; dwelling place
Thy dyng ofspring maid us to syng
worthy
   Befor his tabernakle.
All thing maling we doune thring
malign; thrust down
   Be sicht of his signakle,
sign
Quhilk king us bring unto his ryng
which; kingdom
   Fro dethis dirk umbrakle.
from death's dark shadow
     Ave Maria, gracia plena:
   Haile, moder and maide but makle;
mother; without stain
Bricht syng, gladyng our languissing
sign bringing joy to our sorrow
   Be micht of thi mirakle.
power

Haile, bricht be sicht in hevyn on hicht,
bright to look upon; heaven on high
   Haile, day-sterne orientale!
day-star of the east
Our licht most richt in clud of nycht,
light; true; cloud; night
   Our dirknes for to scale.
darkness to disperse
Hale, wicht in ficht, puttar to flicht
valiant in fight
   Of fendis in battale!
fiends
Haile, plicht but sicht, hale, mekle of mycht,
unclear; unseen; great in power

54

Haile, glorious virgin, hale!
   Ave Maria, gracia plena:
Haile, gentill nychttingale,   *gracious nightingale*
Way stricht, cler dicht, to wilsome wicht   *straight; clearly marked*
   That irke bene in travale.   *are weary in journeying*

Hale, qwene serene, hale, most amene,   *kindly*
   Haile, hevinlie hie empyrs!   *high empress*
Haile, schene, unseyne with carnale eyne,   *beautiful one; unseen; eyes*
   Haile, ros of paradys!
Haile, clene bedene ay till conteyne,   *wholly pure; ever to continue*
   Haile, fair fresche floure-de-lyce,   *lily*
Haile, grene daseyne, haile fro the splene,   *fresh daisy; from the heart*
   Of Jesu genitrice!   *begetter*
   Ave Maria, gracia plena:
   Thow baire the prince of prys,   *bore; glory*
Our teyne to meyne and ga betweyne,   *affliction; mediate*
   As humile oratrice.   *humble intercessor*

Haile, more decore than of before   *beautiful*
   And swetar be sic sevyne!   *sweeter by seven such*
Our glore forlore for to restore   *glory gone*
   Sen thow art quene of hevyn.   *since*
Memore of sore, stern in aurore,   *mindful of our grief; star at dawn*
   Lovit with angellis stevyne,   *praised by angels' voices*
Implore, adore, thow indeflore,   *virgin*
   To mak our oddis evyne!   *forgive our sins*
   Ave Maria, gracia plena:
   With lovingis lowde ellevyn   *praises; eleven*
Quhill store and hore my youth devore,   *adversity; old age; devour*
   Thy name I sall ay nevyne.   *shall; name*

Empryce of prys, imperatrice,   *empress*
   Bricht polist precious stane,   *polished*
Victrice of vyce, hie genitrice   *conqueror*
   Of Jesu lord soverayne,
Our wys pavys fro enemys   *wise; shield*
   Agane the feyndis trayne,   *against the fiend's deception*

Oratrice, mediatrice, salvatrice,   *mediator, saviour*
  To God gret suffragane!   *great assistant*
    Ave Maria, gracia plena;
  Haile, sterne meridiane,   *star of midday*
Spyce, flour-de-lice of paradys,   *spice*
  That baire the gloryus grayne.   *seed*

Imperiall wall, place palestrall   *magnificent palace*
  Of peirles pulcritud,   *peerless beauty*
Tryumphale hall, hie trone regall   *royal throne*
  Of Godis celsitud!   *God's majesty*
Hospitall riall, the lord of all   *royal refuge*
  Thy closet did include,   *chamber; enclose*
Bricht ball cristall, ros virginall,   *globe; crystal*
  Fulfillit of angell fude,   *filled with the food of angels*
    Ave Maria, gracia plena:
  Thy birth has with his blude   *child; blood*
Fra fall mortall originall   *from the first fall which brought death*
  Us raunsound on the rude.   *ransomed; cross*

THE DREGY OF DUNBAR

We that ar heir in hevins glory,
To yow that ar in purgatory,
Commendis us on our hairtly wyis;
I mene we folk in parradyis,
In Edinburch with all mirrines,
To yow of Strivilling in distres,   Stirling
Quhair nowdir plesance nor delyt is,   neither
For pety this epistell wrytis.
O ! ye heremeitis and hankersaidilis,   anchorites
That takis your pennance at your tablis,
And eitis nocht meit restorative,
Nor drynkis no wyn confortative,
Nor aill bot that is thyn and small,
With few coursis into your hall,
But cumpany of lordis and knychtis,   without
Or ony uder gudly wichtis,
Solitar walkand your allone,   walking alone
Seing no thing bot stok and stone;   lifeless things
Out of your panefull purgatory,
To bring yow to the blis and glory
Off Edinburgh, the mirry toun,
We sall begyn ane cairfull soun,
Ane dergy devoit and meik,   dirge
The Lord of blis doing beseik
Yow to delyver out of your noy,   annoyance
And bring yow sone to Edinburgh joy,
For to be mirry amang us;
And sa the dergy begynis thus.

   Lectio prima.
The Fader, the Sone, and Haly Gaist,
The mirthfull Mary virgene chaist,
Of angellis all the ordouris nyne,

And all the hevinly court devyne,
Sone bring yow fra the pyne and wo   pain
Of Strivilling, every court manis fo,
Agane to Edinburghis joy and blis,
Quhair wirschep, welth, and weilfar is,
Pley, plesance, and eik honesty: also
Say ye amen for cheritie.

Responsio, Tu autem Domine.
Tak consolatioun In your pane,
In tribulatioun Tak consolatioun,
Out of vexatioun Cum hame agane,
Tak consolatioun In your pane.

Iube Domine benedicere.
Oute of distress of Strivilling toun
To Edinburch blis, God mak yow boun.   ready

Lectio secunda.
Patriarchis, profeitis, and appostillis deir,
Confessouris, virgynis, and marteris cleir,
And all the saitt celestiall,   assembly
Devotely we upoun thame call,
That sone out of your panis fell,   awful pains
Ye may in hevin heir with us dwell,
To eit swan, cran, pertrik, and plever,   crane, partridge
And every fische that swymis in rever;
To drynk with us the new fresche wyne,
That grew upoun the rever of Ryne,
Fresche fragrant clairettis out of France,
Of Angers and of Orliance,
With mony ane cours of grit dyntie: gourmet's delight
Say ye amen for cheritie.

Responsorium, Tu autem Domine.
God and Sanct Jeill Heir yow convoy   St Giles; convey
Baith sone and weill, God and Sanct Jeill
To sonce and seill, Solace and joy,   plenty and prosperity
God and sanct Geill Heir yow convoy.

Iube Domine benedicere.
Out of Strivilling panis fell,   *pains; cruel*
In Edinburch ioy sone mot ye dwell.   *may*

Lectio tertia
We pray to all the Sanctis of hevin,
That ar aboif the sterris sevin,
Yow to deliver out of your pennance,
That ye may sone play, sing, and dance
Heir in to Edinburch and mak gude cheir,
Quhair welth and weilfair is but weir;   *without war*
And I that dois your panis discryve   *describe*
Thinkis for to vissy yow belyve;   *visit; soon*
Nocht in desert with yow to dwell,
Bot as the angell Sanct Gabriell
Dois go betwene fra hevinis glory
To thame that ar in purgatory,
And in thair tribulatioun
To gif thame consolatioun,
And schaw thame quhen thair panis ar past
They sall till hevin cum at last;
And how nane servis to haif sweitnes
That nevir taistit bittirnes,
And thairfoir how suld ye considdir
Of Edinburch bliss, quhen ye cum hiddir,
Bot gif ye taistit had befoir
Of Strivilling toun the panis soir;
And thairfoir tak in patience
Your pennance and your abstinence,
And ye sall cum, or Yule begyn,   *before*
Into the bliss that we ar in;
Quhilk grant the glorious Trinitie!
Say ye amen for cheritie.

Responsorium.
Cum hame and dwell No moir in Strivilling;
Frome hiddous hell Cum hame and dwell,
Quhair fische to sell Is non bot spirling;   *spratlike*
Cum hame and dwell No moir in Strvilling.

Et ne nos inducas in temptationem de Strivilling:
Sed libera nos a malo illius.
Requiem Edinburgi dona eiis, Domine,
Et lux ipsius luceat eiis.
A porta tristitie de Strivilling,
Erue, Domine, animas et corpora eorum.
Credo gustare statim vinum Edinburgi,
In villa viventium.
Requiescant Edinburgi. Amen.

Deus qui iustos et corde humiles
Ex omni eorum tribulatione liberare dignatus es,
Libera famulos tuos apud villam de Stirling versantes
A penis et tristitiis eiusdem,
Et ad Edinburgi gaudia eos perducas,
Ut requiescat Strivilling. Amen.

NOTE ON 'THE DREGY OF DUNBAR'

The *dregy* or *dirige* was named after the opening antiphon of the Office of the Dead, read at burial or memorial services: *Dirige, Deus meus, in conspectu tuo viam meam* (Direct my path, o God, in Thy sight.' Dunbar partly follows its division into three lessons and their responses in shortened form: *Tu autem, domine* for 'And may you also, Lord, have mercy on us' and *Iube, domine* for 'Send us your blessing, Lord.'

The Latin in the final section opens with a parody of The Lord's Prayer, and proceeds to an ironic version of the conclusion of Lauds, sung after the Matins of the Dead:
'And lead us not into the temptation of Stirling, but deliver us from its evil. The peace of Edinburgh grant unto them, o Lord, and let its light shine upon them. Out of the gates of sadness in Stirling bring forth, O Lord, their bodies and their souls. I know that I shall taste the wine of Edinburgh in the habitation of the living. May they shortly rest in peace in Edinburgh. Amen.

'O God, who art pleased to set free the just and humble of heart from their sufferings, liberate now thy servants who dwell in the town of Stirling from the pain and sorrows of that place, and lead them happily to the joys of Edinburgh. Amen.'

GAVIN DOUGLAS

c.1474–1522

CONSCIENCE

Quhen halie kirk first flurist in youthheid,	the time of youth
Prelatis wer chosin of all perfectioun;	
Off conscience than the brydill had to leid,	bridle
And conscience maid the hale electioun.	choice
Syn eftir that come schrewit correctioun,	cursed
And thocht that conscience had our large ane weid,	too big a coat
And of his habite out cuttit thay ane skreid.	shred
And fra conscience the *con* thay clip away,	
And maid of conscience *science* and a na mair;	learning
Bot yit the kirk stude weill full mony day,	
For it wes rewlit be mene of wit and layre.	knowledge
Sayn eftir that *sciens* began to payr,	grow worse
And thocht at *sciens* was our lang ane iaip.	too long a joke
The *sci* away fast can thay rub and scraip.	did
And fra *scie* of *science* wes adew,	parted
Than left thai nocht bot this sillab *ens*,	
Quhilk in our language singnifies that schrew,	evil creature
Riches and geir, that gart all grace go hens;	made
For *sciens* both and faythfull conscience	
So corruptit ar with this warldis gude	
That falset ioukis in everie clerkis hude.	falsehood lodges
O hungerie *ens*, cursit with caris calde!	cold
All kynd of folk constrenis thow to wirk:	
For the that theif Iudas his maister sald,	thee; sold
For the Symon infectit halie kirk.	
To poysoun Iustis thow dois never irk.	
Thow fals *ens*, go hens, thow monsture peralous!	
God send defens with conscience in till ws.	unto us

GEORGE BUCHANAN

1506–1582

IOANNIS CALVINI EPICEDIUM

Si quis erit nullos superesse a funere manes
qui putet, aut si forte putet, sic vivit ut Orcum
speret et aeternas Stygio sub gurgite poenas,
is merito sua fata fleat, sua funera ploret
vivus, et ad caros luctum transmittat amicos.
at nos, invitis quamquam sis raptus amicis
ante diem, magnis quamvis inviderit ausis
mors, te flere nefas, Calvine, et funera vanae
ludibrio pompae et miseris onerare querelis.
liber enim curis, terrenae et pondere molis,
astra tenes, propiusque Deo, quem mente colebas,
nunc frueris, puroque vides in lumine purum
lumen, et infusi satiatus numinis haustum
exigis aeternam sine sollicitudine vitam;
quam neque deiciunt luctus nec tollit inani
ebria laetitia spes exanimantve timores,
quaeque animo offundit morbi contagia corpus.
hanc ego, quae curis te lux exemit acerbis,
natalem iure appellem, qua raptus in astra
in patriam remeas, et post fastidia duri
exilii, mortis iam mens secura secundae,
fortunae imperio maior, primordia longae
ingreditur vitae. nam ceu per corporis artus
cum subiit animus, pigrae vegetatque movetque
molis onus, funditque agilem per membra vigorem;
cum fugit, exanimum iacet immotumque cadaver,
nec quicquam est luteae nisi putris fabrica massae:

ELEGY ON JEAN CALVIN

Some may think life goes out like snuff: finis.
Other imagine spirits surviving but to hell
With that: literally: they scorn the pains to come,
They live with the roaring Styx on their shoulder.
Both would have a case for fears and tears,
Both ought to shudder and make others shudder.
But to us, Calvin, although you have been filched
In your mid-fifties from your helpless friends,
As if death had seen enough of your achievements,
Weeping and breast-beating are totally inappropriate,
All the oppression of a second burial,
Lachrymose lying verbal *pompes funèbres*.
For the dead weight of your body with its apprehensions
Has left you, you are beyond the stars, you nudge
God, you enjoy the one your mind adored,
You see pure light within pure light, you drink
Divinity poured brimming into you,
Your life has become an everlasting thing
Unanxious, impervious to empty-headed joys
Or devastating fears or the hammer of grief
Or the cancer of disease creeping from body to soul.
As for me, I call that morning which released you
From bitterest cares a very birthday: snatched
To the stars, you re-entered your old homeland,
You left a repellent exile behind, your mind
Scoffs at any second death, rules the supposed
Rule of fate, steps into the vista
Of an immeasurable life. Consider:
As the soul slides through the limbs of the body
At its awakening, impatient with the deadweight flesh,
Jetting its invigoration from head to heel,
So when it leaves, it leaves a stiffening shell
Without breath, leaves nothing but the crumbling

sic animi Deus est animus, quo si caret, atris
obruitur tenebris, specieque illusus inani
fallaces rectique bonique amplectitur umbras.
ast ubi divini concepit numinis haustum,
diffugiunt tenebrae simulacraque vana facessunt,
nudaque se veri facies in luce videndam
exhibet aeterna, quam nullo vespere claudit
saepta caput furvis nox importuna tenebris.
hunc ergo in portum caelo plaudente receptus
tu licet in placida tranquillus pace quiescas,
non tamen omnino potuit mors invida totum
tollere Calvinum terris: aeterna manebunt
ingenii monumenta tui, et livoris iniqui
languida paullatim cum flamma resederit, omnes,
religio qua pura nitet, se fundet in oras
fama tui, ut nuper falso te nomine Clemens,
te Pauli duo, flagitiis et fraude gemelli,
te Iuli timuit rabies, te nobilis una
fraterna impietate Pius: sic nominis umbram
ingeniique tui effigiem post fata timebit
vana superstitio; quique olim in sede Quirini
triste furens flammaque minax ferroque tyrannus
transtulit inferni cuncta in se munia regni,
imperio Pluto, foedis Harpyia rapinis,
Eumenis igne, Charon naulo, triplicique corona
Cerberus, immissi stupefactus lumine veri,
terrificoque tuae deiectus fulmine linguae,
transferet infernas in se post funera poenas:
inter aquas sitiens, referens revolubile saxum,

Of a foul mound of clay: and is that all, all?
But God is the soul of the soul. God absent,
The soul is wrapped in deepest darkness, prey
To mocks and fleers and prestidigitations,
Thinking shadows bright and evil good.
But give it its one great draught of godhead
And the dark dissolves and flickering phantoms go
And the naked face of truth lunges forward
In its eternal light, eternal day,
Resisting every twilight, every shadow
Cruel muffling night might try to bring.
You, Calvin, have earned and reached your haven
Where you rest in peace and calm, but grudging death
Could not but leave some part of you on the earth.
That part is the monuments, untarnishable,
Of your genius, and once the crackle and flash
Of mean-spirited envy has gone dark and dead,
You fame will ripple out to every shore
Where the true faith shines.
                              Where it does not,
Grey superstition will shiver at the mention
Of your ghostly name, at the gleam of the mask
Of your genius, just as in recent times
You struck fear into a wretched brace of mitres:
Clement the Seventh, total stranger to clemency,
Paul the Third, that famous pederast,
Paul the Fourth, more straightforward in viciousness,
Julius the Third, driven raging mad,
Pius the Fourth, from a brotherhood of impiety.
The usurper of the seat of good old Romulus,
The tyrant threatening stake and sword, the assumptor
Of the crown of hell, would-be Pluto of power,
Harpy of godly theft, Fury of heretic flames,
Charon ferrying indulgences, Carberus barking
Under his triple tiara, will be dazzled blind
By the light of invading truth and overthrown
By the thunder and terror of your tongue, and in the end
Will guarantee his own infernal punishments:
Parched with thirst as waters welter round him,

vulturibus iecur exesus, cava dolia lymphis
frustra implens, Ixioneum distentus in orbem.

Pushing back the stone that will not stay there,
Pierced by beaks of liver-riving vultures,
Pouring liquids into sievelike pitchers,
Prostrated on a turning wheel of eternal fire.

translated from the Latin by Edwin Morgan

HYMNUS IN CHRISTI ASCENSIONEM

Io triumphe, Eccelsia,
iam victor hostium tuus
dux templa scandit aetheris,
adversa patri vulnera
it et coronam ostendere,
qualis redit de proelio
tabo decoro sordidus.
demissa nubes se explicat
sub Imperatoris pedes;
reclusa caeli ianua
invitat omnem exercitum;
vox Angelorum cantibus
venire Regem nuntiat;
aether nitescit gaudio,
timore pallent Tartara,
mundus stupet spectaculo
suspensus ante incognito;
Mors victa flet, spes praemii
levat labores militum.
cum Patre Proles unica,
et ex utroque Spiritus,
adeste sic pugnantibus
ut sint triumphi compotes.

FOR CHRIST'S ASCENSION

Heads back and cheer, you crowds of faithful souls!
The enemy's defeated and your hero
Climbs high up to the bailey gates of Heaven,
Like any warrior badged with dust and blood
Straight from the fight, to let his Father hear
What the good wounds on head and torso say.
Clouds like a drawbridge drop to take his stride,
Heaven's gates swing open wide for him and all
His army to pass through, with songs of angels
Heralding their entry. Heaven shines; Hell pales.
The world, drymouthed, watches Death's tears fall.
Now veterans reckon up their just rewards:
Prince, with your Heavenly Father's strength and Spirit,
Help us footsoldiers find room at your feast.

translated from the Latin by James McGonigal

IN IULIUM II PONTIFICEM

Genua cui patrem, genitricem Graecia, partum
   pontus et unda dedit, num bonus esse potes?
fallaces Ligures, et mendax Graecia, ponto
   nulla fides. in te singula solus habes.

OAN PAIP J 2

Daddy a Genoan, Mammy a Greek,
Yer a fushionless son o' the sea.   no good
Tallies, Greeks, an the Med are full o lyin cheek.   Italians
You, pal, are full o aa three.

Scots version of the Latin by Robert Crawford

ATHAIRNE Mac EOGHAIN

fl. c. **1558**

IS MAIRG DO-NI UAILLE AS OIGE

Is mairg do-ní uaille as óige,
    as iasachd deilbhe, a deirc ghlais,
a cruth séimh, a suidhe aoibhinn,
    a céibh bhuidhe chaoimhfhinn chais.

Dá dtiobhradh Dia dhuit, a dhuine,
    – daoine meallta mheallas siad –
déad mar an gcuip is taobh taislim,
    duit a-raon is aisling iad.

Duille an bheatha bhudh bláth bréige,
    baoghal an chuirp cur rén íoc,
ná déan uaill fa cheann na cruinne,
    gearr go buain a duille dhíot.

Dá bhfuighe fós, ni fáth díomais,
    duille an bheatha nach buan seal,
cuimhnigh réd ré dála an duine,
    gurb é námha an uile fhear.

Cuimhnigh ar chnuasach na ngráineog,
    guais dod thionól bheith mar bhíd,
ní bhfuil achd pian ann dot anmuin,
    ná iarr barr don talmhuin tríd.

Ubhall ar gach bior dá mbearaibh
    beirid don taobh dá dtéid siad,
ar ndul ón choill fhádbhuig fhéarchruinn
    fágbhuid fa bhroinn éanphuill iad.

WOE TO THE ONE WHO TAKES PRIDE IN YOUTH

Woe to the one who takes pride in youth,
in a borrowed form, in a grey eye,
in a graceful figure, in comely face,
in shining, soft, yellow, curling locks.

If God should have given to *you*, oh man,
– only deluded people do they deceive –
teeth like foam and a slender waist,
to you alone they are a dream.

The petals of life are false blossom,
it is dangerous for the body to aim to buy them,
do not take pride on account of the world,
all too soon will you be stripped of its leaves.

If even so you gain – no cause for pride –
the petals of life that do not last,
always keep in mind the state of man
that makes the world a foe to every one.

Remember the hoarding of hedgehogs,
dangerous for your garnering to be as they,
it will only entail your soul in pain,
from it do not expect the fruit of the earth.

With an apple on the tip of every spine
they carry them to a special place,
leaving the soft-turfed smooth-grassed wood
they leave them buried in a hole.

Fúigfighthear leat loise an t-saoghail
   mar so, a chuirp, ag cosg do mhian,
fa bhéal na h-uaighe an t-anam,
   sgéal as truaighe, a chalann chriadh.

Gach bhfuarais d'ór agus d'ionnmhus,
   d'eachaibh 's do bhuaibh, giodh beart chlé,
ní léigfighthear lat díbh, a dhuine,
   achd brat lín don chruinne ché.

Ainbhfios an chuirp cuid da uabhar,
   eagal dúinn a dhul ós aird,
daor re dhaoirmheas uaill na h-óige,
   buain re h-aoibhneas móide is mairg.

Thus will the fox of the world find you
oh body, resist spending your desires,
the soul at the mouth of the cave,
the most wretched of stories, oh body of clay.

All you have acquired of gold and wealth,
of horses and cows, though it were a wicked deed,
you will not be allowed any of them with you
but a linen shroud of this world, O man.

The body's ignorance is part of its pride,
our fear to go on up,
pride of youth is an ignoble thing to be despised
to be concerned with happiness is all the greater woe.

translated from the Classical Gaelic by Meg Bateman

JAMES, JOHN AND ROBERT WEDDERBURN

D.1553, 1556, 1557

from THE GUDE AND GODLIE BALLATES (1567)

THE CONCEPTIOUN OF CHRIST

Let vs reioce and sing,
And praise that michtie King,
   Quhilk send his Sone of a Virgine bricht.   *sent*
     La.   Lay.   La.
And on him tuke our vyle nature,
Our deidlie woundis to cure,
   Mankynde to hald in richt.
     La.   Lay.   La.
Sanct Luk wrytis in his Gospell,
God fend his Angell Gabriell,
   Unto that Virgine but defame.   *without stain*
     La.   Lay.   La.
For to fulfill the Prophesie,
Was spousit with Josaph fre,
   Mary scho had to name: *she*
     La.   Lay.   La.
Thir wordis to hir he did reheirs.   *These; rehearse*
Haill Mary! full of grace,
   The Lord God is with thé.
     La.   Lay.   La.
Thow blyssit Virgine mylde,
Thow sall consaue ane Chylde
   The pepill redeme sall he:
     La.   Lay.   La.
Quhais power and greit micht,
Sall be in Goddis sicht,
   Quhilk from the Father of micht is send,
     La.   Lay.   La.
Jesus his name ye call,

Quhilk salbe Prince ouir all
  His Kingdome sall haue nane end.
    La.   Lay.   La.
Than spak that Virgin fre,
Behald, how sall this be,
  Seeing I knaw na man?
    La.   Lay.   La.
Than said the Angell chaist,
Be the power of the Haly Gaist,
  Quhilk all thing wirk he can.
    La.   Lay.   La.
Elizabeth thy cousing also,
Sex monethis with chylde can go,
  At quhais birth greit joy sall be:
    La.   Lay.   La.
Call him Johne, sayis the Angell bricht,
Quihilk is send be Goddis micht,
  The Lordis way prepair sall he.
    La.   Lay.   La.

VSQUE QUO DOMINE. PSAL. XXII, WITH THE TUNE OF EXAUDI, DEUS, ORATIONEM MEAM

O Lord, how lang for euer wil thow forget,
And hyde thy face fra me, or yit how lang
Sall I reheirs thy counsell in my hart?
Quhen sall my hart ceis of this sorie sang?
O Lord, behald, help me, and licht my eine,
That suddand sleip of deid do me na teine.   does not vex me

Or ellis quhen my enemies seis my fall,
We did preuaill, sone will thay say on me:
And gif thay se me be thame brocht in thrall,
Thay will reioyce into thair tyrannie
Bot I in God hes hope, and traist to se
His godly help, than sall I loue the Lord
Quhilk did me saue fra them that had me schord.   menaced

MUSING GREITLIE IN MY MYNDE

Mvsing greitlie in my mynde,
The folie that is in mankynde,
Quhilk is sa brukill and sa blind,   brittle
    And downe sall cum, downe ay, downe ay.

Leuand maist part in all vice,   Living
Nouther sa gracious, nor sa wyse,
As out of wretchitnes to ryse,
    Bot downe to cum, downe ay, downe ay.

And all this warld to weild thow had,
Thy body perfit and properlie maid,
Yit man, as floure, thow sall said,
    And downe thow sall cum, downe ay.

Thocht thow war euer eternall,
As man that neuer fuld haue ane fall,
Yit doutles die thow sall,
    And downe sall cum, downe ay, downe ay.

Thocht thow war man neuer sa thrall   powerful
Remember yit that die thow sall;
Quha hiest clymmis gettis greitest sall,
    And downe sall cum, downe ay, downe ay.

Thocht thow war neuer of sa greit degre,
In riches nor in dignitie,
Remember, man, that thow mon die,   must
    And downe sall cum, downe ay, downe ay.

Thair is na King, nor Empreour,
Duke, nor Lord of greit valure,
Bot he sall faid as lely floure,
    And downe sall cum, downe ay, downe ay.

Quhair is Adam, and Eve his wyfe,
And Hercules, with his lang stryfe,
And Matussalem, with his lang lyfe?   Methuselah
    Thay all ar cum downe ay, downe ay.

WITH HUNTIS VP

With huntis vp, with huntis vp,
　　It is now perfite day,
Jesus, our King, is gane in hunting,
　　Quha lykis to speid thay may.

Ane cursit fox lay hid in rox
　　This lang and mony ane day,
Deuouring scheip, quhill he micht creip,
　　Nane micht him schaip away.　　　　　　　　　　　　　　frighten

It did him gude to laip the blude　　　　　　　　　　　　　lap
　　Of young and tender lammis,
Nane culd he mis, for all was his,
　　The young anis with thair dammis.

The hunter is Christ, that huntis in haist,
　　The hundis ar Peter and Paull,
The Paip is the foxe, Rome is the rox,
　　The rubbis vs on the gall.

That cruell beist, he neuer ceist,
　　Be his vsurpit power,
Under dispens to get our penneis,　　　　　　　　　　　　pennies
　　Our saulis to deuoir.

Quha culd deuyse sic merchandise
　　As he had thair to sell,
Onles it war proud Lucifer,
　　The greit maister of Hell.

He had to sell the Tantonie bell,   *St Anthony's bell*
   And pardonis thairin was;
Remissioun of sinnis in auld scheip skinnis,
   Our saulis to bring from grace.

With bullis of leid, quhyte wax and reid,   *papal Bulls*
   And vther quhylis with grene,
Closit in ane box, this vsit the fox,
   Sic peltrie was neuer sene.   *rubbish*

With dispensatiounis and obligatiounis,
   According to his law,
He wald dispens, for money from hence,
   With thame he neuer saw.

To curs and ban the sempill pure man,
   That had nocht to flé the paine;
Bot quhen he had payit all to ane myte,   *to his last mite*
   He mon be obsoluit than.   *must be absolved then*

To sum, God wot, he gaue tot quot,   *as directed*
   And vther sum pluralitie;   *openly*
Bot first with pennies he mon dispens,
   Or ellis it will nocht be.

Kingis to marie, and sum to tarie,   *marry*
   Sic is his power and micht,
Quha that hes gold, with him will he hold,
   Thocht it be contrair all richt.   *against*

O blissit Peter, the foxe is ane lier,
   Thow knawis weill it is nocht sa,
Quhill at the last, he salbe downe cast
   His peltrie, pardonis, and all.   *rubbish*

WILLIAM KETHE

c.1530–1594

PSALM C

All people that on earth do dwell,
Sing to the Lord with cheerful voice.
Him serve with mirth, his praise forth tell,
Come ye before him and rejoice.

Know that the Lord is God indeed;
Without our aid he did us make:
We are his flock, he doth us feed,
And for his sheep he doth us take.

O enter then his gates with praise,
Approach with joy his courts unto:
Praise, laud, and bless his name always,
For it is seemly so to do.

For why? the Lord our God is good,
His mercy is for ever sure;
His truth at all times firmly stood,
And shall from age to age endure.

ATTRIBUTED TO
MARY, QUEEN OF SCOTS
1542–1587

O Domine Deus! speravi in Te;
O care mi Jesu! nunc libera me.
In dura catena, in misera poena, desidero te;
Languendo, gemendo, et genu flectendo,
Adoro, imploro, ut liberes me!

PRAYER BEFORE EXECUTION

O merciful Father, my hope is in thee!
O Gracious Redeemer, deliver thou me!
My bondage bemoaning, with sorrowful groaning,
   I long to be free;
Lamenting, relenting and humbly repenting,
O Jesu, my Saviour, I languish for thee!

translated from the Latin anonymously

ALEXANDER HUME
c.1556–1609

OF THE DAY ESTIVALL   midsummer

O perfite light, quhilk schaid away   divided
The darkenes from the light,
And set a ruler ou'r the day,
Ane uther ou'r the night;

Thy glorie when the day foorth flies
Mair vively dois appeare   vividly
Nor at midday unto our eyes   than
The shining sun is cleare.

The shaddow of the earth anon
Remooves and drawes by,
Sine in the east. when it is gon,   then
Appeares a clearer sky;

Quhilk sunne perceaves the little larks,   which; soon
The lapwing and the snyp,   snipe
And tunes their sangs like Natures clarks,
Ou'r midow, mure and stryp.   meadow; stream

Bot everie bais'd nocturnall beast   frightened
Na langer may abide;
They hy away, baith maist and least,   hurry
Them selves in house to hide.

They dread the day, fra thay it see,   when
And from the sight of men
To saits and covars fast they flee,   dens and coverts
And lyons to their den.

Oure hemisphere is poleist clein,   polished
And lightened more and more,
While everie thing be clearely sein,   until

86

Quhilk seemed dim before;

Except the glistering astres bright,   *stars*
Which all the night were cleere,
Offusked with a greater light   *obscured*
Na langer dois appeare.

The golden globe incontinent   *immediately*
Sets up his shining head,
And ou'r the earth and firmament
Displays his beims abroad.   *abroad*

For joy the birds with boulden throts,   *swollen*
Agains his visage shein,   *against; bright*
Takes up their kindelie musicke nots   *natural notes*
In woods and gardens grein.

Up braids the carefull husbandman,   *rises; farmer*
His cornes and vines to see,
And everie tymous artisan,   *early*
In buith worke busilie.   *covered stall*

The pastor quits the slouthfull sleepe   *shepherd*
And passis forth with speede,
His little camow-nosed sheepe   *snub*
And rowtting kie to feede.   *lowing cattle*

The passenger from perrels sure   *traveller*
Gangs gladly foorth the way:
Breife, everie living creature   *in brief*
Takes comfort of the day.

The subtile, mottie rayons light *containg motes; beams of light*
At rifts thay are in wonne,   *entered*
The glansing thains and vitre bright *sparkling vanes; glass*
Resplends against the sunne.   *shines*

The dew upon the tender crops,
Lyke pearles white and round

Or like to melted silver drops,
Refreshes all the ground.

The mystie rocke, the clouds of raine,   vapour
From tops of mountaines skails,   evaporates
Cleare are the highest hils and plaine,
The vapors takes the vails.

Begaried is the saphire pend   ornamented; vault
With spraings of skarlet hew,   streaks
And preciously from end till end
Damasked white and blew.   patterned

The ample heaven of fabrik sure   workmanship
In cleannes dois surpas
The chrystall and the silver pure,
Or clearest poleist glas.

The time sa tranquill is and still,
That nawhere sall ye find.
Saife on ane high and barren hill,   except
Ane aire of peeping wind.   piping

All trees and simples, great and small,   herbs
That balmie leife do beir,
Nor thay were painted on a wall,   than if
Na mair they move or steir.   stir

Calme is the deepe and purpour se,
Yee, smuther nor the sand;   Indeed, smoother than
The wals that woltring wont to be   waves; tossing
Are stable like the land.

Sa silent is the cessile air,   yielding
That every cry and call,
The hils and dails and forrest fair
Againe repeates them all.

The rivers fresh, the callor streames.   cool
Ou'r rockes can softlie rin,
The water cleare like chrystall seames,
And makes a pleasant din.

The fields and earthly superfice   surface
With verdure greene is spread,
And naturallie, bur artifice,   without
In partie coulors cled.

The flurishes and fragrant flowres,   blossoms
Throw Phoebus fostring heit,   god of the sun
Refresht with dew and silver showres,
Casts up ane odor sweit.

The clogged, busie, bumming beis,   laden
That never thinks to drowne,
On flowers and flourishes of treis
Collects their liquor browne.

The sunne maist like a speedie post   messenger
With ardent course ascends,
The beautie of the heavenly host
Up to our zenith tends;

Nocht guided be na Phaeton
Nor trained in a chyre   drawn; by; chariot
Bot be the high and haly On,
Quhilk dois allwhere impire.   govern

The burning beims downe from his face
Sa fervently can beat,
That man and beast now seekes a place
To save them fra the heat.

The brethles flocks drawes to the shade
And frechure of their fald,   freshness
The startling nolt, as they were made,   stampeding cattle; mad
Runnes to the rivers cald.

89

The heards beneath some leaffie trie,   *shepherds*
Amids the flowers they lie,
The stabill ships upon the sey   *still*
Tends up their sails to drie.   *stretch*

The hart, the hynd, and fallow deare
Are tapisht at their rest,   *are crouching*
The foules and birdes that made the beare   *noise*
Prepares their prettie nest.

The rayons dures descending downe   *harsh rays*
All kindlis in a gleid,   *low coal*
In cittie nor in borroughstowne   *burgh*
May nane set foorth their heid.

Back from the blew paymented whun   *whinstone pavement*
And from ilk plaister wall
The hote reflexing of the sun
Inflams the aire and all.

The labowrers that timellie raise,   *early*
All weerie, faint and weake,
For heate downe to their houses gaise,
Noone meate and sleepe to take.   *midday meal*

The callowr wine in cave is sought,   *cool; cellar*
Mens brothing breists to cule;   *sweating, cool*
The water cald and cleare is brought,
And sallets steipt in ule.   *salads; oil*

Some plucks the honie plowm and peare,   *plum*
The cherrie and the pesche,   *peach*
Sume likes the reymand London beare,   *foaming*
The bodie to refresh.

Forth of their skepps some raging bees   *hives*
Lyes out and will not cast,   *settle outside; swarm*
Some uther swarmes hyves on the trees,   *make hives*
In knots togidder fast.   *clusters*

The corbeis and the kekling kais   crows; cackling jackdaws
May scarce the heate abide,
Halks prunyeis on the sunnie brais   hawks preen
And wedders back and side.   sun bathes

With gilted eyes and open wings   gilded
The cock his courage shawes,
With claps of joy his breast he dings,   strikes
And twentie times he crawes.

The dow with whisling wings sa blew   dove
The winds can fast collect,
Hir pourpour pennes turnes mony hew,   purple feathers
Against the sunne direct.

Now noone is went, gaine is mid-day,   gone
The heat dois slake at last,
The sunne descends downe west away,
Fra three of clock be past.

A little cule of braithing wind   gentle
Now softly can arise,
The warks throw heate that lay behind
Now men may enterprise.

Furth fairis the flocks to seeke their fude
On everie hill and plaine,
Ilk labourer, as he thinks gude,
Steppes to his turne againe.

The rayons of the sunne, we see,
Diminish in their strength,
The schad of everie towre and tree   shadow
Extended is in length.

Great is the calme, for everiequhair
The wind is sitten downe,   settled
The reik thrawes right up in the air   smoke curls
From everie towre and towne.

Their firdoning the bony birds   *warbling*
In banks they do begin,
With pipes of reides the jolie hirds   *shepherds*
Halds up the mirrie din.

The maveis and the philomeen,   *thrush; nightingale*
The stirling whissilles lowd,   *starling*
The cuschetts on the branches green   *pigeons*
Full quietly they crowd.   *coo*

The gloming comes, the day is spent,   *dusk*
The sun goes out of sight,
And painted is the occident   *west*
With pourpour sanguine bright.   *blood-red*

The skarlet nor the golden threid,   *scarlet cloth*
Who would their beawtie trie,
Are nathing like the colour reid
And beautie of the sky.

Our west horizon circuler,
Fra time the sunne be set,
Is all with rubies (as it wer)
Or rosis reid ou'rfret.   *embroidered*

What pleasour were to walke and see,
Endlang a river cleare,   *along*
The perfite forme of everie tree
Within the deepe appeare!

The salmon out of cruifs and creils   *wickwork traps; basket traps*
Up hailed into skowts,   *pulled; flat-bottomed boats*
The bels and circles on the weills,   *bubbles; pools*
Throw lowpping of the trouts.   *leaping*

O, then it were a seemely thing,
While all is still calme,
The praise of God to play and sing,
With cornet and with shalme.   *woodwind instrument*

Bot now the hirds with mony schout
Cals uther be their name: beasts
'Ga, Billie, turne our gude about,
Now time is to go hame.'

With bellie fow the beastes belive   full; quickly
Are turned fra the corne,
Quhilk soberly they hameward drive,
With pipe and lilting horne.

Throw all the land great is the gild   clamour
Of rustik folk that crie,
Of bleiting sheepe fra they be fild,
Of calves and rowting ky.   lowing cattle

All labourers drawes hame at even,
And can till uther say,
Thankes to the gracious God of heaven,
Quhilk send this summer day.   sent

ELIZABETH MELVILLE OF CULROSS, LADY CUMRIE

c.1574 – c.1630

from ANE GODLIE DREAME

CHRIST SPEAKS TO THE DREAMER
WHO HOPES TO SEE HEAVEN

I am the way, I am the treuth and lyfe,
I am thy spous that brings thee store of grace:
I am thy luif, quohom thou wald faine imbrace,
I am thy joy, I am thy rest and peace.
Ryse up anone and follow efter mee,
I sall the leid into thy dwelling place:
The Land of rest thou langs sa sair to sie
I am thy Lord that sone sall end thy race.

With joyfull heart I thankit him againe,
Reddie am I (said I) and weill content
To follow thee, for heir I leive in paine,
O wretch unworth, my dayes ar vainlie spent.
Nocht ane is just bot all ar fearcelie bent,
To rin to vyce, I have na force to stand:
My sinnes increase quhilk maks me sair lament,
Mak haist, O Lord, I lang to sie that Land.

WILLIAM DRUMMOND OF HAWTHORNDEN

1585–1649

from FLOWRES OF SION

[Sonnet vi]
THE BOOKE OF THE WORLD

Of this faire Volumne which wee World doe name,
If wee the sheetes and leaues could turne with care,
Of Him who it correctes, and did it frame,
Wee cleare might read the Art and Wisedome rare?
Finde out his Power which wildest Pow'rs doth tame,
His Prouidence extending euerie-where,
His Iustice which proud Rebels doeth not spare,
In euerie Page, no, Period of the same:
But sillie wee (like foolish Children) rest
Well pleas'd with colour'd Velame, Leaues of Gold,
Faire dangling Ribbones, leauing what is best,
On the great Writers sense nee'r taking hold;
    Or if by chance our Mindes doe muse on ought,
    It is some Picture on the Margine wrought.

[Sonnet viii]
THE ANGELS FOR THE NATIVITIE OF OUR LORD

Runne (Sheepheards) run where *Bethleme* blest appeares,
Wee bring the best of newes, bee not dismay'd,
A Saviour there is borne, more olde than yeares,
Amidst Heavens rolling hights this Earth who stay'd;
In a poore Cotage Inn'd, a Virgine Maide
A weakling did him beare, who all upbeares,
There is hee poorelie swadl'd, in Manger lai'd,
To whom too narrow Swadlings are our Spheares:
Runne (Sheepheards) runne, and solemnize his Birth,
This is that Night, no, Day growne great with Blisse,

In which the power of *Sathan* broken is,
In Heaven bee glorie, Peace unto the Earth.
    Thus singing through the Aire the Angels swame,
    And Cope of Starres re-echoed the same.

[*Sonnet xi*]
FOR THE BAPTISTE

The last and greatest Herauld of Heauens King,
Girt with rough Skinnes, hyes to the Desarts wilde,
Among that sauage brood the Woods foorth bring,
Which hee than Man more harmlesse found and milde:
His food was Blossomes, and what young doth spring,
With Honey that from virgine Hiues distil'd;
Parcht Bodie, hollow Eyes, some vncouth thing
Made him appeare, long since from Earth exilde.
There burst hee foorth; All yee, whose Hopes relye
On God, with mee amidst these Desarts mourne,
Repent, repent, and from olde errours turne.
Who listned to his voyce, obey'd his crye?
    Onelie the Ecchoes which hee made relent,
    Rung from their Marble Caues, repent, repent.

[*Sonnet xii*]
FOR THE MAGDALENE

These Eyes (deare Lord) once Brandons of Desire,
Fraile Scoutes betraying what they had to keepe,
Which their owne heart, then others set on fire,
Their traitrous blacke before thee heere out-weepe:
These Lockes, of blushing deedes the faire attire,
Smooth-frizled Waues, sad Shelfes which shadow deepe,
Soule-stinging Serpents in gilt curles which creepe,
To touch thy sacred Feete doe now aspire.
In Seas of Care behold a sinking Barke,
By windes of sharpe Remorse vnto thee driuen,
O let mee not expos'd be Ruines marke,
My faults confest (Lord) say they are forgiuen.
    Thus sigh'd to Iesvs the Bethanian faire,
    His teare-wet Feete still drying with her Haire.

SIR WILLIAM MURE OF ROWALLAN

1594–1657

SONNET

O three times happie, if the day of grace
In my darke soule did (though but dimly) dawne,
If to my struggling thoughts proclamd were peace,
If from mine eyes the vaile of darknesse drawne,
If once the seed of true repentance sawne
Made gushing streames leave furrowes on my face;
Sinnes menstruous rags in pure transparent laune
Were chang't, O then how happie were my cace!
So darknesse paths no more my feete should trace,
So ever on a quyet conscience feast
Repentance planted so should vice displace,
So clenst from sinne, sinne's filth I should detest!
Grace, light, repentance, inward peace I crave,
Grant these, good Lord, for mee thy selfe who gave.

DONNCHADH MacRAOIRIDH

D.c.1630

CEITHIR RAINN DO RINNEADH LEIS AN LA A D'EUG SE

Beir mise leat, a Mhic Dè,
   Agad fèin a b'ait leam tàmh;
Cum air do shlighe gu dlùth
   Mo chridhe is mo rùn 's mo ghràdh.

M'ùrnaigh agus m'aithrigh bhuan
   Bhith agad gach uair 's gach tràth;
Nar peacaidh uile leig linn –
   Tuilleadh cha dèan sinn gu bràth.

Achain eile dh'iarrmaid ort,
   Feudaidh do thoil-s' thobhairt dùinn:
An t-anam bhith agad fèin
   'S a' cholann chrè dhol san ùir.

Gu bhith air cathair nan àgh
   Cuide ri càch far a bheil,
Bho is tu as fiosraich mar a tàim
   Beir mise leat tràth is beir.

FOUR VERSES MADE BY HIM THE DAY HE DIED

Take me with You, Son of God,
    with You I'd gladly live;
and keep these three close to Your path:
    my heart, my wish, my love.

May all my prayers be with You now,
    my tears forever flow;
forgive my every sin –
    I can commit no more.

One other gift I ask of You,
    – and grant it soon, I trust:
that You will catch hold of the soul
    when my clay meets earth's dust.

To be standing soon at the throne of joy,
    part of the happy crowd;
since You can see the truth in me,
    Christ, take me with You – now.

translated from the Gaelic by Meg Bateman and James McGonigal

JAMES GRAHAM, MARQUIS OF MONTROSE

1612–1650

ON HIMSELF, UPON HEARING
WHAT WAS HIS SENTENCE

Let them bestow on ev'ry Airth a Limb;
Open all my Veins, that I may swim
To Thee my Saviour, in that Crimson Lake;
Then place my purboil'd Head upon a Stake;
Scatter my Ashes, throw them in the Air:
Lord (since Thou know'st where all these Atoms are)
I'm hopeful, once Thou'lt recollect my Dust,
And confident Thou'lt raise me with the Just.

A COMMITTEE OF THE GENERAL ASSEMBLY OF THE CHURCH OF SCOTLAND

1650

from THE PSALMS OF DAVID IN METRE

PSALM XXIII

The Lord's my shepherd, I'll not want.
    He makes me down to lie
In pastures green: he leadeth me
    the quiet waters by.

My soul he doth restore again;
    and me to walk doth make
Within the paths of righteousness,
    ev'n for his own name's sake.

Yea, though I walk in death's dark vale,
    yet will I fear none ill:
For thou art with me; and thy rod
    and staff me comfort still.

My table thou hast furnished
    in presence of my foes;
My head thou dost with oil anoint,
    and my cup overflows.

Goodness and mercy all my life
    shall surely follow me:
And in God's house for evermore
    my dwelling-place shall be.

PSALM CXXI

I to the hills will lift mine eyes,
 from whence doth come mine aid.
My safety cometh from the Lord,
 who heav'n and earth hath made.
Thy foot he'll not let slide, nor will
 he slumber that thee keeps.
Behold, he that keeps Israel,
 he slumbers not, nor sleeps.

The Lord thee keeps, the Lord thy shade
 on thy right hand doth stay:
The moon by night thee shall not smite,
 nor yet the sun by day.
The Lord shall keep thy soul; he shall
 preserve thee from all ill.
Henceforth thy going out and in
 God keep for ever will.

PSALM CXXVIII

Bless'd is each one that fears the Lord,
   and walketh in his ways;
For of thy labour thou shalt eat,
   and happy be always.
Thy wife shall as a fruitful vine
   by thy house' sides be found:
Thy children like to olive-plants
   about thy table round.

Behold, the man that fears the Lord,
   thus blessed shall he be,
The Lord shall out of Sion give
   his blessing unto thee:
Thou shalt Jerus'lem's good behold
   whilst thou on earth dost dwell.
Thou shalt thy children's children see,
   and peace on Israel.

ANONYMOUS
?17TH CENTURY

URNAIGH

Gum b'ann 'nad ainm, m'eudail,
A laigheas 's a dh'éireas mi,
A thogas mo làmh, a shìneas mo chas,
Buileachas is mathas Mhic Dé
As gach nì bhuineas dhòmhsa.

URNAIGH

Iosa an t-ainm os cionn gach ainm,
    Beatha an anma gu léir:
Ged as tric a thoill mi t'fhearg
    Bidh mi leanmhainn as Do dhéidh.

PRAYER

In thy name, my love,
May I lie down and rise,
Raise my hand and stretch my foot,
And may the bounty and the goodness
Of the Son of God be in everything
That I possess.

translated from the Gaelic by Margaret Fay Shaw

PRAYER

Jesu, the Name above every name,
The entire life of the soul:
Though often I deserved Thy anger,
I will follow after Thee.

translated from the Gaelic by Margaret Fay Shaw

SMALADH AN TEINE

Smàlaidh mise nochd an teine,
Mar a smàladh Muire 'n t-aingeal.
Có bhios air an fhaire nochd?
Muire gheal 's a Mac,
'S aingeal geal an dorus an taighe
Gus an dig a' là màireach.

SMOORING THE FIRE

I shall smoor the fire tonight,
As Mary would smoor the fire.
Who shall be on watch tonight?
Bright Mary and her Son,
And a white angel at the door of the house
Until tomorrow comes.

translated from the Gaelic with note by Margaret Fay Shaw

[Note: The prayer for 'smooring' or smothering the fire is said when covering the burning peats with ashes to keep them alight until morning. The first thought of the housewife is the fire, for, kindling being very scarce, it must not be allowed to go out. At night the live peats were well covered and in the morning they were 'lifted' from the ashes and the new peats added, which soon were ablaze.]

SILEAS NA CEAPAICH/
SILEAS MacDONALD
c. 1660–*c.* 1729

LAOIDH AIR BAS A FIR AGUS A H-IGHNE

'S mór mo mhulad 's mi 'm ònar,
  'S mi 'm shuidhe ann an seòmar gun luaidh,
Is nach faic mi tighinn dachaigh
  Fear cumail mo chleachdaidh a suas,
Fear a dh'fhadadh mo theine
  Is a dh'éigheadh gach deireas a nuas:
Ona chaidh sibh an taisgeadh
  'S goirt a chaochail mo chraiceann a shnuadh.

'S tric mo shùilean ri dòrtadh
  Ona thug iad thu Mhòr-chlaich a suas,
'S nach faic mise 'n t-àite
  'S an do chuir iad mo ghràdh-sa 's an uaigh;
Dh'fhàg sibh Anna aig a' bhaile
  'S bidh mise 'ga ghearan gu cruaidh,
A' sìor-amharc a' bhalla
  Aig na chuir iad i 'm falach gu buan.

'S mór mo mhulad 's mo chùram
  'Nuair a shileas mo shùilean gu làr,
Nach eil spiorad na h-ùmhlachd
  Ann am thaic 'ga mo ghiùlan na's fheàrr;
Gu dol air mo ghlùinibh
  'S 'gam liùbhairt do Phrionnsa nan Gràs,
On tha sgeula ro-chinnteach
  Gu bheil sinn uile fo chìs aig a' Bhàs.

Chan ann gu tighinn a rithisd
  Chaidh cuideachd mo chridhe-sa uam;
Gus an ruig mise iad-san
  Chan fhaicear leam iad gu Là Luain:
On nach tilleadh air ur n-ais duibh,
  Ach ur cnàimhean air seacadh 's an uaigh,

A HYMN ON THE DEATHS OF HER HUSBAND AND DAUGHTER

Great my sorrow and lonesomeness
as I sit in a room without talk,
with no sign of the man returning
who kept me the way I was wont,
a man who kindled my embers,
and sent out orders for anything we lacked,
since you were laid in the graveyard
the appearance of my skin has changed.

Since they took you up to Mortlach,
my eyes have often shed tears,
as I cannot see the resting place
where they laid my love in the grave;
I lament it sorely
that you all left Anna behind
as I stare at the wall
in which they have hidden her forever.

Great my sorrow and my worry
when my tears fall to the ground
that I do not have the spirit of humility
to give me better support
to go down on my knees
and yield myself to the Prince of Grace,
since it is certain knowledge
that we must all pay tribute to Death.

It is with no intention of returning
that I have been deserted by the ones that I love;
not until Doomsday
will I reach them and see them again;
since all that would return of you
were your bones withered in the grave,

Righ dèan iochd ri ur n-anam
    'N comh-chomunn nan Aingeal tha shuas.

'S beag mo ghnothach ri féilltibh
    No dh' amharc na réise ri m' bheò,
No m' aighear ri daoine:
    Chaidh mo chuid-sa dhiùbh cuide fo 'n fhòd;
Ona dh'fhalbh iad le chéile,
    An dithis nach tréigeadh mi beò,
Rìgh thoir dhomh-sa bhith leughadh
    Air an aithreachas gheur a bh' aig Iòb.

'Nuair thig latha a' bhràtha
    'S bhios na trompaidean àghmhor 'gan seinn,
'S thig Crìosd anns a' chathair
    Ghabhail cunntais is taca de chloinn,
Bidh na gobhair 's na caoirich
    An sin air gach taobh dhe 'gan roinn:
'S mairg a théid anns an teine
    Nach teirig 's nach deilich ri 'n druim.

Gheibh na caoirich an deas-làmh,
    'S na gobhair am feasd an làmh chlì,
'S an uair bhios Crìosd a' toirt breith:
    'Thigibh dhachaigh, a chlann a rinn sìth,
Gu rìoghachd ur n-Athar
    Far nach cluinn sibh ach aighear gun strì:
Sgriosar sìos a' chuid eile
    Do 'n teine nach teirig a chaoidh.'

Glòir thoir do Mhac Muire
    Thug 'e ghibht domh gun d'fhuiling mi leòn,
Thug de bhròn 's de leann-dubh dhomh
    Gus na theirig de m' fhuil agus m' fheòil,
Gus an tigeadh mo Shlànair
    A rithisd 'gam shàbhaladh beò;
Rìgh, glac m' anam an latha ud
    'S thoir suas e gu Cathair a' Cheòil.

Lord, have mercy on your souls
in communion with the angels above.

Little my interest in markets
or watching the race anymore
or making merry with others –
my own ones have gone below the sod,
since those two left together
who would never desert me in life,
God, make me start reading
of the bitter penance of Job.

On the day of Judgement
when the glorious trumpets sound,
when Christ takes account of His children
collecting their rents on His throne,
then the sheep and the goats will be parted,
shed off on His either side,
and woe to the ones for the furnace,
whose undying fire will never leave their backs.

The sheep will take the right-hand
and the goats the left
when Christ passes judgement:
'You children who made peace,
come home to your Father's Kingdom
where you will hear joy without strife;
let the others be cast asunder,
down to the eternal fire.'

Glory to the Son of Mary
who gifted me with suffering pain,
with so much grief and dejection
that my blood and my flesh have gone,
until the coming of my Saviour
restores me to life again;
on that day to the City of Music
take up my soul, O King.

translated from the Gaelic by Meg Bateman

ALLAN RAMSAY

1686–1758

THE MARROW BALLAD

*On seeing a stroling congregation going to a
field meeting, May 9th, 1738.*

To the tune of: *Fy let us a' to the bridal.*

O fy, let us a' to the meeting,
    For there will be canting there,   *tale-telling*
Where some will be laughing, some greeting,
    At the preaching of Erskine and Mair.
Then rouze ye up, Robie and Willy!
    The lasies are raiking awa,   *running*
In petty-coats white as the lilly,
    And biggonets prind on fou braw.   *linen caps; pinned; attractively*

And there will be blinkan eyed Bessy,
    Blyth Baby, and sweet lipet Megg,
And mony a rosie cheek'd lassie
    With coats kiltet to their mid-legg.
To gar them gang clever and lightly,
    We'll carry their hose and their shoon;   *stockings; shoes*
Syne kiss them and clap them fou tightly,   *fondle; very*
    As soon as the sermon is done.

The sun will be sunk in the west
    Before they have finished the wark:
Then behind a whin bush we can rest,
    Ther's mekle good done in the dark.   *much*
There Tammy to Tibby may creep,
    Slee Sandy may mool in with Kate;   *make love*
While other dowf sauls are asleep,   *unenergetic*
    We'll handle deep matters of state.

And shou'd we deserve the black stools,   penance stools
    For geting a gamphrell with wean,   fool
We'll answer we're no siccan fools
    To obey them that have the oaths tane.   taken
When the lave's to the parish kirk gawn,   rest's
    On Sundays – we'll rest us at hame,
An' runing to hills now and than
    Makes it nowther a sin nor a shame.   neither

Then up with the brethren true blew,
    Wha lead us to siccan delight,   such
And can prove it, altho they be few,
    That ther is naebody else wha is right,
And doun with all government laws,
    That are made by the Bishops of Baal,
And the thieves wha climb o'er the kirk waws   walls
    And come not in by a right call.

ROB DONN

1714–1778

MARBHRANN DO CHLOINN FHIR TAIGH RUSPAINN

'Nan luighe seo gu h-ìosal
Far na thìodhlaic sinn an triùir
Bha fallain, làidir, inntinneach
Nuair dh' inntrig a' bhliadhn' ùr;
Cha deachaidh seachad fathast
Ach deich latha dhith o thùs;
Ciod fhios nach tig an teachdair-s' oirnn
Nas braise na ar dùil?

Am bliadhna thìm bha dithis diubh
Air tighinn on aon bhroinn,
Bha iad 'nan dà chomrad
O choinnich iad 'nan cloinn,
Cha d' bhris an t-aog an comann ud
Ged bu chomasach dha 'n roinn,
Ach gheàrr e snàth'nn na beath'-s' aca
Gun dàil ach latha 's oidhch'.

Aon duine 's bean on tàinig iad,
Na bràithrean seo a chuaidh,
Bha an aon bheatha thìmeil ac'
'S bha 'n aodach d 'an aon chluaimh,
Mun aon uair a bhàsaich iad
'S bha 'n nàdar d' an aon bhuaidh,
Chaidh 'n aon siubhal dhaoine leo
'S chaidh 'n sìneadh san aon uaigh.

Daoine nach d' rinn briseadh iad
'S e fiosrachail do chàch,
'S cha mhò a rinn iad aon dad
Ris an can an saoghal gràs,
Ach ghineadh iad, is rugadh iad,
Is thogadh iad, is dh' fhàs,

THE RISPOND MISERS

Lying in their lowly state
are three we buried here,
though they were strong and healthy,
and lively at New Year;
ten days only have gone by
since then – who can be sure
that our dread Summoner is not,
unknown to us, as near?

Within one year a pair of them
had come from the one womb,
and they had been close comrades
since their childhood in one room;
their fellowship is still intact,
unsevered by the tomb –
within two days Eternity
has plucked them from Time's loom.

These brothers now departed
came from one man and wife,
their clothes were made from the one fleece,
each lived the self-same life;
their deaths came close together,
their natures were alike,
the one procession bore their dust
and laid it out of sight.

These men broke no commandments,
as far as we can trace,
nor did their deeds show anything
of what the world calls grace;
they were conceived and brought to birth,
were nursed, and grew apace,

Chaidh stràchd d 'an t-saoghal theiris orr',
'S mu dheireadh fhuair iad bàs.

Nach eil an guth seo labhrach
Ris gach aon neach againn beò,
Gu h-àraidh ris na seann daoinibh
Nach d' ionnsaich an staid phòsd',
Nach gabh na tha 'na dhleasdanas
A dheasachadh no lòn,
Ach caomhnadh nì gu falair dhoibh
'S a' falach an cuid òir?

Cha chaith iad fèin na rinn iad,
Agus oighreachan cha dèan,
Ach ulaidhnean air shliabh ac'
Bhios a' biathadh chon is eun.
Tha iad fon aon dìteadh,
Fo nach robh 's nach bi mi fhèin,
Gur duirche, taisgte 'n t-òr ac'
Na 'n uair bha e 'n tòs sa' mhèinn.

Barail ghlic an Aird Rìgh:
Dh' fhàg e pàirt de bhuidheann gann
Gu feuchainn iochd is oileanachd
D 'an dream d 'an tug e meall.
Carson nach tugteadh pòrsan
Dhe 'n cuid stòrais aig gach àm
Do bhochdaibh 'n Aoin a dheònaicheadh
An còrr a chur 'na cheann?

An dèidh na rinn mi rùsgadh dhuibh –
Tha dùil agam gun lochd –
'S a liuthad focal fìrinneach
A dhìrich mi nur n-uchd,
Tha eagal orm nach èisd sibh
Gu bhith feumail don a' bhochd
Nas mò na rinn na fleasgaich ud
A sheachdain gus a-nochd.

a swatch of life passed by them
and Death put them in their place.

Surely this sounds a warning
to each one of us alive,
especially old bachelors,
unlearned in married love:
men who will not spend on food
the cash to which they cleave,
saving for a funeral feast
the gold that they must leave.

They'll never spend what they have made,
and make no heirs besides;
their treasures on the hillsides
are food for dogs and birds;
they stand condemned – though I can plead
'not guilty' in assize –
of hoarding darklier their gold
than ever did the mines.

The High King in His providence
wisely left some men short,
to test the sense of charity
of those who have a lot;
these should surely give a part
of all the wealth they've got
to His poor folk; He's ready
to increase their meagre stock.

In spite of this straight talking –
and I feel it's only right –
and all the words of truth I've put
directly in your sight,
I fear you will not listen,
or give the poor a bite,
any more than these did
a week ago tonight.

translated from the Gaelic by Derick Thomson

DUGHALL BOCHANAN/
DUGALD BUCHANAN
1716–1768

from AN GAISGEACH

Cha bu ghaisgeach Alasdair mòr,
    No Caesar thug an Ròimh gu géill;
Oir ged a thug iad buaidh air càch,
    Dh' fhan iad 'nan tràill' d'a miannaibh féin.

Cha ghaisg' an ni bhi liodairt dhaoin',
    'S cha chliù bhi ann an caonnaig tric;
Cha 'n uaisle inntinn àrdan borb,
    'S cha treubhantas bhi garg gun iochd.

Ach 's gaisgeach esan a bheir buaidh
    Air eagal beatha, 's uamhunn bàis,
'S a chòmh'laicheas le misnich cri',
    A h-uile nì ata dha 'n dàn.

        *   *   *

Tha inntinn daingean mar a' chreag,
    Cha charaich eagal e no fiamh;
Tha shùilean furachair is geur,
    Is léir dha 'n dubhan crom troi 'n bhiadh.

Gu diomhain nochdaidh 'n saogh'l a ghlòir,
    Gach òr is inbhe ata ann;
Ta saoibhreas aig' cho pailt 'na chri',
    'S gur truagh leis rìgh is crùn mu cheann.

        *   *   *

O m' anam! dùisg is deasaich t' airm,
    'S gabh farmad ris a' ghaisgeach threun;

from THE HERO

No hero was Alexander the Great
or Caesar who brought Rome to her knees,
for though they conquered others
they remained as slaves to their own desires.

There's nothing heroic about bullying folk,
it's no boast to be forever caught up in strife,
arrogance is no nobility of mind,
to be brutal and merciless is not to be brave.

But the true hero is he who quells
fear of his life and dread of death,
who faces all that lies in store
with courage and unfailing heart.

* * *

His mind is steadfast like a rock,
neither fear nor dread can him sway,
his eyes ever watchful and sharp,
he sees the bent hook through the bait.

In vain the world reveals its pride –
all its circumstance and gold;
so plentiful the treasure in his heart
he pities a king with a crown on his head.

* * *

Oh my soul, wake, prepare your arms,
and emulate that hero brave,

Is t' anamianna cuir fo chìs,
    Chum rìogh'chd a cheannsach' annad féin.

Biodh t' inntinn àrd os cionn nan speur,
    Cha 'n 'eil fo 'n ghréin ach pòrsan truagh;
Mar tholman ùire faic an saogh'l,
    Is daoin' mar sheangain air mu'n cuairt:

A null 's a nall gun fhois gun tàmh,
    A' cruinneach' as gach àit d'an cist,
Gu lionmhor marcachd thar a chéil',
    'S a' trod gu geur mu bhioran brist'.

'N uair chì thu 'n sealladh so de'n t-sluagh
    Do smuainte cruinnich riut gu léir,
A shealbhach' saoibhreis, sonais, 's sìth,
    Air nach tig crìoch ad anam féin.

and subjugate your every lust
to rule a kingdom in yourself.

Let your mind float above the skies,
what lies below is but the dregs;
see the world like a mound of earth
with people rushing about like ants –

Unceasingly rushing back and forth,
gathering their store from every airt,
trampling each other under foot,
squabbling bitterly over a broken twig.

When you see humanity thus
together muster all your thoughts
in order to gain riches, happiness and peace
to hold without end in your own soul.

translated from the Gaelic by Meg Bateman

from LA A' BHREITHEANAIS

'N sin fàsaidh rudhadh anns an speur,
   Mar fhàir' na maidne 'g èirigh dearg,
Ag innse gu bheil Iosa fèin
   A' teachd 'na dhèidh le latha garbh.

Grad fhosglaidh às a chèil' na neòil,
   Mar dhoras seòmair an Ard-Rìgh,
Is foillsichear am Breitheamh mòr
   Le glòir is greadhnachas gun chrìoch.

Tha 'm bogha-frois mun cuairt d 'a cheann,
   'S mar thuil nan gleann tha fuaim a ghuth,
'S mar dhealanach tha sealladh 'shùl
   A' spùtadh às na neulaibh tiugh.

A' ghrian, àrd-lòcharan nan speur,
   Do ghlòir a phearsa gèillidh grad:
An deàlradh drillseach thig o 'ghnùis,
   A solas mùchaidh e air fad.

Cuiridh si uimpe culaidh bhròin,
   'S bidh 'ghealach mar gun dòirt' oirr' fuil;
Is crathar cumhachdan nan speur
   A' tilgeadh nan reult' às am bun.

Bidh iad air uideal anns an speur
   Mar mheas air gèig ri ànradh garbh,
Tuiteam mar bhraona dh' uisge dlùth,
   'S an glòir mar shùilean duine marbh.

Air carbad-teine suidhidh e,
   'S mun cuairt da beucaidh 'n tàirneanach,
A' dol le 'ghairm gu crìoch nan nèamh
   'S a' reub' nan neul gu doineannach.

from THE DAY OF JUDGEMENT

The heavens have a ruddy glow,
like morning dawn red in the sky,
telling us that Christ himself
comes in its wake with a rough day.

The clouds come suddenly apart,
an opening to the High King's room,
and the great Judge is then revealed,
in endless joy and glory come.

A rainbow placed around his head,
his voice's sound like glens in flood;
like lightning, glances from his eyes
come spouting from each darkling cloud.

The sun, high lantern of the skies,
bows down before the glorious sight;
his countenance's radiant sheen
entirely smothers the sun's light.

It puts the clothes of sorrow on;
the moon seems to be bathed in blood;
and heaven's powers are shaken sore,
wrenching each star out from its root.

Like fruit on branches tossed by storm
they waver weakly in the skies,
falling like drops of water fast,
their glory that of dead men's eyes.

On fiery chariot he sits
as thunder makes its roaring sounds,
ripping the clouds tempestuously
with calls that reach Heaven's outmost bounds.

O chuibhlibh 'charbaid thig a-mach
  Sruth mòr de theine laist' le feirg,
'S sgaoilidh 'n tuil ud air gach taobh
  A' cur an t-saoghail 'na lasair dheirg.

Leaghaidh na dùile nuas le teas,
  Ceart mar a leaghas teine cèir;
Na cnuic 's na sléibhtean lasaidh suas,
  'S bidh teas-ghoil air a' chuan gu lèir.

Na beannta iargalt' nach tug seach
  An stòras riamh do neach d' an deòin,
Ta iad gu fialaidh 'taosgadh mach
  An ionmhais leaght' mar abhainn mhòir.

Gach neach bha sgrìobadh cruinn an òir
  Le sannt, le dò-bheart no le fuil,
Làn chaisgibh nis bhur n-ìota mòr
  'S an asgaidh òlaibh dheth on tuil.

O sibhse rinn ur bun den t-saoghal,
  Nach tig sibh 's caoinibh e gu geur,
Nuair tha e gleacadh ris a' bhàs
  Mar dhuine làidir dol don eug.

A' chuisle chleachd bhith fallain fuar
  Ri mireag uaibhreach feadh nan gleann,
Tha teas a chlèibh ga smùidreadh suas
  Le goilibh buaireis feadh nam beann.

Nach faic sibh 'chrith tha air mun cuairt,
  'S gach creag a' fuasgladh anns gach sliabh!
Nach cluinn sibh osnaich throm a bhàis
  'S a chridhe sgàineadh staigh 'na chliabh!

An cùrtain gorm tha nunn on ghrèin,
  'S mun cuairt don chruinne-chè mar chleòc,
Crupaidh an lasair e r 'a chèil'
  Mar bheilleig air na h-èibhlibh beò.

Out from beneath his chariot's wheels
    fire lit with wrath comes in a stream,
and that flood spreads on every side
    till the whole world is a red flame.

The elements all melt with heat
    as fire melts wax with its hot breath;
the hills and moors are all aflame
    and all the oceans boil and seethe.

The fearsome mountains that by choice
    never gave anyone their stores
now let their molten treasure out
    as a great river freely pours.

All you who scraped with ploughs for gold,
    greed-driven, prone to vice and blood,
now you can slake your desperate thirst
    and drink your fill from out the flood.

O you who set on world your store,
    come and lament with every breath,
as now it wrestles with its end
    like a strong man approaching death.

The rill that once was hale and cold,
    and bubbled proudly through the glens,
now has its hot and smoky breath
    and fiercely boils among the bens.

Can you not see it trembling there
    as the rocks gape on the high ground?
As its heart splits within its chest
    can you not hear death's doleful sound?

The blue drape spread out from the sun,
    cloaking the universe entire,
is wrinkled up by that red flame
    like birch-tree bark in living fire.

translated from the Gaelic by Derick Thomson

ROBERT FERGUSSON

1750–1774

TO THE TRON-KIRK BELL

Wanwordy, crazy, dinsome thing,　　　　　　　　　*Worthless; noisy*
As e'er was fram'd to jow or ring,　　　　　　　　　　　　*toll*
What gar'd them sic in steeple hing　　　　　　　　　　　*made*
　　They ken themsel',
But weel wat I they coudna bring
　　War sounds frae hell.　　　　　　　　　　　　　　　*Worse*

What de'il are ye? that I shud ban,　　　　　　　　　　　*curse*
Your neither kin to pat nor pan;　　　　　　　　　　　　*pot*
Not uly pig, nor master-cann,　　　　　　　*oil-vessel; piss-vessel*
　　But weel may gie
Mair pleasure to the ear o' man
　　Than stroak o' thee.

Fleece merchants may look bald, I trow,　　　　　　　　*confident*
Sin a' Auld Reikie's childer now　　　　　　　*Edinburgh's children*
Maun stap their lugs wi' teats o' woo,　　　　　　　　　　*wool*
　　Thy sound to bang,　　　　　　　　　　　　　　*overcome*
And keep it frae gawn thro' and thro'
　　Wi' jarrin' twang.

Your noisy tongue, there's nae abideint,　　　　　　　　*abiding*
Like scaulding wife's, there is nae guideint;　　　　　　*guiding*
Whan I'm 'bout ony bus'ness eident,　　　　　　　　　　*eager*
　　It's sair to thole;
To deave me, than, ye tak' a pride in't　　　　　　　　　*stun*
　　Wi' senseless knoll.

O! war I provost o' the town,
I swear by a' the pow'rs aboon,　　　　　　　　　　　　*above*
I'd bring ye wi' a reesle down;　　　　　　　　　　　*clatter*
　　Nor shud you think

(Sae sair I'd crack and clour your crown)   _batter_
    Again to clink.

For whan I've toom'd the muckle cap,   _emptied; cup_
An' fain wud fa' owr in a nap,   _eagerly_
Troth I cud doze as sound's a tap,   _top_
    Wer't na for thee,
That gies the tither weary chap   _the other_
    To waukin me.

I dreamt ae night I saw Auld Nick;
Quo he, 'this bell o' mine's a trick,
A wylie piece o' politic,
    A cunnin snare
To trap fock in a cloven stick,   _folk_
    'Ere they're aware.

As lang's my dautit bell hings there,   _fondled_
A' body at the kirk will skair;   _take fright_
Quo they, 'gif he that preaches there
    Like it can wound,
We douna care a single hair
    For joyfu' sound.'

If magistrates wi' me wud 'gree,
For ay tongue-tackit shud you be,   _with a speech impediment_
Nor fleg wi' antimelody   _frighten_
    Sic honest fock,
Whase lugs were never made to dree   _suffer_
    Thy doolfu' shock.

But far frae thee the bailies dwell,
Or they wud scunner at your knell,
Gie the foul thief his riven bell,
    And than, I trow,
The by-word hads, 'the de'il himsel'   _proverb holds_
    Has got his due.'

JOB, CHAPTER III PARAPHRASED

Perish the fatal Day when I was born,
The Night with dreary darkness be forlorn;
The loathed, hateful, and lamented night
When Job, 'twas told, had first perceiv'd the light;
Let it be dark, nor let the God on high
Regard it with the favour of his eye;
Let blackest darkness and death's awful shade
Stain it, and make the trembling earth afraid;
Be it not join'd unto the varying year,
Nor to the fleeting months in swift career.
Lo! Let the night in solitude's dismay
Be dumb to joy, and waste in gloom away;
On it may twilight stars be never known;
Light let it wish for, Lord! but give it none;
Curse it let them who curse the passing day,
And to the voice of mourning raise the lay;
Nor ever be the face of dawning seen
To ope its lustre on th' enamel'd green;
Because it seal'd not up my *mother's womb*,
Nor hid from me the Sorrows doom'd to come.
Why have I not from *mother's womb* expir'd?
My life resign'd when life was first requir'd?
Why did supporting knees prevent my death,
Or suckling breasts sustain my infant breath?
For now my soul with quiet had been blest,
With kings and counsellors of earth at rest,
Who bade the house of desolation rise,
And awful ruin strike tyrannic eyes,
Or with the princes unto whom were told
Rich store of silver and corrupting gold;
Or, as untimely birth, I had not been,
Like infant who the light hath never seen;
For there the wicked from their trouble cease,

And there the weary find their lasting peace;
There the poor prisoners together rest,
Nor by the hand of injury opprest;
The small and great together mingl'd are,
And free the servant from his master there;
Say, Wherefore has an over-bounteous heaven
Light to the comfortless and wretched given?
Why should the troubl'd and oppress'd in soul
Fret over restless life's unsettled bowl,
Who long for death, who lists not to their pray'r,
And dig as for the treasures hid afar;
Who with excess of joy are blest and glad,
Rejoic'd when in the tomb of silence laid?
Why then is grateful light bestow'd on man,
Whose life is darkness, all his days a span?
For 'ere the morn return'd my sighing came,
My mourning pour'd out as the mountain stream;
Wild visag'd fear, with sorrow-mingled eye,
And wan destruction piteous star'd me nigh;
For though nor rest nor safety blest my soul,
New trouble came, new darkness, new controul.

JOHN MORISON
1750–1798

FROM HOSEA VI. 1–4

Come, let us to the Lord our God
    With contrite hearts return:
Our God is gracious, nor will leave
    The desolate to mourn.

His voice commands the tempest forth,
    And stills the stormy wave;
And though His arm be strong to smite,
    'Tis also strong to save.

Long hath the night of sorrow reigned,
    The dawn shall bring us light:
God shall appear, and we shall rise
    With gladness in His sight.

Our hearts, if God we seek to know,
    Shall know Him, and rejoice;
His coming like the morn shall be,
    Like morning songs His voice.

As dew upon the tender herb,
    Diffusing fragrance round;
As showers that usher in the spring,
    And cheer the thirsty ground:

So shall His presence bless our souls,
    And shed a joyful light;
That hallowed morn shall chase away
    The sorrows of the night.

ROBERT BURNS
1759–1796

HOLY WILLIE'S PRAYER

'And send the Godly in a pet to pray.' –Pope

Argument.

Holy Willie was a rather oldish batchelor Elder in the parish of Mauchline, and much and justly famed for that polemical chattering which ends in tippling Orthodoxy, and for that Spiritualized Bawdry which refines to Liquorish Devotion.—In a Sessional process with a gentleman in Mauchline, a Mr Gavin Hamilton, Holy Willie, and his priest, father Auld, after full hearing in the Presbytry of Ayr, came off but second best; owing partly to the oratorical powers of Mr Robert Aiken, Mr Hamilton's Counsel; but chiefly to Mr Hamilton's being one of the most irreproachable and truly respectable characters in the county.—On losing his Process, the Muse overheard him at his devotions as follows—

O Thou, wha in the heavens dost dwell,
Wha, as it pleases best thysel',
Sends ane to heaven and ten to hell,
   A' for thy glory,
And no for ony guid or ill
   They've done afore thee!

I bless and praise thy matchless might,
Whan thousands thou hast left in night,
That I am here afore thy sight,
   For gifts an' grace,
A burnin' an' a shinin' light,
   To a' this place.

What was I, or my generation,
That I should get such exaltation,
I wha deserve sic just damnation,
   For broken laws,
Five thousand years ere my creation,
   Thro' Adam's cause.

When frae my mither's womb I fell,
Thou might ha'e plunged me in hell,
To gnash my gums, to weep and wail,
    In burnin' lake,
Whar damned devils roar and yell,
    Chain'd to a stake.

Yet I am here a chosen sample,
To show thy grace is great an' ample;
I'm here a pillar in thy temple,
    Strong as a rock,
A guide, a buckler, an' example
    To a' thy flock.

But yet, O Lord! confess I must,
At times I'm fash'd wi' fleshly lust   *troubled*
An' sometimes too, wi' warldly trust,
    Vile Self gets in;
But thou remembers we are dust,
    Defil'd in sin.

O Lord! yestreen, thou kens, wi' Meg –   *yesterday; knows*
Thy pardon I sincerely beg –
O may't ne'er be a living plague
    To my dishonor!
An' I'll ne'er lift a lawless leg
    Again upon her.

Besides, I farther maun avow –   *must*
Wi' Leezie's lass, three times, I trow –
But, Lord, that Friday I was fou,   *drink*
    When I cam near her,
Or else, thou kens, thy servant true
    Wad never steer her.

Maybe thou lets this fleshly thorn
Buffet thy servant e'en and morn,
Lest he owre proud and high should turn
    That he's sae gifted:
If sae, thy han' maun e'en be borne

Until thou lift it.

Lord, bless thy Chosen in this place,
For here thou has a chosen race!
But God confound their stubborn face
    An' blast their name,
Wha bring thy elders to disgrace
    An' open shame!

Lord mind Gaun Hamilton's deserts,
He drinks, an' swears, an' plays at carts,   *cards*
Yet has sae mony taking' arts,
    Wi' great an' sma'
Frae God's ain priest the people's hearts
    He steals awa'.

An' whan we chasten'd him therefore,
Thou kens how he bred sic a splore,   *commotion*
As set the warld in a roar
    O laughin' at us;
Curse thou his basket and his store,
    Kail an' potatoes.   *cabbage*

Lord hear my earnest cry an' pray'r
Against that presbyt'ry o' Ayr;
Thy strong right hand, Lord make it bare,
    Upo' their heads,
Lord weigh it down, and dinna spare,
    For their misdeeds.

O Lord my God, that glib-tongu'd Aiken,
My very heart an' soul are quakin',
To think how we stood, sweatin', shakin',
    An' pissed wi' dread,
While Auld wi' hingin lip gaed sneakin',
    And hid his head.

Lord in the day of vengeance try him,
Lord visit them wha did employ him,
And pass not in thy mercy by 'em,

Nor hear their prayer;
But for thy people's sake destroy 'em,
    And dinna spare.

But Lord remember me and mine
Wi' mercies temp'ral and divine,
That I for gear and grace may shine,
    Excell'd by nane,
An' a' the glory shall be thine,
    Amen, Amen.

KIRKCUDBRIGHT GRACE

Some have meat and cannot eat,
    Some cannot eat that want it:
But we have meat and we can eat,
    Sae let the Lord be thankit.

ADDRESS TO THE DEIL

O Prince, o chief of many throned pow'rs,
That led th' embattl'd Seraphim to war
– Milton

O Thou, whatever title suit thee!
Auld Hornie, Satan, Nick, or Clootie!
Wha in yon cavern grim an' sootie,
 Clos'd under hatches,
Spairges about the brunstane cootie,   *scatters; brimstove tub*
 To scaud poor wretches!   *scald*

Hear me, *auld Hangie*, for a wee,
An' let poor, *damned bodies* bee;
I'm sure sma' pleasure it can gie,
 Ev'n to a *deil*,
To skelp an' scaud poor dogs like me,   *strike*
 An' hear us squeel!

Great is thy pow'r, an' great thy fame;
Far kend an' noted is thy name;
An' tho' yon *lowan heugh's* thy hame,   *blazing pit*
 Thou travels far;
An' faith! thou's neither lag nor lame,   *tardy*
 Nor blate nor scaur.   *shy; timid*

Whyles, ranging like a roaran lion,   *sometimes*
For prey, a' holes an' corners trying;
Whyles, on the strong-wing'd tempest flyin,
 Tirlan the *kirks*;   *rattling*
Whyles, in the human bosom pryin,
 Unseen thou lurks.

I've heard my rev'rend *Graunie* say,
In lanely glens ye like to stray;

Or where auld, ruin'd castles, gray,
    Nod to the moon,
Ye fright the nightly wand'rer's way,
    Wi' eldritch croon.   *eerie*

When twilight did my *Graunie* summon,
To say her prayers, douse, honest woman!   *genteel*
Aft 'yont the dyke she's heard you bumman,   *humming*
    Wi' eerie drone;
Or, rustling, thro' the boortries coman,   *elder trees*
    Wi' heavy groan.

Ae dreary, windy, winter night,
The stars shot down wi' sklentan light,   *slanting*
Wi' you, *myself*, I gat a fright,
    Ayont the lough;   *loch*
Ye, like a *rass-buss*, stood in sight,   *clump of rushes*
    Wi' waving sugh.   *murmur*

The cudgel in my nieve did shake,   *fist*
Each bristl'd hair stood like a stake,
When wi' an eldritch, stoor *quaick, quaick*,   *harsh*
    Amang the springs,
Awa ye squatter'd like a *drake*,   *fluttered in water*
    On whistling wings.

Let *Warlocks* grim, an' wither'd *Hags*,
Tell how wi' you on ragweed nags,   *ragwort*
They skim the muirs an' dizzy crags,
    Wi' wicked speed;
And in kirk-yards renew their leagues,
    Owre howcket dead.   *exhumed*

Thence, countra wives, wi' toil an' pain,   *country*
May plunge an' plunge the *kirn* in vain;   *churn*
For Oh! the yellow treasure's taen
    By witching skill;
An' dawtet, twal-pint *Hawkie's* gane   *petted; giving 12 pints at a milking*
    As yell's the bill.   *dry; bull*

Thence, mystic knots mak great abuse,
On *Young-Guidmen*, fond, keen an' croose;   bold
When the best *wark-lume* i' the house,   penis
    By cantraip wit,   magic
Is instant made no worth a louse,
    Just at the bit.

When thowes dissolve the snawy hoord,   thaws
An' float the jinglan icy boord,
Then *water-kelpies* haunt the foord,
    By your direction,
An' nighted trav'llers are allur'd
    To their destruction.

An' aft your moss-traversing *spunkies*   spirits
Decoy the wight that late an' drunk is: man
The bleezan, curst, mischievous monkies   blazing
    Delude his eyes,
Till in some miry slough he slunk is,
    Ne'er mair to rise.

When Mason's mystic *word* an' *grip*,
In storms an' tempests raise you up,
Some cock or cat, your rage maun stop,
    Or, strange to tell!
The *youngest brother* ye wad whip
    Aff straught to Hell.

Lang syne in Eden's bonie yard,
When youthfu' lovers first were pair'd,
An' all the Soul of Love they shar'd,
    The raptur'd hour,
Sweet on the fragrant, flow'ry swaird,
    In shady bow'r.

Then you, ye auld, snick-drawing dog!
Ye cam to Paradise incog,
An' play'd on man a cursed brogue,   trick
    (Black be your fa'!)
An' gied the infant warld a shog,   shake

'Maist ruin'd a'.

D'ye mind that day, when in a bizz,   state of commotion
Wi' reeket duds, an' reestet gizz,   smoking clothes; cured wig
Ye did present your smoutie phiz,   smutty face
   'Mang better folk,
An' sklented on the *man of Uzz*,   aimed
   Your spitefu' joke?

An how ye gat him i' your thrall,
An' brak him out o' house an' hal',
While scabs an' botches did him gall,
   Wi' bitter claw,
An' lows'd his ill-tongu'd, wicked *scrawl*
   Was warst ava?

But a' your doings to rehearse,
Your wily snares an' fechtin fierce,
Sin' that day Michael did you pierce,
   Down to this time,
Wad ding a *Lallan* tongue, or *Erse*,
   In Prose or Rhyme.

An' now, auld *Cloots*, I ken ye're thinkan,
A certain *Bardie's* rantin, drinkin,
Some luckless hour will send him linkan,   walking quickly
   To your black pit;
But faith! he'll turn a corner jinkan,
   An' cheat you yet.

But fare-you-weel, auld *Nickie-ben*!
O wad ye tak a thought an' men'!
Ye aiblens might – I dinna ken –   perhaps
   Still hae a *stake* –
I'm wae to think upo' yon den,
   Ev'n for your sake!

THE COTTER'S SATURDAY NIGHT
INSCRIBED TO R. AIKEN, ESQ

Let not Ambition mock their useful toil,
Their homely joys, and destiny obscure;
Nor Grandeur hear, with a disdainful smile,
The short and simple annals of the Poor. – Gray

My lov'd, my honor'd, much respected friend,
    No mercenary Bard his homage pays;
With honest pride, I scorn each selfish end,
    My dearest meed, a friend's esteem and praise:
To you I sing, in simple Scottish lays,
    The *lowly train* in life's sequester'd scene;
The native feelings strong, the guileless ways,
    What Aiken in a *cottage* would have been;
Ah! tho' his worth unknown, far happier there I ween!

November chill blaws loud wi' angry sugh;   gale
    The short'ning winter-day is near a close;
The miry beasts retreating frae the pleugh;
    The black'ning trains o' craws to their repose:
The toil-worn Cotter frae his labor goes,
    This night his weekly moil is at an end,
Collects his *spades*, his *mattocks* and his *hoes*,
    Hoping the *morn* in ease and rest to spend,
And weary, o'er the moor, his course does hameward bend.

At length his lonely *Cot* appears in view,
    Beneath the shelter of an aged tree;
The expectant *wee-things*, toddlan, stacher through
    To meet their *Dad*, wi' flichterin noise and glee.
His wee-bit ingle, blinkan bonilie,
    His clean hearth-stane, his thriftie *Wifie's* smile,
The *lisping infant*, prattling on his knee,

Does a' his weary *kiaugh* and care beguile,   carking anxiety [Burns's note]
And makes him quite forget his labor and his toil.

Belyve, the *elder bairns* come drapping in,   soon
    At *service* out, amang the farmers roun';
Some ca' the pleugh, some herd, some tentie rin   watchful
    A cannie errand to a neebor town:
Their eldest hope, their *Jenny*, woman-grown,
    In youthfu' bloom, love sparkling in her e'e,
Comes hame, perhaps, to shew a braw new gown,
    Or deposite her sair-won penny-fee,
To help her *Parents* dear, if they in hardship be.

Wi' joy unfeign'd, *brothers* and *sisters* meet,
    And each for other's weelfare kindly spiers:
The social hours, swift-wing'd, unnotic'd fleet;
    Each tells the uncos that he sees or hears;   news
The Parents partial eye their hopeful years;
    Anticipation forward points the view;
The *Mother*, wi' her needle and her sheers,
    Gars auld claes look amaist as weel's the new;   makes
The *Father* mixes a' wi' admonition due.

Their Master's and their Mistress's command,
    The *younkers* a' are warned to obey;   young folk
And mind their labors wi' an eydent hand,   diligent
    And ne'er, tho' out o' sight, to jauk or play: trifle
'And O! be sure to fear the Lord alway!
    And mind your *duty*, duely, morn and night!
Lest in temptation's path ye gang astray,
    Implore His *counsel* and assisting *might*:
They never sought in vain that sought the Lord aright.'

But hark! a rap comes gently to the door;
    Jenny, wha kens the meaning o' the same,
Tells how a neebor lad came o'er the moor,
    To do some errands, and convoy her hame.
The wily Mother sees the *conscious flame*
    Sparkle in *Jenny's* e'e, and flush her cheek,
With heart-struck, anxious care enquiries his name,

While *Jenny* hafflins is afraid to speak;   nearly
Weel-pleas'd the Mother hears, it's nae wild, worthless *Rake*.

With kindly welcome, *Jenny* brings him ben;
    A *strappan youth*; he takes the Mother's eye;
Blythe *Jenny* sees the *visit's* no ill taen;
    The Father cracks of horses, pleughs and kye.
The *Youngster's* artless heart o'erflows wi' joy,
    But blate and laithfu', scarce can weel behave;   diffident; bashful
The Mother, wi' a woman's wiles, can spy
    What makes the *youth* sae bashfu' and sae grave;
Weel-pleas'd to think her *bairn's* respected like the lave.   rest

O happy love! where love like this is found!
    O heart-felt raptures! bliss beyond compare!
I've paced much this weary, *mortal round,*
    And sage Experience bids me this declare –
    'If Heaven a draught of heavenly pleasure spare,
    One *cordial* in this melancholy *Vale,*
'Tis when a youthful, loving, *modest* pair,
    In other's arms, breathe out the tender tale,
Beneath the milk-white thorn that scents the ev'ning gale.'

Is there, in human form, that bears a heart –
    A Wretch! a Villain! lost to love and truth!
That can, with studies, sly, ensnaring art,
    Betray sweet Jenny's unspecting youth?
Curse on his perjur'd arts! dissembling smooth!
    Are *Honor, Virtue, Conscience,* all exil'd?
Is there no pity, no relenting ruth,
    Points to the parents fondling o'er their child?
Then paints the *ruin'd Maid,* and *their* distraction wild!

But now the supper crowns their simple board,
    The healsome *porritch,* chief of Scotia's food:
The soupe their *only Hawkie* does afford,   cow
    That 'yont the hallan snugly chows her cood: partition
The *Dame* brings forth, in complimental mood,
    To grace the lad, her weel-hain'd kebbuck, fell,   hoarded cheese, strong
And aft he's prest, and aft he ca's it guid;

The frugal *Wifie*, garrulous, will tell,
How 'twas a towmond auld, sin' lint was i' the bell.   year, flax

The chearfu' supper done, wi' serious face,
    They, round the ingle, form a circle wide;
The sire turns o'er, with patriarchal grace,
    The big *ha'–Bible*, ance his *Father's* pride:
His bonnet rev'rently is laid aside,
    His *lyart haffets* wearing thin and bare;   grey temples
Those strains that once did sweet in Zion glide,
    He wales a portion with judicious care;   chooses
'And let us worship God!' he says with solemn air.

They chant their artless notes in simple guise;
    They tune their *hearts*, by far the noblest aim:
Perhaps *Dundee's* wild warbling measures rise,
    Or plaintive *Martyrs*, worthy of the name;
Or noble *Elgin* beets the heaven-ward flame,   kindles
    The sweetest far of Scotia's holy lays:
Compar'd with these, *Italian trills* are tame;
    The tickl'd ears no heart-felt raptures raise;
Nae unison hae they, with our Creator's praise.

The priest-like Father reads the sacred page,
    How *Abram* was the Friend of God on high;
Or, *Moses* bade eternal warfare wage,
    With *Amalek's* ungracious progeny;
Or how the *royal Bard* did groaning lye,
    Beneath the stroke of Heaven's avenging ire;
Or *Job's* pathetic plaint, and wailing cry;
Or rapt *Isaiah's* wild, seraphic fire;
    Or other *Holy Seers* that tune the *sacred lyre*.

Perhaps the *Christian volume* is the theme,
    How *guiltless blood* for *guilty man* was shed;
How He, who bore in heaven the second name,
    Had not on earth whereon to lay His head;
How His first *followers* and *servants* sped;
    The *precepts sage* they wrote to many a land:
How *he*, who lone in *Patmos* banished,

Saw in the sun a mighty angel stand;
And heard great *Bab'lon's* doom pronounc'd by Heaven's command.

Then kneeling down to Heaven's Eternal King,
 The *Saint*, the *Father*, and the *Husband* prays:
Hope 'springs exultant on triumphant wing,'   Pope's *Windsor Forest* [Burns's note]
 That *thus* they all shall meet in future days:
There, ever bask in *uncreated rays*,
 No more to sigh, or shed the bitter tear,
Together hymning their Creator's praise,
 In *such society*, yet still more dear;
While circling time moves round in an eternal sphere.

Compar'd with *this*, how poor Religion's pride,
 In all the pomp of *method*, and of *art*,
When men display to congregations wide,
 Devotion's ev'ry grace, except the *heart*!
The Power, incens'd, the pageant will desert,
 The pompous strain, the sacredotal stole;
But haply, in some *cottage* far apart,
 May hear, well pleas'd, the language of the *soul*;
And in His *Book of Life* the inmates poor enroll.

Then homeward all take off their sev'ral way;
 The youngling *cottagers* retire to rest:
The parent-pair their *secret homage* pay,
 And proffer up to Heaven the warm request,
That He who stills the *raven's* clam'rous nest,
 And decks the *lily* fair in flow'ry pride
Would, in the way His *Wisdom* sees the best,
 For *them* and for their *little ones* provide;
But chiefly, in their hearts with *Grace divine* preside.

From scenes like these, old Scotia's grandeur springs,
 That makes her lov'd at home, rever'd abroad:
Princes and lords are but the breath of kings,
 'An honest man's the noblest work of God.'
And *certes*, in fair virtue's heavenly road,   certainly
 The *Cottage* leaves the *Palace* far behind:
What is a lordling's pomp? a cumbrous load,

Disguising oft the *wretch* of human kind,
Studied in arts of Hell, in wickedness refin'd!

O Scotia! my dear, my native soil!
    For whom my warmest wish to heaven is sent!
Long may thy hardy sons of *rustic toil*,
    Be blest with health, and peace, and sweet content!
And O may Heaven their simple lives prevent
    From *luxury's* contagion, weak and vile!
Then howe'er *crowns* and *coronets* be rent,
    A *virtuous populace* may rise the while,
And stand a wall of fire around their much-lov'd Isle.

O Thou! who pour'd the *patriotic tide*,
    That stream'd thro' great, unhappy Wallace' heart;
Who dar'd to, nobly, stem tyrannic pride,
    Or *nobly die*, the second glorious part:
(The Patriot's God, peculiarly thou art,
    His *friend, inspirer, guardian* and *reward!*)
O never, never Scotia's realm desert,
    But still the *Patriot*, and the *Patriot–Bard*,
In bright succession raise, her *Ornament* and *Guard!*

JAMES GRAHAME

1765–1811

from THE SABBATH

O blissful days!
When all men worship God as conscience wills.
Far other times our fathers' grandsires knew,
A virtuous race, to godliness devote.
What tho' the sceptic's scorn hath dar'd to soil
The record of their fame! What tho' the men
Of worldy minds have dared to stigmatize
The sister-cause, Religion and the Law,
With Superstition's name! yet, yet, their deeds
Their constancy in torture, and in death,
These on tradition's tongue still live, these shall
On history's honest page be pictur'd bright
To latest times. Perhaps some bard, whose muse
Disdains the servile strain of Fashion's quire,
May celebrate their unambitious names.
With them each day was holy, every hour
They stood prepared to die, a people doom'd
To death;– old men, and youths, and simple maids,
With them each day was holy; but that morn
On which the angel said, '*See where the Lord
Was laid,*' joyous arose; to die that day
Was bliss. Long ere the dawn, by devious ways,
O'er hills, thro' woods, o'er dreary wastes, they sought
The upland muirs, where rivers there but brooks
Dispart to different seas: fast by such brooks,
A little glen is scoop'd, a plat
With green sward gay, and flowers that strangers seem
Amid the heathery wild, that all around
Fatigues the eyes in solitudes like these,
Thy persecuted children, SCOTIA, foil'd
A tyrant's and a bigot's bloody laws:
There leaning on his spear (one of the grove
That held at bay the invading Charles's peers,

Yet rang'd itself to aid his son dethroned),
The lyart veteran heard the word of God,   grizzled
By CAMERON thundered, or by RENWICK poured
In gentle stream; then rose the sound, the loud
Acclaim of praise; the whistling plover ceased
Her plaint; the solitary place was glad,
And on the distant cairns the watcher's ear*
Caught doubtfully at times the breeze-borne note.
But years still sadder followed; and no more
The assembled people dared, in face of day,
To worship God, or even at the dead
Of night, save when the wintry storm raved fierce,
And thunder-peals compelled the men of blood
To couch within their dens; then dauntlessly
The scattered few would meet, in some deep dell
By rocks o'er-canopied, to hear the voice,
Their faithful pastor's voice: he by the gleam
Of sheeted lightning oped the sacred book,
And words of comfort spake: O'er their souls
His accents soothing came,– as to her young
The heathfowl's plumes, when at the close of eve
She mournful, gathers in her brood, dispersed
By the murderous sport, and o'er the remnant spreads
Fondly her wings; close nestling 'neath her breast
They cherish'd cow'r amidst the purple blooms.

*Sentinels were placed on the surrounding hills, to give warning of the approach of the military.
[Grahame's note]

A COMMITTEE OF THE GENERAL ASSEMBLY OF THE CHURCH OF SCOTLAND

1781

from TRANSLATIONS AND PARAPHRASES, IN VERSE, OF SEVERAL PASSAGES OF SACRED SCRIPTURE

IX. JOB XXVI. 6, TO THE END

Who can resist th' Almighty arm
    that made the starry sky?
Or who elude the certain glance
    of God's all-seeing eye?
From him no cov'ring vails our crimes;
    hell opens to his sight;
And all Destruction's secret snares
    lie full disclos'd in light.

Firm on the boundless void of space
    he pois'd the steady pole,
And in the circle of his clouds
    bade secret waters roll.
While nature's universal frame
    its Maker's pow'r reveals,
His throne, remote from mortal eyes,
    an awful cloud conceals.

From where the rising day ascends,
    to where it sets in night,
He compasses the floods with bounds,
    and checks their threat'ning might.
The pillars that support the sky
    tremble at his rebuke;
Through all its caverns quakes the earth,
    as though its centre shook.

He brings the waters from their beds,
    although no tempest blows,
And smites the kingdom of the proud
    without the hand of foes.
With bright inhabitants above
    he fills the heav'nly land,
And all the crooked serpent's breed
    dismay'd before him stand.

Few of his works can we survey;
    these few our skill transcend:
But the full thunder of his pow'r
    what heart can comprehend?

XIX. ISAIAH IX. 2–8

The race that long in darkness pin'd
    have seen a glorious light;
The people dwell in day, who dwelt
    in death's surrounding night.
To hail thy rise, thou better Sun!
    the gath'ring nations come,
Joyous, as when the reapers bear
    the harvest treasures home.

For thou our burden hast remov'd,
    and quell'd th' oppressor's sway,
Quick as the slaughter'd squadrons fell
    in Midian's evil day.
To us a Child of hope is born;
    to us a Son is giv'n;
Him shall the tribes of earth obey,
    him all the hosts of heav'n.

His name shall be the Prince of Peace,
    for evermore ador'd,
The Wonderful, the Counsellor,
    the great and mighty Lord.
His pow'r increasing still shall spread,
    his reign no end shall know:
Justice shall guard his throne above,
    and peace abound below.

LIV. 2 TIMOTHY I.12

I'm not asham'd to own my Lord,
    or to defend his cause,
Maintain the glory of his cross,
    and honour all his laws.
Jesus, my Lord! I know his name,
    his name is all my boast;
Nor will he put my soul to shame,
    nor let my hope be lost.

I know that safe with him remains,
    protected by his pow'r,
What I've committed to his trust,
    till the decisive hour.
Then will he own his servant's name
    before his Father's face,
And in the new Jerusalem
    appoint my soul a place.

CAROLINA OLIPHANT
1766–1845

THE LAND O' THE LEAL

I'm wearin' awa', John,
Like snaw-wreaths in thaw, John –
I'm wearin' awa'
    To the land o' the leal.   loyal
There's nae sorrow there, John;
There's neither cauld nor care, John –
The day is aye fair
    In the land o' the leal.

Our bonnie bairn's there, John;
She was baith guid and fair, John;
And, oh! we grudged her sair
    To the land o' the leal.
But sorrow's sel' wears past, John,
And joy is coming fast, John –
The joy that's aye to last
    In the land o' the leal.

Ye were aye leal and true, John;
Your task's ended now, John,
And I'll welcome you
    To the land o' the leal.
Now fare-ye-weel, my ain John:
This warld's cares are vain, John; –
We'll meet and we'll be fain   glad
    In the land o' the leal.

ANNA NIC EALAIR

fl.c. 1800

LUINNEAG ANNA NIC EALAIR

Is ann am bothan bochd a' bhròin
    A chuir mi eòlas ort an toiseach;
As thug mi thu gu tigh mo mhàth'r
    'S an d' rinn mi d' àrach car tamuill.

  'S e do ghaol-sa, a ghaoil,
    'S e do ghaol-sa rinn mo tharruing;
  'S e do ghràdh-sa, a rùin,
    Rinn mo dhùsgadh 's a' mhadainn.

Tha thu mar dhubhar carraig mhòir
    Am fearann sgìth is mi làn airsneil;
'N uair a thionndaidh riut mo shùil
    'S ann bha thu an rùn mo ghlacadh.

'S ann a thug thu dhomh do ghaol
    Fo dhubhar craobh an aiteil;
As comh-chomunn do rùin
    Ann an gàradh nan ubhall.

Is mìllse leam do ghaol na'm fion,
    Seadh am fion, 'nuair is treis' e,
'S 'n uair a thug thu dhomh do ghràdh
    'S ann a dh' fhàilnich mo phearsa.

'S ann a thug thu dhomh do d' ghràdh
    Gus an d'fhàilnich mo phearsa;
'S gus am b' éigin domh a ràdh
    'Cùm air do làmh a charaid.'

'S ann a dh' éirich thu le buaidh
    As an uaigh suas le cabhaig,
Amhluidh dhùisgeas do shluagh
    Suas le buaidh anns a' mhadainn.

ANNA NIC EALAIR'S SONG

It was in the wretched poor stall
that I first came to know you;
and I took you to my mother's house
where for a while I nursed you.

It was your love, my love,
it was your love that drew me,
it was your love, my dear,
that awoke me in the morning.

You're like the shade of a great rock
in a troubled land where I walk in sadness;
when I looked to you for help
you desired my encapture.

You gave me your love
in the juniper's shadow,
and the company of your regard
in the garden of apples.

Sweeter to me your love than wine,
even wine at its strongest;
when you showed me your esteem
it made my body falter.

You gave me of your love
until it overwhelmed me
and I had to call out
'Friend, stop your caresses.'

You have risen up with haste
from the grave, victorious;
likewise will your host awake,
triumphant in the morning.

'S chaidh thu suas air ionad àrd
    Dh' ullach' àite do m' anam;
'S tha thu 'g ràdh gu 'n tig thu rìs
    A choimh-lìonadh do gheallaidh.

And you went up to a place on high
to prepare my soul a lodging,
and you say you'll come back again
to bring about your promise.

Translated from the Gaelic by Meg Bateman

JAMES HOGG

1770–1835

CORPUS CHRISTI CAROL

The heron flew east, the heron flew west,
The heron flew to the fair forest;
She flew o'er streams and meadows green
And a' to see what could be seen:
And when she saw the faithful pair,
Her breast grew sick, her head grew sair;
For there she saw a lovely bower,
Was a' clad o'er wi' lilly-flower;
And in the bower there was a bed
With silken sheets, and weel down spread
And in the bed there lay a knight,
Whose wounds did bleed both day and night,
And by the bed there stood a stane,
And there was a set a leal maiden,
With silver needle and silken thread,
Stemming the wounds when they did bleed.

(from the recitation of his mother, Margaret Laidlaw)

A CAMERONIAN BALLAD

'O what is become o' your leel goodman,
   That now you are a' your lane?
If he has joined wi' the rebel gang,
   You will never see him again.'

'O say nae 'the rebel gang,' ladye,
   It's a term nae heart can thole,
For they wha rebel against their God,
   It is justice to control.

When rank oppression rends the heart,
   'An' rules wi' stroke o' death,
Wha wadna spend their dear heart's blood
   For the tenets o' their faith?

Then say nae 'the rebel gang,' ladye,
   For it gi'es me muckle pain;
My John went away with Earlston,
   And I'll never see either again.'

'O wae is my heart for thee, Janet,
   O sair is my heart for thee!
These covenant men were ill advised,
   They are fools, you may credit me.

Where's a' their boastfu' preaching now,
   Against their king and law,
When mony a head in death lies low,
   An' mony mae maun fa'?'

more

'Ay, but death lasts no for aye, ladye,
   For the grave maun yield its prey;
And when we meet on the verge of heaven,

We'll see wha are fools that day:

We'll see wha looks in their Saviour's face
   With holiest joy and pride,
Whether they who shed his servants' blood,
   Or those that for him died.

I wadna be the highest dame
   That ever this country knew,
And take my chance to share the doom
   Of that persecuting crew.

Then ca' us nae rebel gang, ladye,
   Nor take us fools to be,
For there is nae ane of a' that gang,
   Wad change his state wi' thee.'

'O weel may you be, my poor Janet,
   May blessings on you combine!
The better you are in either state,
   The less shall I repine.

But wi' your fightings an' your faith,
   Your ravings an' your rage,
There you have lost a leel helpmate,   *loyal*
   In the blossom of his age.

An' what's to come o' ye, my poor Janet,
   Wi' these twa babies sweet?
Ye hae naebody now to work for them,
   Or bring you a meal o' meat;

It is that which makes my heart sae wae,
   An' gars me, while scarce aware,
Whiles say the things I wadna say,
   Of them that can err nae mair.'

Poor Janet kissed her youngest babe,
   And the tears fell on his cheek,
And they fell upon his swaddling bands,

For her heart was like to break.

'O little do I ken, my dear, dear babes,
    What misery's to be thine!
But for the cause we hae espoused,
    I will yield thy life and mine.

O had I a friend, as I hae nane,
    For nane dare own me now,
That I might send to Bothwell brigg,
    If the killers wad but allow,

To lift the corpse of my brave John,
    I ken where they will him find,
He wad meet his God's foes face to face,
    And he'll hae nae wound behind.'

'But I went to Bothwell brigg, Janet,
    There was nane durst hinder me,
For I wantit to hear a' I could hear,
    An' to see what I could see;

And there I found your brave husband,
    As viewing the dead my lane,   by myself
He was lying in the very foremost rank,
    In the midst of a heap o' slain.'

Then Janet help up her hands to heaven,
    An' she grat, an' she tore her hair,
'O sweet ladye, O dear ladye,
    Dinna tell me ony mair!

There is a hope will linger within
    When earthly hope is vain,
But when ane kens the very worst,
    It turns the heart to stane!'

'O wae is my heart, John Carr, said I,
    That I this sight should see!

And when I said these waefu' words,
　　He liftit his een to me.

"O art thou there, my kind ladye,
　　The best o' this warld's breed,
And are you gangin' your liefu' lane,　　　　　　　　quite alone
　　Amang the hapless dead?"

I hae servants within my ca', John Carr,
　　And a chariot in the dell,
An' if there is ony hope o' life,
　　I will carry you hame mysel'.

"O lady, there is nae hope o' life –
　　And what were life to me!
Wad ye save me frae the death of a man,
　　To hang on a gallows tree?

I hae nae hame to fly to now,
　　Nae country an' nae kin,
There is not a door in fair Scotland
　　Durst open to let me in.

But I hae a loving wife at hame,
　　An' twa babies dear to me;
They have naebody now that dares favour them,
　　An' of hunger they a' maun dee.　　　　　　　　must

Oh, for the sake of thy Saviour dear,
　　Whose mercy thou hopest to share,
Dear lady take the sackless things　　　　　　　　blameless
　　A wee beneath thy care!

A long fareweel, my kind ladye,
　　O'er weel I ken thy worth;
Gae send me a drink o' the water o' Clyde,
　　For my last drink on earth."'

'O dinna tell ony mair, ladye,
　　For my heart is cauld as clay;

There is a spear that pierces here,
    Frae every word ye say.'

'He was nae feared to dee, Janet,
    For he gloried in his death,
And wished to be laid with those who had bled
    For the same enduring faith.

There were three wounds in his boardly breast,
    And his limb was broke in twain.
An' the sweat ran down wi' his red heart's blood,
    Wrung out by the deadly pain.

I rowed my apron round his head,   rolled
    For fear my men should tell,
And I hid him in my lord's castle,
    An' I nursed him there mysel' –

An' the best leeches in a' the land   doctors
    Have tended him as he lay,
And he never has lacked my helping hand,
    By night nor yet by day.

I durstna tell you before, Janet,
    For I feared his life was gane,
But now he's sae well, ye may visit him,
    An' ye's meet by yoursels alane.'

Then Janet she fell at her lady's feet,
    And she claspit them ferventlye,
And she steepit them a' wi' the tears o' joy,
    Till the good lady wept to see.

'Oh, ye are an angel sent frae heaven,
    To lighten calamitye!
For in distress, a friend or foe
    Is a' the same to thee.

If good deeds count in heaven, ladye,
    Eternal bliss to share,
Ye hae done a deed will save your soul,
    Though ye should never do mair.'

'Get up, get up, my kind Janet,
    But never trow tongue or pen,   *believe*
That a' the warld are lost to good,
    Except the covenant men.'

Wha wadna hae shared that lady's joy,
    When watching the wounded hind,
Rather than those of the feast and the dance,
    Which her kind heart resigned?

Wha wadna rather share that lady's fate,
    When the stars melt away,
Than that of the sternest anchorite,
    That can naething but graen an' pray?

WALTER SCOTT
1771–1832

DIES IRAE

That day of wrath, that dreadul day,
When heaven and earth shall pass away,
What power shall be the sinner's stay?
How shall he meet that dreadful day?

When, shrivelling like a parchèd scroll,
The flaming heavens together roll;
When, louder yet, and yet more dread,
Swells the high trump that wakes the dead;

O, on that day, that wrathful day,
When man to judgment wakes from clay,
Be Thou the trembling sinner's stay,
Though heaven and earth shall pass away!

ROBERT ALLAN

1774–1841

THE TWA MARTYRS' WIDOWS

Sit down, sit down by thy martyr's side,
And I'se sit down by mine:
And I shall speak o' him to my Gude,
And thou may speak o' thine.

It's wae to thee, and it's wae wi me,
For our day o' peace is gane,
And we maun sit wi a tearfu ee,
In our bouroch-ha' alane.   hall

O Scotland, Scotland, it's wae to thee,
When thy lichts are taen awa;
And it's wae, it's wae to a sinfu' lan'
When the righteous sae maun fa'.   must

It was a halie covenant aith
We made wi our Gude to keep;
And it's for the halie covenant vow
That we maun sit and weep.

O wha will gang to yon hill-side,
To sing the psalm at een?
And wha will speak o' the luve o' our Gude?
For the covenant reft hath been.

The gerse may grow on yon bonnie hill-tap,   grass
And the heather sweetly bloom;
But there nae mair we sall sit at een,
For our hearts are in the tomb.

The hectic glow is upo' my cheek,
And the lily hue on thine,
Thou soon will lie by thy martyr's side,
And soon I sall sleep by mine.

JOHN LEYDEN

1775–1811

THE SABBATH MORNING

With silent awe I hail the sacred morn,
That slowly wakes while all the fields are still.
A soothing calm on every breeze is borne.
A graver murmer gurgles from the rill;
And echo answers softer from the hill;
And sweeter sings the linnet from the thorn.
The skylark warbles in a tone less shrill:
Hail, light serene! hail, sacred Sabbath morn!
The rooks float silent by in airy drove.
The sun a placid yellow lustre throws.
The gales that lately sighed along the grove
Have hushed their downy wings in dead repose.
The hovering rack of clouds forgets to move –
So smiled the day when the first morn arose.

WILLIAM TENNANT
1 7 8 4 – 1 8 4 8

from PAPISTRY STORM'D

As they cam' to the Prior-muir,
And saw Sanct Androis town and towr
   Atween them and the sea,
A wee they haltit to look down
Upon the multi-towred town,
That on her mountain o' renown
   Sat in her majestie;
Her sindry steeples, shootin' high,
Amid the schimmer o' the sky,
They set themsels, wi' curious eye,
   To reckon up and tell:
Her goodlie, great cathedral, spread
Upon the mountain's lordlie head,
In leviathan length, becrown'd
I' the middle, and at ilka bound,
Wi towr and spindyl turrets round,
   They mark'd and noted well;
The gowd that glitter'd on ilk spire,
The capper roofs that flared like fire,
Heigh sarklin' ower kirk and quire,
Wi' langsame gaze they did admire:
   But whan they thocht upon
The idolatries and sins confest,
That there did brood as in their nest;
The monie murder't saints that there,
Thro' persecutions sharp and sair,
   Had to their Maker gone;
How poor Paul Craw, for speakin' true,
Was burnt wi' brass-ba' in his mou';
How Wishart, gentle, guid, and kind,
The friend and favourite o' mankind,
   Had, frae her causey-crown,
Ascendit upwarts frae his pyre

In chariot of whirlin' fire:
  Ah! martyr-murderin' town!
Thus thocht they in their hearts, and said
And cry'd, 'Aha!' and shook the head
  Wi' bannin' and wi' frown;
'Thy end is come!' cry'd Barns aloud,
'Thou Scottish Babel lewd and proud!
Thou Rome o' Scotland! ah, the day
Is come; or just upon its way,
Whan Retribution, dour but just,
Thy gawcy glorie down shall thrust,   jolly
To rot amang the kirkyard dust
  Like carrion-corp for aye;
As asks and dragons now abide   newts
Whare Babylon, in gowden pride
  Ance like a queen did ring;
Sae whair thy altars glister now,
Shall craps o' gosky dockens grow,
And jag-arm'd nettles soon, I know,
  The passer-by shall sting;
And schule-bairns, on a future day,
Shall be rampagin' in their play
Whare ance thy priests, in lang array,
Their matin-sangs did sing!'

GEORGE GORDON, LORD BYRON

1788–1824

from THE VISION OF JUDGMENT

Saint Peter sat by the celestial gate,
   And nodded o'er his keys: when, lo! there came
A wondrous noise he had not heard of late –
   A rushing sound of wind, and stream, and flame;
In short, a roar of things extremely great,
   Which would have made aught save a Saint exclaim;
But he, with first a start and then a wink,
Said, 'There's another star gone out, I think!'

But ere he could return to his repose,
   A Cherub flapped his right wing o'er his eyes –
At which Saint Peter yawned, and rubbed his nose:
   'Saint porter,' said the angel, 'prithee rise!'
Waving a goodly wing, which glowed, as flows
   An earthly peacock's tail, with heavenly dyes:
To which the saint replied, 'Well, what's the matter?
'Is Lucifer come back with all this clatter?'

'No,' quoth the Cherub: 'George the Third is dead.'
   'And who *is* George the Third?' replied the apostle:
'*What George? what Third?*' 'The King of England,' said
   The angel. 'Well! he won't find kings to jostle
Him on his way; but does he wear his head?
   Because the last, we saw here had a tustle,   [Louis XVI (beheaded)]
And ne'er would have got into Heaven's good graces,
Had he not flung his head in all our faces.

'He was – if I remember – King of France;
   That head of his, which could not keep a crown
On earth, yet ventured in my face to advance
   A claim to those of martyrs – like my own:
If I had had my sword, as I had once
   When I cut ears off, I had cut him down;

But having but my *keys*, and not my brand,
I only knocked his head from out his hand.

'And then he set up a headless howl,
    That all the Saints came out and took him in;
And there he sits by Saint Paul, cheek by jowl;
    That fellow Paul – the parvenu! The skin
Of Saint Bartholomew, which makes his cowl
    In heaven, and upon earth redeemed his sin,
So as to make a martyr, never sped
Better than did this weak and wooden head.

'But had it come up here upon its shoulders,
    There would have been a different tale to tell:
The fellow-feeling in the Saint's beholders
    Seems to have acted on them like a spell;
And so this very foolish head Heaven solders
    Back on its trunk: it may be very well,
And seems the custom here to overthrow
Whatever has been wisely done below.'

The Angel answered, 'Peter! do not pout:
    The King who comes has head and all entire,
And never knew much what is was about –
    He did as doth the puppet – by its wire,
And will be judged like all the rest, no doubt:
    My business and your own is not to inquire
Into such matters, but to mind our cue –
Which is to act as we are bid to do.'

While thus they spake, the angelic caravan,
    Arriving like a rush of mighty wind,
Cleaving the fields of space, as doth the swan
    Some silver stream (say Ganges, Nile, or Inde,
Or Thames, or Tweeed), and midst them an old man
    With an old soul, and both extremely blind,
Halted before the gate, and, in his shroud,
Seated their fellow-traveller on a cloud

But bringing up the rear of this bright host
   A Spirit of a different aspect waved
His wings, like thunder-clouds above some coast
   Whose barren beach with frequent wrecks is paved;
His brow was like the deep when tempest-tossed;
   Fierce and unfathomable thoughts engraved
Eternal wrath on his immortal face,
And *where* he gazed a gloom pervaded space.

As he drew near, he gazed upon the gate
   Ne'er to be entered more by him or Sin,
With such a glance of supernatural hate,
   As made Saint Peter wish himself within;
He pottered with his keys at a great rate,
   And sweated through his Apostolic skin:
Of course his perspiration was but ichor,
Or some such other spiritual liquor.

The very Cherubs huddled all together,
   Like birds when soars the falcon; and they felt
A tingling to the tip of every feather,
   And formed a circle like Orion's belt
Around their poor old charge; who scarce knew whither
   His guards had led him, though they gently dealt
With royal Manes (for by many stories,
And true, we learn the Angels all are Tories).

As things were in this posture, the gate flew
   Asunder, and the flashing of its hinges
Flung over space an universal hue
   Of many-coloured flame, until its tinges
Reached even our speck of earth, and made a new
   Aurora borealis spread its fringes
O'er the North Pole; the same seen, when ice-bound,
By Captain Parry's crew, in 'Melville's Sound.'

And from the gate thrown open issued beaming
    A beautiful and mighty Thing of Light,
Radiant with glory, like a banner streaming
    Victorious from some world-o'erthrowing fight:
My poor comparisons must needs be teeming
    With earthly likenesses, for here the night
Of clay obscures our best conceptions, saving
Johanna Southcote, or Bob Southey raving.   [a religious fanatic; a poet]

'Twas the Archangel Michael: all men know
    The make of Angels and Archangels, since
There's scarce a scribbler has not one to show,
    From the fiends' leader to the Angels' Prince.
There also are some altar-pieces, though
    I really can't say that they much evince
One's inner notions of immortal spirits;
But let the connoisseurs explain *their* merits.

Michael flew forth in glory and in good;
    A goodly work of him from whom all Glory
And Good arise; the portal past – he stood;
    Before him the young Cherubs and Saints hoary –
(I say *young*, begging to be understood
    By looks, not years; and should be very sorry
To state, they were not older than St. Peter,
But merely that they seemed a little sweeter).

The Cherubs and the Saints bowed down before
    That arch-angelic Hierarch, the first
Of Essences angelical who wore
    The aspect of a god; but this ne'er nursed
Pride in his heavenly bosom, in whose core
    No thought, save for his Maker's service, durst
Intrude, however glorified and high;
He knew him but the Viceroy of the sky.

He and the sombre, silent Spirit met –
    They knew each other both for good and ill;
Such was their power, that neither could forget

His former friend and future foe; but still
There was a high, immortal, proud regret
   In either's eye, as if 'twere less their will
Than destiny to make the eternal years
Their date of war, and their 'Champ Clos' the spheres.   [Tournament ground]

But here they were in neutral space: we know
   From Job, that Satan hath the power to pay
A heavenly visit thrice a-year or so;
   And that the 'Sons of God,' like those of clay,
Must keep him company; and we might show
   From the same book, in how polite a way
The dialogue is held between the Powers
Of Good and Evil – but t'would take up hours.

And this is not a theologic tract,
   To prove with Hebrew and with Arabic,
If Job be allegory or a fact,
   But a true narrative; and thus I pick
From out the whole but such and such an act
   As sets aside the slightest thought of trick.
'Tis every tittle true, beyond suspicion,
And accurate as any other vision.

The spirits were in neutral space, before
   The gate of Heaven: like eastern thresholds is
The place where Death's grand cause is argued o'er,
   And souls despatched to that world or to this;
And therefore Michael and the other wore
   A civil aspect: though they did not kiss,
Yet still between his Darkness and his Brightness
There passed a mutual glance of great politeness.

THOMAS CARLYLE
1795–1881

CUI BONO?

What is hope? A smiling rainbow
   Children follow through the wet;
'Tis not here, still yonder, yonder:
   Never urchin found it yet.

What is life? A thawing iceboard
   On a sea with sunny shore: –
Gay we sail; it melts beneath us;
   We are sunk, and seen no more.

What is man? A foolish baby,
   Vainly strives, and fights, and frets;
Demanding all, deserving nothing; –
   One small grave is what he gets.

GOBHA NA HEARADH/
JOHN MORISON
THE BLACKSMITH OF HARRIS

c.1796–1852

from AN NUADH BHREITH
no GLEACHD AN T-SEANN DUINE
AGUS AN DUIN' OIG

Gu'n cuir sibh dhibh, thaobh a' cheud chaithe-beatha, an seann duine, a tha truaillidh a
rèir nan ana-miann cealgach; agus gu 'm bi sibh air bhur n-ath-nuadhachadh ann an
Spiorad bhur n-inntinn; agus gu 'n cuir sibh umaibh an nuadh-dhuine, a tha air a
chruthachadh a rèir Dhè am fireantachd agus am fìor-naomhachd.
– Ephesianaich iv. 22–24.

Seann duin' mi o leasraidh Adhaimh
O 'n do shìolaich mi thaobh nàduir,
Ach duin' òg tre Léigh na slàinte
Shaor o 'n bhàs mi tre ghràs naisgte.
    Nach robh 'n seana duin' na ghràin domh
    S an duin' òg na ghràdh ni 's faisge.

Rinn an seana duin' daor-thràill dhiom
Thug mi 'm bràighdeanas do Shàtan,
'S e 'n duin' òg a shaor o mhàig mi
Dh 'ionnsuidh slàint o phlàigh a' pheacaidh.
    Leag an seann duin' anns an ùir mi
    S e 'n duin' òg a dhùisg a mach mi.

                    *

Dithis iad nach còrd an càraid
Ged tha 'n còmhnuidh san aon àros,
Gus a leagar nuas am pàilliun
Anns na ghabh iad tàmh mar chairteal.
    'N seana duin' gu carach lùbach
    'S an duin' ùr to'airt cùis gach gleachd deth.

                    *

from THE REBIRTH
or THE STRUGGLE BETWEEN THE OLD MAN
AND THE NEW MAN

That ye put off concerning the former conversion the old man, which is corrupt according
to the deceitful lusts; And be renewed in the spirit of your mind; And that ye put on the new
man, which after God is created in righteousness and true holiness.
– Ephesians iv, 22–24

I am an old man from the loins of Adam,
descended from him in regard to my nature,
but I am a young man through the Great Physician
freed from death by Grace under warrant.
    The old man was an object of loathing,
    the young man, beloved, much nearer.

The old man made a slave of me
and gave me into Satan's bondage;
the young man saved me from his paw,
set me for health from the plague of sinning.
    The old man dropped me in the grave-mould;
    it was the young man who there awoke me.

                    *

These are two who do not agree as a couple
though they must live in the one dwelling
until the time the tent is brought down
which has fallen to them to be their quarters:
    The old man treacherous and twisted
    and the new man overcoming him in battle.

                    *

Is e 'n seann duin' neach a's gòraich,
Ach 's e Aosd' nan làithean m' òig-fhear,
An seana duin' na rìogh an tòs orm,
'S nì an t-òig-fhear na stòl-chas e.
    An seana duin' s a lùs ga 'fhàgail
    'S an duin' òg a' fàs ni 's neartmhoir.

*

Tha mi bàit' an cuan an t-seann duin',
Fo gheur fhuar-dhealt 's fuachd a' gheamhraidh
Thig an t-òg na ghlòir gu 'theampull
Chuireas mis' a' dhanns' le m' chasaibh.
    Is e 'n seann duin' chuir fo neòil mi
    S e 'n duin' òg mo lòchran laiste.

*

Is mòr ioghnadh e le reusan
Teagasg dìomhair seo mo sgeula:
Na leth-aona seo bhi 'm' chreubhaigh
'S gur mi féin le chéil' mu seach iad:
    Is mi seann duin' do thaobh nàduir
    Ach duin' òg tre ghràs a nasgaidh.

The most foolish of men is the old man
while the Ancient of Days is my young hero;
over me, the old man first was monarch
while the young man acted as his footstool.
    The old man with his strength is departing
    and the young man is getting stronger.

*

I am drowned in the old man's ocean,
covered by the bitter cold dew of winter,
the young man comes in his glory to his temple,
up on my feet he sets me dancing.
    It is the old man who made me gloomy,
    the young man who is my blazing lantern.

*

The mysterious message of this, my story,
is with every reason a great wonder
that this pair of twins inhabits my body
and in turn I become each one of them:
    I am the old man in regard to nature
    but the young man through Grace under warrant.

translated from the Gaelic by Meg Bateman

CHARLES, LORD NEAVES
1800–1876

LET US ALL BE UNHAPPY ON SUNDAY:
A LYRIC FOR SATURDAY NIGHT

We zealots, made up of stiff clay,
   The sour-looking children of sorrow,
While not over-jolly today,
   Resolve to be wretched tomorrow.
We can't for a certainty tell
   What mirth may molest us on Monday;
But, at least, to begin the week well,
   Let us all be unhappy on Sunday.

That day, the calm season of rest,
   Shall come to us freezing and frigid;
A gloom all our thoughts shall invest,
   Such as Calvin would call over-rigid,
With sermons from morning to night,
   We'll strive to be decent and dreary:
To preachers a praise and delight,
   Who ne'er think that sermons can weary.

All tradesmen cry up their own wares;
   In this they agree well together:
The Mason by stone and lime swears;
   The Tanner is always for leather;
The Smith still for iron would go;
   The Schoolmaster stands up for teaching;
And the Parson would have you to know,
   There's nothing on earth like his preaching.

The face of kind Nature is fair;
   But our system obscures its effulgence:
How sweet is a breath of fresh air!
   But our rules don't allow the indulgence.
These gardens, their walks and green bowers,

Might be free to the poor man for one day;
But no, the glad plants and gay flowers
    Mustn't bloom or smell sweetly on Sunday.

What though a good precept we strain
    Till hateful and hurtful we make it!
What though, in thus pulling the rein,
    We may draw it as tight as to break it!
Abroad we forbid folks to roam,
    For fear they get social or frisky;
But of course they can sit still at home,
    And get dismally drunk upon whisky.

Then, though we can't certainly tell
    How mirth may molest us on Monday;
At least, to begin the week well,
    Let us all be unhappy on Sunday.

HORATIUS BONAR
1808–1889

LOVE IS OF GOD

Beloved, let us love: love is of God;
In God alone hath love its true abode.

Beloved, let us love: for they who love,
They only, are His sons, born from above.

Beloved, let us love: for love is rest,
And he who loveth not abides unblest.

Beloved, let us love: for love is light,
And he who loveth not dwelleth in night.

Beloved, let us love: for only thus
Shall we behold that God Who loveth us.

GO, LABOUR ON

Go, labour on: spend and be spent,
   Thy joy to do the Father's will;
It is the way the Master went;
   Should not the servant tread it still?

Go, labour on while it is day:
   The world's dark night is hastening on;
Speed, speed thy work; cast sloth away;
   It is not thus that souls are won.

Men die in darkness at thy side,
   Without a hope to cheer the tomb;
Take up the torch and wave it wide,
   The torch that lights time's thickest gloom.

Toil on, faint not, keep watch and pray;
   Be wise the erring soul to win;
Go forth into the world's highway,
   Compel the wanderer to come in.

Toil on, and in thy toil rejoice;
   For toil comes rest, for exile home;
Soon shalt thou hear the Bridegroom's voice,
   The midnight peal, 'Behold, I come!'

NORMAN MACLEOD

1812–1872

Courage, brother! do not stumble,
　Though thy path be dark as night;
There's a star to guide the humble:
　'Trust in God, and do the right.'
Let the road be rough and dreary,
　And its end far out of sight,
Foot it bravely, strong or weary,
　Trust in God, and do the right.

Perish policy and cunning,
　Perish all that fears the light!
Whether losing, whether winning,
　Trust in God, and do the right.
Some will hate thee, some will love thee,
　Some will flatter, some will slight;
Cease from man, and look above thee:
　Trust in God, and do the right.

Simple rule, and safest guiding,
　Inward peace, and inward might,
Star upon our path abiding, –
　Trust in God, and do the right.
Courage, brother! do not stumble,
　Though thy path be dark as night,
There's a star to guide the humble:
　'Trust in God, and do the right.'

WILLIAM EDMONDSTOUNE AYTOUN
1813–1865

from THE SCOTTISH CHRISTMAS

In truth it was a solemn show,
   The ancient Scottish Christmas tide:
The holly and the mistletoe.
   With other boughs as green beside,
Within the altar and the rail;
   The offering of the stainless flowers,
And all the grateful heart's avail,
   For hope and promise such as ours.

But these have long since pass'd away
   Beneath the cold Geneva ban;
No message brings that sacred day
   Of what was done and wrought for man.
A cheerless day! – A gloomy time!
   Whereon no grateful thanks are given;
Unhallow'd by the holy chime
   That ought to rise and welcome heaven.

A frost more deep than winter brings,
   Hath fallen on the Northern moor,
And no glad voice the Christmas brings
   To stay the labours of the poor.
No anthem, in the dead of night,
   Awakes the shepherd from afar,
Nor can he see the radiant light
   That flashes from the promised Star.

MAIRI DHOMHNALLACH/ MARY MACDONALD

1817 – *c*. 1890

LEANABH AN AIGH

Leanabh an àigh, an leanabh aig Màiri,
Rugadh san stàball, Rìgh nan Dùl;
Thàinig don fhàsach, dh'fhuiling nar n-àite –
Son' iad an àireamh bhitheas dhà dlùth!

Ged a bhios leanabain aig rìghrean na talmhainn
An greadhnachas garbh is anabarr mùirn,
'S geàrr gus am falbh iad, 's fàsaidh iad anfhann,
An àilleachd 's an dealbh a' searg san ùir.

Cha b 'ionann 's an t-Uan thàinig gur fuasgladh –
Iriosal, stuama ghluais e'n tùs;
E naomh gun truailleachd, Cruithfhear an t-sluaigh,
Dh'èirich e suas le buaidh on ùir.

Leanabh an àigh, mar dh'aithris na fàidhean;
'S na h-àinglean àrd', b'e miann an sùl;
'S E 's airidh air gràdh 's air urram thoirt dhà –
Sona an àireamh bhitheas dhà dlùth.

CHILD IN THE MANGER

Child in the manger,
  Infant of Mary;
Outcast and stranger,
  Lord of all!
Child who inherits
  All our transgressions,
All our demerits
  On Him fall.

Once the most holy
  Child of salvation
Gently and lowly
  Lived below;
Now, as our glorious
  Mighty Redeemer,
See Him victorious
  O'er each foe.

Prophets foretold Him,
  Infant of wonder;
Angels behold Him
  On His throne;
Worthy our Saviour
  Of all their praises;
Happy for ever.
  Are His own.

translated from the Gaelic by Lachlan MacBean

JOHN R. MacDUFF

1818–1895

from DAVID LIVINGSTONE

His Death and Burial
Chitambo, May 1st, 1873:
Westminster Abbey, April 18th, 1874.

Now the end of all was nearing
Underneath the tattered awning;
Angels would relieve their vigils
Ere another morrow's dawning.
First they raised him from the mud-floor,
Leaves and grass his pallet only,
Then they smoothed a downless pillow
In that desert drear and lonely;
While the faithful boy Majwara
Lay close by his dying master,
Knowing well how helpless was he
To avert the dire disaster.
As the waves of life were ebbing,
Thoughts about the past were ever
Mingling in the feverish wanderings
Over mountain, lake, and river.
'Say, is this the Luapula?
This the chill Loinko's water?'
'No, my Bwana,' answered Susi,
Nursing like a tender daughter; –
'We are near the Mulilamo,
We are in Chitambo's village,
You may sleep assured of safety,
Fearing neither blood nor pillage.'

Then he sank in broken slumber;
Who can tell what he was dreaming?
Of his childhood days at Blantyre;
Of the golden sunlight gleaming

Through old Bothwell's storied castle,
Lighting its umbrageous meadows;
Or when in the silver moonlight
He had watched the tender shadows?
Or it may be of the mother
Who the mission torch first lighted,
Which her son had borne to regions
By the direst curse benighted?
Or, perchance, the sainted partner
Who in life had shared his dangers,
Dreaming she had closed his eyelids
In the far-off land of strangers.

Now his sight is quickly fading, –
'Susi – come and light the candle;
Fill my med'cine-cup with water,
Guide my fingers to the handle.'
Promptly were his wishes answered,
Half were guessed from speech so broken;
'You can go,' in feeble whispers,
Were the last words that were spoken.

GEORGE MacDONALD

1824–1905

MARTIN ELGINBRODDE

Here lie I, Martin Elginbrodde
Ha'e mercy o' my soul Lord God,
As I wad do, were I Lord God
And ye were Martin Elginbrodde.

ANNE ROSS COUSIN
1824–1906

THE DOUBLE SEARCH

There are two gone out in the starless wild –
   Gone out on the desert night;
Earth's sad and weary and homeless child,
   And heaven's fair Lord of Light.

And one is seeking forlorn and blind,
   Can give to his loss no name;
But the other knows well what He stoops to find –
   Knows well what He comes to claim.

Though the hills are dark, though the torrents roll
   By each must his path be trod;
Both seek, for the Saviour has lost a soul,
   And the soul has lost its God.

That piteous cry and that tender call
   Come each from a yearning heart;
Through storm and stillness they rise and fall,
   And they seem not far apart.

I can hear the sound of their nearing feet
   By a sure attraction drawn:
Those night-long seekers shall timely meet,
   As the darkness dies in the dawn.

JAMES MACFARLAN

1832–1862

THE LORDS OF LABOUR

They come, they come, in a glorious march,
   You can hear their steam-steeds neigh,
As they dash through Skill's triumphal arch,
   Or plunge 'mid the dancing spray.
Their bale-fires blaze in the mighty forge,
   Their life-pulse throbs in the mill,
Their lightnings shiver the gaping gorge,
   And their thunders shake the hill.
     Ho! these are the Titans of toil and trade,
      The heroes who wield no sabre;
     But mightier conquests reapeth the blade
      That is borne by the lords of labour.

Brave hearts like jewels light the sod,
   Through the mists of commeree shine,
And souls flash out, like stars of God,
   From the midnight of the mine.
No palace is theirs, no castle great,
   No princely pillar'd hall,
But they well may laugh at the roofs of state,
   'Neath the heaven which is over all.
     Ho! these are the Titans of toil and trade,
      The heroes who wield no sabre;
     But mightier conquests reapeth the blade
      Which is borne by the lords of labour.

Each bares his arm for the ringing strife
   That marshals the sons of the soil,
And the sweat-drops shed in their battle of life
   Are gems in the crown of Toil.
And better their well-won wreaths, I trow,
   Than laurels with life-blood wet;
And nobler the arch of a bare bold brow,

Than the clasp of a coronet.
    Then hurrah for each hero, although his deed
      Be unblown by the trump or tabor.
    For holier, happier far is the meed
      That crowneth the lords of labour.

ALEXANDER CARMICHAEL

1832–1912

from CARMINA GADELICA
(collected and edited by Carmichael)

AN STRINGLEIN

'Each 's an stringlein,'
Orsa Calum-cille.

'Tillidh mis e,'
Thubhairt Crìosd.

'Moch Di-dòmhnaich?'
Orsa Calum-cille.

'Romh èirigh ghrèine,'
Thubhairt Crìosd.

'Trì postachan anns an tobar,'
Orsa Calum-cille.

'Togaidh mis iad,'
Thubhairt Crìosd.

'An leighis sin e?'
Ors Eòin Baistidh.

'Barantaich e,'
Thubhairt Crìosd.

THE STRANGLES

'A horse in strangles,'
Quoth Columba.

'I will turn it,'
Said Christ.

'On Sunday morning?'
Quoth Columba.

'Ere rise of sun,'
Said Christ.

'Three pillars in the well,'
Quoth Columba.

'I will lift them,'
Said Christ.

'Will that heal him?'
Quoth John the Baptist.

'Assuredly,'
Said Christ.

translated from the Gaelic by Alexander Carmichael

CUIRIM FIANAIS
(fuidheall)

Cuirim fianais gu Moire,
   Màthair chobhair an t-sluaigh;
Cuirim fianais gu Brìghde,
   Muime mhìn-ghil an Uain;

Cuirim fianais gu Peadail,
   Ostal eagail is suain;
Cuirim fianais gu Calum,
   Ostal airin is cuain;

Cuirim fianais gu Flathas,
   Dh'fhios na Cathair tha shuas;
Cuirim fianais gu Mìcheil,
   Ard-mhìlidh nam buadh;

Cuirim fianais gu Athair,
   A dh'altaich gach cré;
Cuirim fianais gu Crìosda,
   Fhuair mìostath is péin;

Cuirim fianais gu Spiorad,
   A ligheas mo chreuchd,
'S a dh'fhàgas mi gile
   Mar chanach an t-sléibh.

I SEND WITNESS
(a fragment)

I send witness to Mary,
Mother who aids men;
I send witness to Brigit,
Pure tender Nurse of the Lamb;

I send witness to Peter,
Apostle of fear and of sleep;
I send witness to Columba,
Apostle of shore and sea;

I send witness to Heaven,
To the City on high;
I send witness to Michael,
Noble warrior triumphant;

I send witness to Father,
Who formed all flesh;
I send witness to Christ,
Who suffered scorn and pain;

I send witness to Spirit,
Who will heal my wound,
Who will make me as white
As the cotton-grass of the moor.

translated from the Gaelic by Alexander Carmichael

ACHAN CHADAIL

Laighim sìos a nochd
  Le Brìghde nam brot,
Le Muire nan sìth,
  Le Iosa nam bochd.

Laighim sìos a nochd
  Le Brìghde na ciùin,
Le Muire na toirt,
  Le Mìchael mo rùin.

Laighim sìos a nochd
  Am fochair Rìgh nan dùl,
Am fochair Crìosd nan nochd,
  Am fochair Spioraid Nùmh.

Laighim sìos a nochd
  Le na naoi croisean fionn,
O bharra mo chinn
  Gu traighean mo bhonn;
    O bharra mo chinn
      Gu traighean mo bhonn.

SLEEP INVOCATION

I lie down this night
With Brigit of the mantles,
With Mary of peace,
With Jesus of the poor.

I lie down this night
With Brigit of calmness,
With Mary revered,
With Michael of my love.

I lie down this night
Near the King of life,
Near Christ of the destitute,
Near the Holy Spirit.

I lie down this night
With the nine angels,
From the crown of my head
To the soles of my feet;
    From the crown of my head
    To the soles of my feet.

translated from the Gaelic by Alexander Carmichael

SITH

Sìth Dhé dhomh, sìth dhaoine,
Sìth Chaluim Chille chaomha,
Sìth Mhoire mhìn na gaoldachd,
Sìth Chrìosda Rìgh na daondachd,
   Sìth Chrìosda Rìgh na daondachd,

Air gach uinneig, air gach doras,
Air gach toll a leigeas solas,
Air ceithir oiseannan mo thaighe,
Air ceithir oiseannan mo leaba,
   Air ceithir oiseannan mo leaba;

Air gach nì a chì mo shùil,
Air gach sìon a tha dha m' bhrù,
Air mo chorp a tha dh'an ùir
Is air m'anam thàin os cionn,
   Air mo chorp a tha dh'an ùir
   Is air m'anam thàin os cionn.

PEACE

The peace of God, the peace of men,
The peace of Columba kindly,
The peace of Mary mild, the loving,
The peace of Christ, King of tenderness,
   The peace of Christ, King of tenderness,

Be upon each window, upon each door,
Upon each hole that lets in light,
Upon the four corners of my house,
Upon the four corners of my bed,
   Upon the four corners of my bed;

Upon each thing my eye takes in,
Upon each thing my mouth takes in,
Upon my body that is of earth
And upon my soul that came from on high,
   Upon my body that is of earth
   And upon my soul that came from on high.

translated from the Gaelic by Alexander Carmichael

JAMES THOMSON ('B. V.')
1834–1882

from THE CITY OF DREADFUL NIGHT

'Per me si va nella città dolente.' – Dante

*'Poi di tanto adoprar, di tanti moti
D'ogni celeste, ogni terrena cosa,
Girando senza posa,
Per tornar sempre là donde son mosse;
Uso alcuno, alcun frutto
Indovinar non so.'*

*'Sola nel mondo eterna, a cui si volve
Ogni creata cosa,
In te, morte, si posa
Nostra ignuda natura;
Lieta no, ma sicura
Dell' antico dolor ...
Però ch' esser beato
Nega ai mortali e nega a' morti il fato.'* – Leopardi

PROEM

Lo, thus, as prostrate, 'In the dust I write
   My heart's deep languor and my soul's sad tears.'
Yet why evoke the spectres of black night
   To blot the sunshine of exultant years?
Why disinter dead faith from mouldering hidden?
Why break the seals of mute despair unbidden,
   And wail life's discords into careless ears?

Because a cold rage seizes one at whiles
   To show the bitter old and wrinkled truth
Stripped naked of all vesture that beguiles,
   False dreams, false hopes, false masks and modes of youth;

Because it gives some sense of power and passion
In helpless impotence to try to fashion
  Our woe in living words howe'er uncouth.

Surely I write not for the hopeful young,
  Or those who deem their happiness of worth,
Or such as pasture and grow fat among
  The shows of life and feel nor doubt nor dearth,
Or pious spirits with a God above them
To sanctify and glorify and love them,
  Or sages who foresee a heaven on earth.

For none of these I write, and none of these
  Could read the writing if they deigned to try:
So may they flourish, in their due degrees,
  On our sweet earth and in their unplaced sky.
If any cares for the weak words here written,
It must be some one desolate, Fate-smitten,
  Whose faith and hope are dead, and who would die.

Yes, here and there some weary wanderer
  In that same city of tremendous night,
Will understand the speech, and feel a stir
  Of fellowship in all-disastrous fight;
'I suffer mute and lonely, yet another
Uplifts his voice to let me know a brother
  Travels the same wild paths though out of sight.'

O sad Fraternity, do I unfold
  Your dolorous mysteries shrouded from of yore?
Nay, be assured; no secret can be told
  To any who divined it not before:
None uninitiate by many a presage
Will comprehend the language of the message,
  Although proclaimed aloud for evermore.

I

The City is of Night; perchance of Death,
  But certainly of Night; for never there

Can come the lucid morning's fragrant breath
   After the dewy dawning's cold grey air;
The moon and stars may shine with scorn or pity;
The sun has never visited that city,
   For it dissolveth in the daylight fair.

Dissolveth like a dream of night away;
   Though present in distempered gloom of thought
And deadly weariness of heart all day.
   But when a dream night after night is brought
Throughout a week, and such weeks few or many
Recur each year for several years, can any
   Discern that dream from real life in aught?

For life is but a dream whose shapes return,
   Some frequently, some seldom, some by night
And some by day, some night and day: we learn,
   The while all change and many vanish quite,
In their recurrence with recurrent changes
A certain seeming order; where this ranges
   We count things real; such is memory's might.

A river girds the city west and south,
   The main north channel of a broad lagoon,
Regurging with the salt tides from the mouth;
   Waste marshes shine and glister to the moon
For leagues, then moorland black, then stony ridges;
Great piers and causeways, many noble bridges,
   Connect the town and islet suburbs strewn.

Upon an easy slope it lies at large,
   And scarcely overlaps the long curved crest
Which swells out two leagues from the river marge.
   A trackless wilderness rolls north and west,
Savannahs, savage woods, enormous mountains,
Bleak uplands, black ravines with torrent fountains;
   And eastward rolls the shipless sea's unrest.

The city is not ruinous, although
   Great ruins of an unremembered past,

With others of a few short years ago
   More sad, are found within its precincts vast.
The street-lamps always burn; but scarce a casement
In house or palace front from roof to basement
   Doth glow or gleam athwart the mirk air cast.

The street-lamps burn amidst the baleful glooms,
   Amidst the soundless solitudes immense
Of rangèd mansions dark and still as tombs.
   The silence which benumbs or strains the sense
Fulfils with awe the soul's despair unweeping:
Myriads of habitants are ever sleeping,
   Or dead, or fled from nameless pestilence!

Yet as in some necropolis you find
   Perchance one mourner to a thousand dead,
So there; worn faces that look deaf and blind
   Like tragic masks of stone. With weary tread,
Each wrapt in his own doom, they wander, wander,
Or sit foredone and desolately ponder
   Through sleepless hours with heavy drooping head.

Mature men chiefly, few in age or youth,
   A woman rarely, now and then a child:
A child! If here the heart turns sick with ruth
   To see a little one from birth defiled,
Or lame or blind, as preordained to languish
Through youthless life, think how it bleeds with anguish
   To meet one erring in that homeless wild.

They often murmur to themselves, they speak
   To one another seldom, for their woe
Broods maddening inwardly and scorns to wreak
   Itself abroad; and if at whiles it grow
To frenzy which must rave, none heeds the clamour,
Unless there waits some victim of like glamour,
   To rave in turn, who lends attentive show.

The City is of Night, but not of Sleep;
   There sweet sleep is not for the weary brain;

The pitiless hours like years and ages creep,
　　A night seems termless hell. This dreadful strain
Of thought and consciousness which never ceases,
Of which some moments' stupor but increases,
　　This, worse than woe, makes wretches there insane.

They leave all hope behind who enter there:
　　One certitude while sane they cannot leave,
One anodyne for torture and despair;
　　The certitude of Death, which no reprieve
Can put off long; and which, divinely tender,
But waits the outstretched hand to promptly render
　　That draught whose slumber nothing can bereave.[*]

II

Because he seemed to walk with an intent
　　I followed him; who, shadowlike and frail,
Unswervingly though slowly onward went,
　　Regardless, wrapt in thought as in a veil:
Thus step for step with lonely sounding feet
We travelled many a long dim silent street.

At length he paused: a black mass in the gloom,
　　A tower that merged into the heavy sky;
Around, the huddled stones of grave and tomb:
　　Some old God's-acre now corruption's sty:
He murmured to himself with dull despair,
Here Faith died, poisoned by this charnel air.

Then turning to the right went on once more,
　　And travelled weary roads without suspense;
And reached at last a low wall's open door,
　　Whose villa gleamed beyond the foliage dense:
He gazed, and muttered with a hard despair,
Here Love died, stabbed by its own worshipped pair.

---

*Though the Garden of thy Life be wholly waste, the sweet flowers withered, the fruit-trees barren, over its wall hang ever the rich dark clusters of the Vine of Death, within easy reach of thy hand, which may pluck of them when it will [J. T.'s note.]

Then turning to the right resumed his march,
  And travelled streets and lanes with wondrous strength,
Until on stooping through a narrow arch
  We stood before a squalid house at length:
He gazed, and whispered with a cold despair,
Here Hope died, starved out in its utmost lair.

When he had spoken thus, before he stirred,
  I spoke, perplexed by something in the signs
Of desolation I had seen and heard
  In this drear pilgrimage to ruined shrines:
When Faith and Love and Hope are dead indeed,
Can Life still live? By what doth it proceed?

As whom his one intense thought overpowers,
  He answered coldly, Take a watch, erase
The signs and figures of the circling hours,
  Detach the hands, remove the dial-face;
The works proceed until run down; although
Bereft of purpose, void of use, still go.

Then turning to the right paced on again,
  And transversed squares and travelled streets whose glooms
Seemed more and more familiar to my ken;
  And reached that sullen temple of the tombs;
And paused to murmur with the old despair,
Here Faith died, poisoned by this charnel air.

I ceased to follow, for the knot of doubt
  Was severed sharply with a cruel knife:
He circled thus for ever tracing out
  The series of the fraction left of Life;
Perpetual recurrence in the scope
Of but three terms, dead Faith, dead Love, dead Hope.[*]

[*]Life divided by that persistent three $\frac{LXX}{333}$ = .$\overset{.}{2}1\overset{.}{0}$. [J.T.'s note]

GEORGE MATHESON
1842–1906

O Love that wilt not let me go,
  I rest my weary soul in Thee:
I give Thee back the life I owe,
That in Thine ocean depths its flow
  May richer fuller be.

O Light that followest all my way,
  I yield my flickering torch to Thee:
My heart restores its borrowed ray,
That in Thy sunshine's blaze its day
  May brighter, fairer be

O Joy that seekest me through pain,
  I cannot close my heart to Thee:
I trace the rainbow through the rain,
And feel the promise is not vain,
  That morn shall tearless be.

O Cross that liftest up my head,
  I dare not ask to fly from Thee:
I lay in dust life's glory dead,
And from the ground there blossoms red
  Life that shall endless be.

ANONYMOUS

c. 1850

A DISRUPTION RHYME

The Wee Kirk,
The Free Kirk,
The Kirk withoot the steeple;
The Auld Kirk,
The cauld Kirk,
The Kirk withoot the people.

ROBERT LOUIS STEVENSON
1850–1894

IF THIS WERE FAITH

God, if this were enough,
That I see things bare to the buff
And up to the buttocks in mire;
That I ask nor hope nor hire,
Nut in the husk,
Nor dawn beyond the dusk,
Nor life beyond death:
God, if this were faith?

Having felt thy wind in my face
Spit sorrow and disgrace,
Having seen thine evil doom
In Golgotha and Khartoum,
And the brutes, the work of thine hands,
Fill with injustice lands
And stain with blood the sea:
If still in my veins the glee
Of the black night and the sun
And the lost battle, run:
If, an adept,
The iniquitous lists I still accept
With joy, and joy to endure and be withstood,
And still to battle and perish for a dream of good:
God, if that were enough?

If to feel, in the ink of the slough,
And the sink of the mire,
Veins of glory and fire
Run through and transpierce and transpire,
And a secret purpose of glory in every part,
And the answering glory of battle fill my heart;
To thrill with the joy of girded men

To go on forever and fail and go on again,

And be mauled to the earth and arise,

And contend for the shade of a word and a thing not seen with the eyes:

With the half of a broken hope for a pillow at night

That somehow the right is the right

And the smooth shall bloom from the rough:

Lord, if that were enough?

TO MOTHER MARYANNE

(A Sister who worked among lepers)

To see the infinite pity of this place,
The mangled limb, the devastated face,
The innocent sufferer smiling at the rod –
A fool were tempted to deny his God.
He sees, he shrinks. But if he gaze again,
Lo, beauty springing from the breast of pain!
He marks the sisters on the mournful shores;
And even a fool is silent and adores.

REQUIEM

Under the wide and starry sky,
Dig the grave and let me lie.
Glad did I live and gladly die,
    And I laid me down with a will.

This be the verse you grave for me:
Here he lies where he longed to be;
Home is the sailor, home from sea,
    And the hunter home from the hill.

JOHN DAVIDSON

1857–1909

THE REV. HABAKKUK McGRUTHER
OF CAPE WRATH, IN 1879

God save old Scotland! Such a cry
    Comes raving north from Edinburgh.
It shakes the earth, and rends the sky,
    It thrills and fills true hearts with sorrow.
'There's no such place, by God's good grace,
    As smoky hell's dusk-flaming cavern?'
Ye fools, beware, or ye may share
    The hottest brew of Satan's tavern.

Ye surely know that Scotland's fate
    Controls the whole wide world's well-being;
And well ye know her godly state
    Depends on faith in sin's hell-feeing.
And would ye then, false-hearted men,
    From Scotland rape her dear damnation?
Take from her hell, then take as well
    From space the law of gravitation.

A battle-cry for every session
    In these wild-whirling, heaving last days:
'Discard for ever the Confession;
    Abolish, if you choose, the Fast-days;
Let Bible knowledge in school and college
    No more be taught – we'll say, 'All's well.'
'Twill scarcely grieve us, if you but leave us
    For Scotland's use, in Heaven's name, Hell.'

TO THE GENERATION KNOCKING AT THE DOOR

Break – break it open; let the knocker rust:
Consider no 'shalt not', and no man's 'must':
And, being entered, promptly take the lead,
Setting aside tradition, custom, creed;
Nor watch the balance of the huckster's beam;
Declare your hardiest thought, your proudest dream:
Await no summons; laugh at all rebuff;
High hearts and youth are destiny enough.
The mystery and the power enshrined in you
Are old as time and as the moment new:
And none but you can tell what part you play,
Nor can you tell until you make assay,
For this alone, this always, will succeed,
The miracle and magic of the deed.

JESSIE ANNE ANDERSON
1861–c.1930

AT SWEET MARY'S SHRINE

I'll sleep me soun' the nicht while sigh
    The saughs an' tender Ythan: *willows*
They're singin' tae the sairest he'rt
    That e'er Luve aince was blythe in.

Luve broke my he'rt, an' got within –
    He only tried tae pain it: –
How could Luve brak' sae saft a he'rt? –
    I never socht tae hain it.   *protect*

I tak' the simple, ae-fauld thing   *honest*
    That's been sae sairly siftit,   *sieved*
An' lay it on sweet Mary's shrine,
    An' leave her grace tae lift it.

VIOLET JACOB
1863–1946

TAM I' THE KIRK

O Jean, my Jean, when the bell ca's the congregation
O'er valley and hill wi' the ding frae its iron mou',
When a'body's thochts is set on their ain salvation,
    Mine's set on you.

There's a reid rose lies on the Buik o' the Word afore ye   dawn
That was growin' braw on its bush at the keek o' day,
But the lad that pu'd yon flower i' the mornin's glory
    He canna pray.

He canna pray, but there's nane i' the kirk will heed him
Whaur he sits sae still his lane at the side o' the wa',   by himself
For nane but the reid rose kens what my lassie gied him –
    It and us twa.

He canna sing for the sang that his ain he'rt raises,
He canna see for the mist that's afore his een,   eyes
And a voice droons the hale o' the psalms and the paraphrases
    Crying 'Jean! Jean! Jean!'

CHARLES MURRAY
1864–1941

GIN I WAS GOD

Gin I was God, sittin' up there abeen,	If; above
Weariet nae doot noo a' my darg was deen,	slog; over
Deaved wi' the harps an' hymns oonendin' ringin',	deafened
Tired o' the flockin' angels hairse wi' singin',	
To some clood-edge I'd daunder furth an', feth,	stroll
Look ower an' watch hoo things were gyaun aneth.	going below
Syne, gin I saw hoo men I'd made mysel'	Then
Had startit in to pooshan, sheet an' fell,	poison; shoot; slaughter
To reive an' rape, an' fairly mak' a hell	steal
O' my braw birlin' Earth, – a hale week's wark –	
I'd cast my coat again, rowe up my sark,	roll; shirt
An', or they'd time to lench a second ark,	before; launch
Tak' back my word an' sen' anither spate,	flood
Droon oot the hale hypothec, dicht the sklate,	concern; wipe the slate
Own my mistak', an', aince I'd cleared the brod,	board
Start a'thing ower again, gin I was God.	

MARION ANGUS
1866–1946

THE TREE

Happy walking it is when
Laughing girls go up the glen;
Grasses nodding, bluebells shy,
They were wishing they were I,
And one ancient thorny tree
It was watching, watching me.

Weary walking is it when
Sighing girls go down the glen;
Lonely cloud in evening sky
Was not lonelier than I,
Yet the strange and solemn tree
Still was watching, watching me.

Could I find some hidden bay
Many and many a mile away,
On the wet and salty strand
When the wind blows from the land
There would rise a hoary tree,
Always watching, watching me.

ANDREW YOUNG

1885–1971

THE FEAR

How often I turn round
To face the beast that bound by bound
Leaps on me from behind,
Only to see a bough that heaves
With sudden gust of wind
Or blackbird raking withered leaves.

A dog may find me out
Or badger toss a white-lined snout;
And one day as I softly trod
Looking for nothing stranger than
A fox or stoat I met a man
And even that seemed not too odd.

And yet in any place I go
I watch and listen as all creatures do
For what I cannot see or hear,
For something warns me everywhere
That even in my land of birth
I trespass on the earth.

HERE AND THERE

Eyes that are black like bramble-berries
   That lustre with light the rank hedgerows
Are kindly eyes and within them there is
   Love of the land where the bramble grows.

But mine are blue as a far-off distance
   And grey as the water beneath the sea;
Therefore they look with a long insistence
   For things that are not and cannot be.

DOMHNALL RUADH CHORUNA/
DONALD MACDONALD
1887–1967

CHUALA MI 'N DAMH DONN

Chuala mi 'n damh donn sa mhòintich.
Chuala mi 'n damh donn sa bhùireadh.
'S gun do dh'ùraich e dhomh m'òige.
Chuala mi 'n damh donn sa mhòintich.

Sheas mi agus chuir mi cluas ris,
'S bhiodh e tuath air Fuaran Dhòmhnaill.
Chuala mi 'n damh donn sa mhòintich.

Shil na deòir air bàrr mo ghruadhach
'S rinn mi 'n suathadh 's ghluais mi brònach.
Chuala mi 'n damh donn sa mhòintich.

Bha mis' uair a chaogainn sùil ris
'S a thàirninn gu chùl an t-òrd ris.
Chuala mi 'n damh donn sa mhòintich.

Ach a-nis cha dèan mi feum ann,
On dhalladh mo lèirsinn còmhla.
Chuala mi 'n damh donn sa mhòintich.

Bu lìonmhor madainn mhoch sa gheamhradh
A leag mi sa ghleann fear cròiceach.
Chuala mi 'n damh donn sa mhòintich.

Cha dìrich mi nis an fhèithe
Air an cuirinn leum nam òigear.
Chuala mi 'n damh donn sa mhòintich.

Beannachd le gach cnoc is gleann ann,
Le gach loch is allt is òban.
Chuala mi 'n damh donn sa mhòintich.

I HEARD THE BROWN STAG

I heard the brown stag on the moor.
I heard the brown stag bellow,
and it renewed my youth for me.
I heard the brown stag on the moor.

I stood still and listened
and placed him north of Fuaran Dhòmhnaill.
I heard the brown stag on the moor.

Tears streamed down my cheeks.
I brushed them off and moved away sadly.
I heard the brown stag on the moor.

There was a time I would have aimed at him
and cocked the hammer.
I heard the brown stag on the moor.

But now I am useless at that,
since I am blind in both eyes.
I heard the brown stag on the moor.

Times without number, early in the winter mornings,
I used to fell an antlered one in the glen.
I heard the brown stag on the moor.

Now I am not able to clamber across the gully
which I used to leap as a young man.
I heard the brown stag on the moor.

Goodbye to every hill and glen,
to every loch and river and bay.
I heard the brown stag on the moor.

translated from the Gaelic by Fred MacAulay

EDWIN MUIR
1887–1959

THE WAY

Friend, I have lost the way.
The way leads on.
Is there another way?
The way is one.
I must retrace the track.
It's lost and gone.
Back, I must travel back!
None goes there, none.
Then I'll make here my place,
(The road run on),
Stand still and set my face,
(The road leaps on),
Stay here, for ever stay.
None stays here, none.
I cannot find the way.
The way leads on.
Oh places I have passed!
That journey's done.
And what will come at last?
The road leads on.

SCOTLAND 1941

We were a tribe, a family, a people.
Wallace and Bruce guard now a painted field,
And all may read the folio of our fable,
Peruse the sword, the sceptre and the shield.
A simple sky roofed in that rustic day,
The busy corn-fields and the haunted holms,
The green road winding up the ferny brae,
But Knox and Melville clapped their preaching palms
And bundled all the harvesters away,
Hoodicrow Peden in the blighted corn
Hacked with his rusty beak the starving haulms.
Out of that desolation we were born.

Courage beyond the point and obdurate pride
Made us a nation, robbed us of a nation.
Defiance absolute and myriad-eyed
That could not pluck the palm plucked our damnation.
We with such courage and the bitter wit
To fell the ancient oak of loyalty,
And strip the peopled hill and the altar bare,
And crush the poet with an iron text,
How could we read our souls and learn to be?
Here a dull drove of faces harsh and vexed,
We watch our cities burning in their pit,
To salve our souls grinding dull lucre out,
We, fanatics of the frustrate and the half,
Who once set Purgatory Hill in doubt.
Now smoke and dearth and money everywhere,
Mean heirlooms of each fainter generation,
And mummied housegods in their musty niches,
Burns and Scott, sham bards of a sham nation,
And spiritual defeat wrapped warm in riches,
No pride but pride of pelf. Long since the young

Fought in great bloody battles to carve out
This towering pulpit of the Golden Calf,
Montrose, Mackail, Argyle, perverse and brave,
Twisted the stream, unhooped the ancestral hill.
Never had Dee or Don or Yarrow or Till
Huddled such thriftless honour in a grave.

Such wasted bravery idle as a song,
Such hard-won ill might prove Time's verdict wrong,
And melt to pity the annalist's iron tongue.

THE CHILD DYING

Unfriendly friendly universe,
I pack your stars into my purse,
And bid you, bid you so farewell.
That I can leave you, quite go out,
Go out, go out beyond all doubt,
My father says, is the miracle.

You are so great, and I so small:
I am nothing, you are all:
Being nothing, I can take this way.
Oh I need neither rise nor fall,
For when I do not move at all
I shall be out of all your day.

It's said some memory will remain
In the other place, grass in the rain,
Light on the land, sun on the sea,
A flitting grace, a phantom face,
But the world is out. There is no place
Where it and its ghost can ever be.

Father, father, I dread this air
Blown from the far side of despair,
The cold cold corner. What house, what hold,
What hand is there? I look and see
Nothing-filled eternity,
And the great round world grows weak and old.

Hold my hand, oh hold it fast –
I am changing! – until at last
My hand in yours no more will change,
Though your change on. You here, I there,
So hand in hand, twin-leafed despair –
I did not know death was so strange.

ONE FOOT IN EDEN

One foot in Eden still, I stand
And look across the other land.
The world's great day is growing late,
Yet strange these fields that we have planted
So long with crops of love and hate.
Time's handiworks by time are haunted,
And nothing now can separate
The corn and tares compactly grown.
The armorial weed in stillness bound
About the stalk; these are our own.
Evil and good stand thick around
In the fields of charity and sin
Where we shall lead our harvest in.

Yet still from Eden springs the root
As clean as on the starting day.
Time takes the foliage and the fruit
And burns the archetypal leaf
To shapes of terror and of grief
Scattered along the winter way.
But famished field and blackened tree
Bear flowers in Eden never known.
Blossoms of grief and charity
Bloom in these darkened fields alone.
What had Eden ever to say
Of hope and faith and pity and love
Until was buried all its day
And memory found its treasure trove?
Strange blessings never in Paradise
Fall from these beclouded skies.

HUGH MacDIARMID

1892–1978

O JESU PARVULE

'Followis ane sang of the birth of Christ, with the tune of Baw lu la law.'
– Godly Ballates

His mither sings to the bairnie Christ
Wi' the tune o' *Baw lu la law.*
The bonnie wee craturie lauchs in His crib   laughs
An' a' the starnies an' he are sib.   stars; kin
    Baw, baw, my loonikie, baw, balloo.   wee lad

'Fa' owre, ma hinny, fa' owre, fa' owre,
A' body's sleepin' binna oorsels.'   except
She's drawn Him in tae the bool o' her breist   curve
But the byspale's nae thocht o' sleep i' the least.   child likely to amaze
    Balloo, wee mannie, balloo, balloo.

THE INNUMERABLE CHRIST

'Other stars may have their Bethlehem, and their Calvary, too.'
– Professor J. Y. Simpson

Wha kens on whatna Bethlehems
Earth twinkles like a star the nicht,
An' whatna shepherds lift their heids
   In its unearthly licht?

'Yont a' the stars oor een can see   *eyes*
An' farther than their lichts can fly
I' mony an unco warl' the nicht   *alien*
   The fatefu' bairnies cry.

I' mony an unco warl' the nicht
The lift gaes black as pitch at noon,   *sky*
An' sideways on their chests the heids
   O' endless Christs roll doon.

An' when the earth's as cauld's the mune
An' a' its folk are lang syne deid,
On coontless stars the Babe maun cry   *must*
   An' the Crucified maun bleed.

NAN SHEPHERD
1893–1981

O, LICHT AMO' THE HILLS

O, licht amo' the hills,
S'uld ye gang oot,
To whatna dark the warld'll fa'.

Nae mair the thochts o' men
'll traivel 'yont the warld
Frae aff some shinin' Ben.

Nae mair the glint o' snaw
Oot ower the warld's wa'
'll mak men doot
Gin they've their e'en or na.   If; eyes

O, licht amo' the hills!

JOE CORRIE
1894–1968

THE IMAGE O' GOD

Crawlin' aboot like a snail in the mud,
  Covered wi' clammy blae,   *blue muck*
Me, made after the image o' God –
  Jings! but it's laughable, tae.

Howkin' awa' 'neath a mountain o' stane,   *Digging*
  Gaspin' for want o' air,
The sweat makin' streams doon my bare back-bane
  And my knees a' hauckit and sair.   *hacked*

Strainin' and cursin' the hale shift through,
  Half-starved, half-blin', half-mad;
And the gaffer he says, 'Less dirt in that coal
  Or ye go up the pit, my lad!'

So I gi'e my life to the Nimmo squad
  For eicht and fower a day;
Me! made after the image o' God –
  Jings! but it's laughable, tae.

NAOMI MITCHISON

1897–1997

THE HOUSE OF THE HARE

At the time I was four years old
I went to glean with the women,
Working the way they told;
My eyes were blue like blue-bells,
Lighter than oats my hair;
I came from the house of the Haldanes
Of work and thinking and prayer
To the God who is crowned with thorn,
The friend of the Boar and the Bear,
But oh when I went from there,
In the corn, in the corn, in the corn,
I was married young to a hare!

We went to kirk on the Sunday
And the Haldanes did not see
That a Haldane had been born
To run from the Boar and the Bear,
And the thing had happened to me
The day that I went with the gleaners,
The day that I built the corn-house,
That is not built with prayer.
For oh I was clean set free,
In the corn, in the corn, in the corn,
I had lived three days with the hare!

WILLIAM SOUTAR
1898–1943

FAITH

Look up; and yonder on the brae,
Like a sang in silence born,
Wi' the dayspring o' the day
Walks the snaw-white unicorn.

Sae far awa he leams in licht;   gleams
And yet his glitter burns atween
The darkness hung ahint the hicht
And hidden in the lifted e'en.   eyes

Look doun and doun; frae ilka airt
The flutherin worlds through darkness fa':
But yon bricht beast walks, in the hert,
Sae far awa; sae far awa.

FRANCISCAN EPISODE

Francis, wha thocht the gospel-words
Guid-news for ilka body,
Aince preach'd a sermon to the birds
And catechis'd a cuddie   horse

He was the haliest saint o' a'
Be grace and be affliction;
And kent God's craturs, great or sma',
Were ane in their election.

But ae day, when he was fell thrang   very busy
Confabbin wi' a gander,
A course gleg stug him sic a stang   cleg; sting
As fair rous'd up his dander.

'Be aff!' yapp't Francis wi' a yowt,   roar
'To Beelzebub your maister:'
And gied the gutsy beast a clowt
To gar it gang the faster.

AM PUILEAN/ANGUS CAMPBELL
1903–1982

from *AM FEAR NACH AINMICH MI*

A Dhòmhnuill Dhuibh na clìchd,
   Fear nan ìnnleachdan, Bràidean,
Cula-sheachant' na tìr,
   ìongnan ort mar an gràp;
Cha bhi sìth air do shàil
   far an tàrr thu thoirt sgrìob,
Amhailtear carach, clì,
   Mìlltear nan spuir 's nan spàg.

*

'S tusa sheòid a thug an taig
   dhan a' bhad tha seo seach chàich;
'S ann as dòch' gur e Ghàidhlig
   an cànan a th'agad,
Gun aig céinich bho thairis
   ach a' mhabadaich gun stàth,
Nach tuig céilidh, no fàd,
   no buntàta na sgadan.

*

'S mùirneach leat do chuid fhéin,
   eucoirich dhubh na mallachd,
Bheir thu déirce nam bochd
   do fhear nan sochairean le riadh,
'S oific dhuit bhith ga liacradh
   le siabunn a' mholaidh,
Bloinig dhiadhaidh mu'n choguis,
   'S blas a' chrogain air a' ghnìomh.

*

from THE ONE I SHALL NOT NAME

Black Donald of the tricks,
Wily Planner, thieving Rascal,
most to-be-avoided here,
nails on you like a hay-fork;
peace you never leave behind
where you happen to visit,
strategist who's cunning, sly,
hooved and taloned destroyer.

*

How attached you are, my lad,
to this place beyond others;
it may be that Gaelic
is the language you know,
all these foreigners there
with their purposeless stammer,
hardly know about peats,
ceilidhs, tatties and herring.

*

But you dearly love your own,
black accursed evil-doers;
giving alms from the poor,
with interest, to the well-to-do;
what you do is to clart him
with soft-soap of applause,
conscience sealed in holy blubber
though the deeds he does stink.

*

Sud a Dhòmhnuill ort fhéin,
    cha b'e m' fheum a bhith mach ort;
Eisdidh tu ri dibhersion
    's bheir thu mathanas dhomh 'n dràsd;
Ma tha rath-air-mhath dhomh 'n dàn
    nuair a thàrras mi dhachaidh
Thèid mi dhrabhadh mo ghloine
    gan a' Chailidh air do shlàint'.

Here's a health to you, Donald,
I'd be better not to quarrel;
you can listen to a leg-pull
and forgive me after all;
if my luck and fortune hold,
when I reach my home again
I'll drink my glass off to the dregs
in the *Caley* to your health.

translated from the Gaelic by Derick Thomson

KATHLEEN RAINE

1908 –

HEIRLOOM

She gave me childhood's flowers,
Heather and wild thyme,
Eyebright and tormentil,
Lichen's mealy cup
Dry on wind-scored stone,
The corbies on the rock,
The rowan by the burn.

Sea-marvels a child beheld
Out in the fisherman's boat,
Fringed pulsing violet
Medusa, sea gooseberries,
Starfish on the sea-floor,
Cowries and rainbow-shells
From pools on a rocky shore,

Gave me her memories,
But kept her last treasure:
'When I was a lass,' she said,
'Sitting among the heather,
'Suddenly I saw
'That all the moor was alive!
'I have told no one before.'

That was my mother's tale.
Seventy years had gone
Since she saw the living skein
Of which the world is woven,
And having seen, knew all;
Through long indifferent years
Treasuring the priceless pearl.

KIRKPATRICK DOBIE
1908–1998

ROUND ABOUT CHRISTMAS

Round about Christmas nineteen eighteen,
just after the end of the war
that was to end war,
an elder who had to speak at a soirée
in the Lower Hall Irish Street
on some aspect of church work,
pronouced it impossible.
'For who', he shouted,
'can doubt after all that has happened
Christianity has failed?'

Later it turned out
his son was reported
'Died of wounds'
and at once a reaction
set in in his favour
among those waiting
for refreshment.

To me – I was only eleven –
it seemed extraordinary
that for several years –
four, to be exact –
millions had been dying of wounds
without anybody –
including the elder –
noticing.

Not only that,
but there was also the fact
that centuries earlier,
Christ had died of wounds.

NORMAN MacCAIG
1910–1996

IN A LEVEL LIGHT

Sheep wander haloed, birds at their plainsong shed
Pure benedictions on water's painted glass.
The gentle worm rears up her hooded head
And weaves hot sermons under her steeple of grass.
Saints objurgate from thickets, angels bank
Over the sea: and its crisp texts unfold,
Silvering the sand's ecclesiastic gold.

Accepted in it all, one of its moods,
The human mind sits in its sense of sin,
Hacking a cross from gross beatitudes,
The price to pay warm in its purse of skin,
And sees out in that bliss, and out of its,
An angel tilt, dive into texts and float,
Working his god down his rebelling throat.

JULY EVENING

A bird's voice chinks and tinkles
Alone in the gaunt reedbed –
     Tiny silversmith
Working late in the evening.

I sit and listen. The rooftop
With a quill of smoke stuck in it
     Wavers against the sky
In the dreamy heat of summer.

Flowers' closing time: bee lurches
Across the hayfield, singing
     And feeling its drunken way
Round the air's invisible corners.

And grass is grace. And charlock
Is gold of its own bounty.
     The broken chair by the wall
Is one with immortal landscapes.

Something has been completed
That everything is part of,
     Something that will go on
Being completed forever.

SOMHAIRLE MacGILL-EAIN/ SORLEY MacLEAN

1911–1996

BAN-GHAIDHEAL

Am faca Tu i, Iùdhaich mhóir,
ri 'n abrar Aon Mhac Dhé?
Am fac' thu 'coltas air Do thriall
ri strì an fhìon-lios chéin?

An cuallach mhiosan air a druim,
fallus searbh air mala is gruaidh;
's a' mhios chreadha trom air cùl
a cinn chrùibte bhochd thruaigh.

Chan fhaca Tu i, Mhic an t-saoir,
ri 'n abrar Rìgh na Glòir,
a miosg nan cladach carrach siar,
fo fhallus cliabh a lòin.

An t-earrach so agus so chaidh
's gach fichead earrach bho 'n an tùs
tharruing ise 'n fheamainn fhuar
chum biadh a cloinne 's duais an tùir.

'S gach fichead foghar tha air triall
chaill i samhradh buidh nam blàth;
is threabh an dubh-chosnadh an clais
tarsuinn mìnead ghil a clàir.

Agus labhair T' eaglais chaomh
mu staid chaillte a h-anama thruaigh;
agus leag an cosnadh dian
a corp gu sàmhchair dhuibh an uaigh.

A HIGHLAND WOMAN

Hast Thou seen her, great Jew,
who art called the One Son of God?
Hast Thou seen on Thy way the like of her
labouring in the distant vineyard?

The load of fruits on her back,
a bitter sweat on brow and cheek,
and the clay basin heavy on the back
of her bent poor wretched head.

Thou hast not seen her, Son of the carpenter,
who art called the King of Glory,
among the rugged western shores
in the sweat of her food's creel.

This Spring and last Spring
and every twenty Springs from the beginning,
she has carried the cold seaweed
for her children's food and the castle's reward.

And every twenty Autumns gone
she has lost the golden summer of her bloom,
and the Black Labour has ploughed the furrow
across the white smoothness of her forehead.

And Thy gentle church has spoken
about the lost state of her miserable soul,
and the unremitting toil has lowered
her body to a black peace in a grave.

Is thriall a tìm mar shnighe dubh
a' drùdhadh tughaidh fàrdaich bochd;
mheal ise an dubh-chosnadh cruaidh;
is glas a cadal suain an nochd.

And her time has gone like a black sludge
seeping through the thatch of a poor dwelling:
the hard Black Labour was her inheritance;
grey is her sleep tonight.

translated from the Gaelic by the author

CALBHARAIGH

Cha n-eil mo shùil air Calbharaigh
no air Bethlehem an àigh
ach air cùil ghrod an Glaschu
far bheil an lobhadh fàis
agus air seòmar an Dun-éideann,
seòmar bochdainn 's cràidh
far am bheil an naoidhean creuchdach
ri aonagraich gu bhàs.

MY EEN ARE NAE ON CALVARY

eyes

My een are nae on Calvary
or the Bethlehem they praise,
but on shitten back-lands in Glesca toun
whaur growan life decays,
and a stairheid room in an Embro land,
a chalmer o puirtith and skaith,
whaur monie a shilpet bairnikie
gaes smoorit doun til daith.

houses set back from the street

Edinburgh tenement
room; poverty; loss
puny wee child
smothered

Scots version of the Gaelic by Douglas Young

TIODHLACADH SA CHLACHAN

Dh' fhàg sinn an corp anns a' Chlachan
ach càit an deachaidh an t-anam?

Cha duirt bial a' Cheisteir guth
an robh an t-slighe geal no dubh.

Ach, a réir teagaisg 's aidmheil
cha robh an còrr ann ri chantainn.

Cha robh aon chomharradh air a ghiùlan
gun dàinig a' Bhreith as Ur air.

Agus, a réir an Abstoil Pòl
cha d' fhuaire e gràs ged a bha e còir.

Bha an duine ceart is bàigheil,
teò-chridheach, onorach is càirdeil.

Ach dé b' fhiach gach beus a b' fheàrr dhiubh
ma dh' fhalbh an duine an Staid Nàduir?

B' e chuibhrionn sìorruidheachd gun dòchas
corruich Dhé san t-sloc dhòbhaidh.

Lasraichean mu 'n cheann liath ud,
a' chnuimh bhreun 's an dosgainn shìorruidh.

Bha chàirdean a thaobh na feòla
ag cur nan ceap air gu dòigheil.

Ach nuair a dh' fhàg iad réidh am fàl
b' e 'n còmhradh iasgach, stoc is bàrr.

FUNERAL IN CLACHAN

We left the corpse in Clachan
but where did the soul go?

The Catechist's mouth said not a word
whether the way was white or black,

but according to preaching and confession
there was no more to be said:

there was not a sign on his bearing
that he was born anew.

And according to the Apostle Paul
he did not get Grace though he was kind.

The man was just and generous,
warm-hearted, honourable and friendly,

but what was the good of the best virtue of them
if the man went in the state of Nature?

His lot was an eternity without hope,
the wrath of God in the fearful pit,

flames about that grey head,
the foul worm and the eternal woe.

His kinsmen in the flesh were
putting the turfs on him decently,

but when they left the turf smooth
their talk was fishing, stock and crops.

Agus ged a thuit na deòir
cha b'e cor an anama 'm bròn.

Ach bròn teaghlaich agus chàirdean,
bròn a chinnich a Staid Nàduir.

Cha robh duine anns an éisdeachd
nach tug a chreud á Sineubha;

Cha robh duine anns a' bhuidhinn
nach do dh' aidich an creud uile.

Ach mun d' fhàg iad an cladh
thuig iad fhéin an fhìor dhragh.

Agus thuig gach fear sa chòmhlan
nì nach seanaiseadh e ri ònrachd:

Nach eil trian de thrian ag creidsinn
ann an Ifrinn bhuan na h-aidmheil.

And though the tears fell
the state of the soul was not their grief,

but the grief of family and kin,
a grief that grew from the state of Nature.

There was not a man in the audience
but took his creed from Geneva.

There was not a man in the band
who did not subscribe to the whole creed;

but before they left the graveyard
many a man understood the real distress.

Almost all the company understood
a thing that one would not whisper to himself alone:

that not a third of a third believed
in the lasting Hell of their creed.

translated from the Gaelic by the author

DOUGLAS YOUNG

1913-1973

THE TWENTY-THIRD PSALM O KING DAUVIT
Composed on St Andrew's Day, 1942, in Edinburgh Prison

The Lord's my herd, I sall nocht want.
   Whaur green the gresses grow
sall be my fauld. He caas me aye
   whaur fresh sweet burnies rowe.   *roll*

He gars my saul be blyth aince mair
   that wandert was frae hame,
and leads me on the straucht smaa gait
   for sake o His ain name.

Tho I suld gang the glen o mirk
   I'ld grue for nae mischance,
Thou bydes wi me, Thy kent and cruik   *staff*
   maks aye my sustenance.

Thou spreids ane brod and gies me meat   *board*
   whaur aa my faes may view,
Thou sains my heid wi ulyie owre   *You bless; oil*
   and pours my cogie fou.   *bowl*

Nou seil and kindliness sall gae   *blessing*
   throu aa my days wi me,
and I sall wone in God's ain hous   *dwell*
   at hame eternallie.

THE SHEPHERD'S DOCHTER

Lay her and lea her here i the gantan grun,   *leave, gaping*
 the blythest, bonniest lass o the countryside,
 crined in a timber sark, hapt wi the pride   *shrivelled; nightdress; clothed*
o hothous flouers, the dearest that could be fund.

Her faither and brithers stand, as suddentlie stunned
 wi the wecht o dule; douce neebours side by side   *weight of sorrow*
 wriest and fidge, sclent-luikan, sweirt tae bide   *
while the Minister's duin and his threep gane wi the wind.   *done; assertion*

The murners skail, thankfu tae lea thon place   *scatter*
 whar the blythest, bonniest lass liggs i the mouls,   *lies; soil*
 Lent lilies lowp and cypresses stand stieve,   *throb; stiff*
Time tae gae back tae the darg, machines and tools   *job*
 and beasts and seeds, the things men uis tae live,
and lea the puir lass there in her state o Grace.

*twist and fidget, looking sideways, reluctant to stay

DEORSA Mac IAIN DEORSA/ GEORGE CAMPBELL HAY
1915–1984

PRIOSAN DA FHEIN AN DUINE?

Seall an t-amshan clis 'na shaighead
o' fhaire fo na neòil,
s an t-eun a' luasgan air a shlataig,
ag cur a bhith air fad 'na cheòl.
Their gnìomh is guth gach creutair ruinn,
ach éisdeachd riu air chòir:
'Cha chuir ceann is cridh' air iomrall thu.
Bi iomlan is bi beò.'

Cò air bith a chruthaich sinn,
cha d'rinn E'n cumadh ceàrr,
is mar thig air tùs gach duine
air bheag uireasbhuidh o 'làimh.
A bheil nì nach biodh air chomas da,
ach cothrom a thoirt dhà,
is a bhuadhan uile còmhla ann
ag còrdach 'nan comfhàs?

Ach nì e tric de 'bhuadhanna
bròg chuagach fo 'shail,
cuid dhuibh fo'n chuip, gun srian riu,
is an dà thrian diubh 'nan tàmh.
Bidh an cridhe 'na thìoran aimhreiteach,
s an ceann aige 'na thràill,
no bidh an corp 'na phrìosanach,
s an inntinn air 'na geàrd.

Ceann is cridhe, teine s coinneal
a thoirt soluis duinn is blàiths,
an corp treun s an t-anam maothsgiathach
air aoigheachd ann car tràth,

LOCKED IN THE HUMAN CAGE?

See the gannet like an arrow
shoot from his watchtower in the cloud,
or that bird locking on a twig
to sing his heart and soul aloud!
Hear their voices and join in
the chorus all creation's singing:
'Head and heart in harmony: sufficient, good.'

Whoever it was created us
worked with a steady hand,
so few the blemishes we start with –
nothing on earth could lie beyond
our powers, given the chance, if only
seeds so generously scattered
could flower at last in fertile ground.

But we wear away our talents
like old lopsided shoes,
or like workers chained whose idle hands
have years of skill to lose.
The tyrant heart enslaves the head,
or else a stronger mind stands guard
and hears the shackled body bruised.

Head and heart, fire and candle
offer their warmth and light
to rooms of sinew where the soul rests,
delicate wings held tight.
These, and two feet firmly planted
on the earth, while eyes look up and outwards
checking the compass sight.

fhuair sinn, s dà chois a shiubhal
gu ceart cunbhalach air làr,
is dà shùil a shealladh suas uaith,
no 'ruith cuairt nan ceithir àird.

An cridhe fialaidh misneachail,
na bu chiomach e am fròig,
ùraich cridh' an t-saoghail leis –
cuir mu sgaoil e – cuir gu stròdh.
Biodh do dhruim s do shealladh dìreach,
agus t'inntinn geur gun cheò;
lean gach beò a th'ann mar thiomnadh,
is bi iomlan is bi beò.

Is seall an triochshluagh dàicheil rianail,
nach robh riamh ach lethbheò,
is beachdan chàich 'nan gàradh-crìche dhaibh
'gan crìonadh ann an crò.
Nigh snidhe mall an àbhaistich
an sgarlaid as an clò,
is thug e breacan ùr an nàduir
gus a' ghnàthach ghlas fadheòidh.

Ma's seabhag bhras no smeòrach thu,
mìn no ròmach clò do ghnè,
na dèan a' Chruitheachd a nàrachadh
le nàir' á cridhe s á cré.
Mar thaing do'n Tì 'chuir deò annad,
ma tha do dhòigh 'na Chreud,
no mar fhialachd do d'chomhdhaoine,
bi beò is bi thu fhéin.

Your generous spirited heart, don't let it
cower like a prisoner in a wood.
Freshen the heart of the world:
release it, spend it all – no shrewd
or twisted backward glances,
only the keen clear eye of every simple
living thing: sufficient, good.

Avoid those half-dead dwarves you see
queuing to enter the pen
they've built of other folks' opinions
while day by day the rain
washes the scarlet from their cloth,
till the fresh tartan of their nature
fades to grey again.

Headlong hawk or mouse-brown thrush,
whatever you favour, smooth or rough,
fly from all shame of the heart and body
made by the One who put the stuff
of life inside you (if you say that Creed)
or in simplehearted human kindness –
just be yourself: sufficient, good enough.

English version of the Gaelic by James McGonigal

W. S. GRAHAM
1918–1986

A NOTE TO THE DIFFICULT ONE

This morning I am ready if you are,
To hear you speaking in your new language.
I think I am beginning to have nearly
A way of writing down what it is I think
You say. You enunciate very clearly
Terrible words always just beyond me.

I stand in my vocabulary looking out
Through my window of fine water ready
To translate natural occurrences
Into something beyond any idea
Of pleasure. The wisps of April fly
With light messages to the lonely.

This morning I am ready if you are
To speak. The early quick rains
Of Spring are drenching the window-glass.
Here in my words looking out
I see your face speaking flying
In a cloud wanting to say something.

MURIEL SPARK

1918 –

LIKE AFRICA

He is like Africa in whose
White flame the brilliant acres lie,
And all his nature's latitude
Gives measure of the simile.

His light, his stars, his hemisphere
Blaze like a tropic, and immense
The moon and leopard stride his blood
And mark in him their opulence.

In him the muffled drums of forests
Inform like dreams, and manifold
Lynx, eagle, thorn, effect about him
Their very night and emerald.

And like a river his Zambesi
Gathers the swell of seasons' rains,
The islands rocking on his breast,
The orchid open in his loins.

He is like Africa and even
The dangerous chances of his mind
Resemble the precipice whereover
Perpetual waterfalls descend.

ELMA MITCHELL
1919 –

COMPARATIVE RELIGION

It's so much easier now.
                  Once, it was blood
The stricken
Yell of the victim
And the horrible, holy, sticky hands of the priest.

But now, just press the button.
The god comes down at once
Clean, prompt and deferential
As electricity
Not even inquiring
What it is we want to destroy.

EDWIN MORGAN

1920 –

COLUMBA'S SONG

Where's Brude? Where's Brude?
So many souls to be saved!
The bracken is thick, the wildcat is quick,
the foxes dance in the moonlight,
the salmon dance in the waters,
the adders dance in the thick brown bracken.
Where's Brude? Where's man?
There's too much nature here,
eagles and deer,
but where's the mind and where's the soul?
Show me your kings, your women, the man of the plough.
And cry me to your cradles.
It wasn't for a fox or an eagle I set sail!

MESSAGE CLEAR

```
    am              i
                          if
i am                      he
        he r           o
        h      ur    t
        the re          and
        he       re    and
        he re
    a               n   d
        the r               e
i am      r                 ife
                  i n
            s        ion and
i                     d      i e
    am    e res    ect
    am    e res    ection
                      o           f
        the                      life
                      o           f
    m     e           n
            sur e
        the                  d      i e
i         s
            s     e t    and
i am the   sur          d
    a    t    res    t
                      o        life
i am  he r                      e
i a           ct
i       r  u      n
i  m    e  e      t
i             t              i e
```

```
i          s      t    and
i am th              o        th
i am    r            a
i am the  su     n
i am the  s         on
i am the  e    rect on       e if
i am     re          n     t
i am       s         a           fe
i am       s    e    n     t
i     he  e               d
i    t  e   s      t
i      re            a  d
  a   th  re         a  d
  a        s    t on            e
  a    t   re         a  d
  a   th  r        on           e
i         resurrect
                         a      life
i am              i  n         life
i am      resurrection
i am the resurrection and
i am
i am the resurrection and the life
```

THE FIFTH GOSPEL

I have come to overthrow the law and the prophets: I have not come to fulfil, but to overthrow.

Listen: a sower went out to sow. And when he sowed, some seeds fell by the wayside, and they sprang up and gave good fruit. Some fell on stony places, where they had not much earth, and they too grew up and flourished well. And some fell among thistles, and they in turn sprang and gave fruit in the very heart of the thistles. But others fell into good ground, and died, and produced neither leaf nor fruit. He who has ears to hear, let him hear.

It is not those that are sick who need a doctor, but those that are healthy. I have not come to call sinners, but the virtuous and law-abiding, to repentance.

A good tree can produce bad fruit, and a poor tree can produce good fruit. It is by their fruit that you will know them.

(And Jesus went into the temple, and brought in those who wanted to buy and sell goods there, and threw together some tables for the money-changers, and put in seats for those who had pigeons and were looking for fanciers. And he said to them: This temple will no doubt be called a den of thieves, but you can make it a house of prayer. And they marvelled at this saying. But Jesus turned to his disciples and said: In my kingdom there are no temples. Work, and pray.)

Each of you by taking thought will someday add a foot to his height.

Give nothing to Caesar, for nothing is Caesar's.

Listen: this is what the kingdom is about. Ten girls took their lamps and went out to meet the bridegroom. Five of them were sensible, and five were thoughtless. The thoughtless ones failed to check if they had enough oil, the sensible ones made sure. The bridegroom was very late in arriving, so they all snatched some sleep. At midnight there was a shout: the bridegroom is here – go and meet him! All the girls got up and trimmed their lamps. And the thoughtless ones said to the sensible ones: Give us some of your oil, for our lamps are nearly out. And the sensible ones answered: Certainly, here is the oil. And if there is not enough to go round, why then, that will teach the bridegroom to keep ten servants waiting for five hours. Sisters, the sensible must help the thoughtless, and all must stand together against those who would exploit their willingness and keep them from the kingdom.

Think about tomorrow: for tomorrow will not look after itself.

(And Jesus crossed the lake and came ashore in the country of the Gadarenes. And a schizophrenic who lived there among the tombs came wildly up to him. His body was bleeding from many wounds where he had slashed himself with stones, and broken chains hung jangling from his arms and legs. He was so strong that no one could hold him. He believed that he was inhabited by demons, who forced him to cry out, and run from place to place, day and night without rest. And he threw himself at the feet of Jesus, and the voice of his demons begged Jesus not to torment them. And Jesus said: But what do you want me to do? The demonic voice replied: Send us into that huge herd of pigs feeding on the hillside. But Jesus refused, and said: Why should I kill two thousand pigs? For being animals they would go frantic and rush headlong into the lake and be drowned. Am I to bring these farmers and their families into destitution in order that you may sit clothed and in your right mind, sipping wine and paying your taxes? Go back to the tombs and cry into the darkness; and men shall learn from you, and you from the wilderness.)

My yoke is not easy, and my burden is not light.

GEORGE MACKAY BROWN
1921–1996

THEY CAME TO AN INN

They came to an inn
    And they reined in the horses
Sat down with crusts and beer

They came to a river
    And they reined in the horses
A ferryman stood with a lantern

They came to a garden
    And they reined in the horses
A hand bled in a rosebush

They came to a smithy
    And they reined in the horses
Three nails and a long lance

They came to a mountain
    And they reined in the horses
Shepherds broke ice in the pass

They came to a palace
    And they reined in the horses
The eyes of the king were thorns

They came to a fair
    And they reined in the horses
They bargained for gold and a jar and a web of silk

They came to a prison
    And they reined in the horses
The chains rang out like bells

They came to an island
        And they reined in the horses
Storm-watchers stood on the shore

And they came to a chapel

HEALER

Gift of wholeness, blossoming, the dance
Of air, stone, rain.

I think of Eck, his blundering
With pen and scroll – such blots – in the library.
No, he could not wash a floor
But the bucket was upset.
The voice of Eck a crow at Matins and Vespers.
Weed the herb garden, Eck. Weeds only
Infected the plot.
We must send Eck back soon
To his father and the fishing boat at Catterline.

In the diversity of gifts, for Eck
Nothing, a stone on his palm.

At Foresters' Hill, our infirmary there,
Eck found rare roots in the burn
We hadn't known before.
Virtue flowed from Eck's fingers
Into abscess and lesion.
The lepers cry, 'We'll have Eck for bandaging, brothers.'

So we may see, dear people,
Blessings may break from stone, who knows how.

RUARAIDH MacTHOMAIS/
DERICK THOMSON

1921–

from AIRC A' CHOIMHCHEANGAIL

3. AN CEISTEAR

'An dùil,'
ars an duine caomh rium,
'am bi sinn còmhla ri chèile
anns an t-sìorraidheachd?'
Ceist fhuar ann am meadhon an t-samhraidh.
Bha i na b'fhaisg aire-san,
's bha e 'n geall oirr';
bha an t-àit' ud
dha mar dhachaigh nach do dh'fhidir e
bho thùs òige,
tlàth ann an suaineadh na cuimhne,
seasgair ann am brù mac-meanmain,
ach mireanach mar adhar earraich;
bha e coiseachd thuice
troimh mhàgh sheargte,
troimhn an fhàsach
ás an èireadh na beanntan,
's air chùl fàire
bha tobar is teinntean.
Bha e 'g iarraidh
gu lorgadh a chàirdean an t-slighe,
's gu ruigeadh iad air an socair fhèin;
cha robh e cur cabhaig orra,
chan eil dùil no cabhag anns an t-sìorraidheachd.

from THE ARK OF THE COVENANT

3. THE CATECHIST

'Do you expect,'
said the kindly man to me,
'we shall be together
in eternity?'
A cold question in midsummer.
It was closer to him
and he longed for it;
that place
was to him like a home he had not known
since early youth,
warm in the folds of memory,
sheltered in the imagination's womb,
but merry like a spring night-sky;
he was walking towards it
over a withered plain,
through the wilderness
out of which the mountains would rise,
and beyond the horizon
there was a well, and a hearth.
He wanted
his friends to find the way,
and they would arrive in their own good time;
he did not hustle them,
there is neither expectation nor hustling in eternity.

translated from the Gaelic by the author

LEODHAS AS T-SAMHRADH

An iarmailt cho soilleir tana
mar gum biodh am brat-sgàile air a reubadh
's an Cruthaidhear 'na shuidhe am fianuis a shluaigh
aig a' bhuntàt 's a sgadan,
gun duine ris an dèan E altachadh.
'S iongantach gu bheil iarmailt air an t-saoghal
tha cur cho beag a bhacadh air daoine
sealltainn a-steach dha'n an t-sìorruidheachd;
chan eil feum air feallsanachd
far an dèan thu chùis le do phrosbaig.

LEWIS IN SUMMER

The atmosphere clear and transparent
as though the veil had been rent
and the Creator were sitting in full view of His people
eating potatoes and herring,
with no man to whom He can say grace.
Probably there's no other sky in the world
that makes it so easy for people
to look in on eternity;
you don't need philosophy
where you can make do with binoculars.

translated from the Gaelic by the author

SRATH NABHAIR

Anns an adhar dhubh-ghorm ud,
àirde na sìorraidheachd os ar cionn,
bha rionnag a' priobadh ruinn
's i freagairt mireadh an teine
ann an cabair taigh m' athar
a' bhlianna thugh sinn an taigh le bleideagan sneachda.

Agus siud a' bhlianna cuideachd
a shlaod iad a' chailleach don t-sitig,
a shealltainn cho eòlach 's a bha iad air an Fhìrinn,
oir bha nid aig eunlaith an adhair
(agus cròthan aig na caoraich)
ged nach robh àit aice-se anns an cuireadh i a ceann fòidhpe.

A Shrath Nabhair 's a Shrath Chill Donnain,
is beag an t-iongnadh ged a chinneadh am fraoch àlainn oirbh,
a' falach nan lotan a dh' fhàg Pàdraig Sellar 's a sheòrsa,
mar a chunnaic mi uair is uair boireannach cràbhaidh
a dh' fhiosraich dòrainn an t-saoghail-sa
is sìth Dhè 'na sùilean.

STRATHNAVER

In that blue-black sky,
as high above us as eternity,
a star was winking at us,
answering the leaping flames of fire
in the rafters of my father's house,
that year we thatched the house with snowflakes.

And that too was the year
they hauled the old woman out on to the dung-heap,
to demonstrate how knowledgeable they were in Scripture,
for the birds of the air had nests
(and the sheep had folds)
though she had no place in which to lay down her head.

O Strathnaver and Strath of Kildonan,
it is little wonder that the heather should bloom on your slopes,
hiding the wounds that Patrick Sellar, and such as he, made,
just as time and time again I have seen a pious woman
who has suffered the sorrow of this world,
with the peace of God shining from her eyes.

translated from the Gaelic by the author

CATRIONA NicDHOMHNAILL/
CATRIONA MacDONALD
1925–

MO CHALMAN

Mo chalman tha falach an sgoltadh nan creag,
'N ionad dìomhair a' bhruthaich nis cluinneam do ghuth;
Na fuirich air d'aineol, 's na deòir air do ghruaidh,
'S mi sireadh do thàladh le cridhe làn truais.

Is mise d'fhear-pòsd', 's tha mo ghràdh dhuit toirt bàrr
Air gràdh athar no màthar, piuthair no bràth'r;
Is àill leam thu thilleadh gu m'ionnsaigh gu saor
Gus an dèan mi do phasgadh' nam ghàirdeanan caomh'.

Ged chaidh thu air seachran, cha d' dh'fhàs mi dhiot sgìth;
'S ged dhiùlt thu rium éisdeachd, 's mi bualadh an sìth,
Dealt na h-oidhch' air mo chiabhan, 's do dhorus orm dùint' –
O, nach cluinn thu mo ghearain, mo chalman, mo rùn!

Do pheacannan lìonmhor gun dubh mi a cuimhn',
'S chan éirich iad tuilleadh a mhilleadh do shaors':
Nì mi'n tilgeadh gu domhain an cuan mo dhiochuimhn',
'S bidh mo ghàirdeanan tharad mar fhasgadh o'n ghaoith.

Air deàrna mo làimhe bidh d'ainm agam sgrìobht'
'S nì mi d'fhalach ri m'bhroilleach, 's bidh tu tèaraint' 'nam ghaol;
Chaidh mi mach thar nam beanntan gus an dèanainn do lorg,
'S tu 'san fhàsach air seachran 'san oidhche dhubh dhorch.

Nis freagair, mo chalman, 's tu gam chluinntinn a' caoidh:
Tionndaidh do shùil rium is faiceam do ghnùis –
Dh'fhuiling mi'm bàs dhuit air crann Chalbhari
Is dh'ullaich mi àit' dhuit am Pàrras gun chrìch.

MY DOVE

My dove that is hiding in a cleft in the rocks,
In a secret place in the cliff, let me now hear your voice,
Don't be a stranger with the tears on your cheeks
While I seek to draw you with a full pitying heart.

I am your spouse, and my love for you exceeds
Love of father, or mother, sister or brother,
I want you to turn to me of your own free will,
So I may take you tenderly into my arms.

I have not tired of you though you have gone astray,
And though you refused to hear me, I quietly knock
With your door closed before me and the night dew on my hair –
Will you not hear my plea, O my dove, O my love!

I will blot from the record your manifold sins
And they will rise no more to spoil your peace,
Deep in the ocean of oblivion I will them cast
With my arms around you as a shelter from the wind.

Your name will be written in the palm of my hand,
I will hide you in my bosom; you will be safe in my love;
I went out to seek you in the hills till I found you
Astray in the wilderness in the deep dark night.

Now answer, my dove, as you hear me cry:
Turn towards me and let me see your face –
I suffered death for your sake on Calvary's Tree
And I've prepared you a place in the eternity of Heav'n.

'N sin fhreagair mo chalman: 'Mo Shlànuighear caomh,
Có dh'ionnsaigh an téid mi, no thairgeas dhomh saors'?
Chan eil neach air an talamh no 'sna nèamhan tha shuas –
'S tu cuibhrionn mo bheatha 'san t-siorruidheachd bhuan.

'Cha d' dh'fhàg mi 's cha d'thréig mi, ach thog thu mi suas
A sloc domhain a' pheacaidh 's an robh mi car uair;
Chuir thu plàsd air mo lotan 's chuir thu blàths 'na mo ghruaidh,
'S thug thu ùrachadh slàinteil do m'anam le buaidh.

'Halleluia gu bràth do mo Shlànuighear caomh,
Halleluia gu sìorruidh fad saoghal nan saogh'l;
Bidh mi seinn dhuit 'sa bhith-bhuantachd mhór tha gun chrìch,
'S cha sgar beatha no bàs mi o'n ghràdh tha cho sìor.'

'My gentle Saviour', my dove then spoke,
'Who can I go to, who can offer me peace?
There is no one on earth or in heaven above –
But You – the portion of my life in the eternity of God.

'You never left me nor forsook me, but have lifted me up
From the deep pit of sinning where I was for a while;
You put a dressing on my wounds and warmth in my cheek
And in triumph You gave renewed health to my soul.

'Halleluia forever to my Redeemer kind,
Halleluia forever throughout the World of worlds,
I will sing to You for all eternity without end
And neither life nor death will part me from Your love.'

translated from the Gaelic by Meg Bateman

ALASTAIR REID

1926 –

SCOTLAND

It was a day peculiar to this piece of the planet,
when larks rose on long thin strings of singing
and the air shifted with the shimmer of actual angels.
Greenness entered the body. The grasses
shivered with presences, and sunlight
stayed like a halo on hair and heather and hills.
Walking into town, I saw, in a radiant raincoat,
the woman from the fish-shop. 'What a day it is!'
cried I, like a sunstruck madman.
And what did she have to say for it?
Her brow grew bleak, her ancestors raged in their graves
as she spoke with their ancient misery:
'We'll pay for it, we'll pay for it, we'll pay for it!'

IAIN CRICHTON SMITH
1928–1998

WHEN THEY REACHED THE NEW LAND

When they reached the new land they rebuilt the old one,
they called the new mountains by old names,

they carved a Presbyterian church on the hill.
Nevertheless there was a sort of slantness,

a curious odd feeling in the twilight
that the mountain had shifted, had cast off its name

and even the Christ in the window seemed different
as if he had survived deserts and was not

a shepherd whom they imagined with his sheep
and his long staff high on the rainy hills.

It was much later before they made it all fit
and by then it was a new land.

They could have changed the names of the mountains
and could have walked in the familiar streets

built by their own strivings. It was then
that their old land was swallowed by the new;

and Christ a haunter of their own deserts,
the birds the colourful haunters of their own

trees and gardens. And they were at peace
among their settled, naturalised names.

DOMHNALL MacAMHLAIGH/
DONALD MacAULAY

1930 –

SOISGEUL 1955

Bha mi a raoir anns a' choinneamh;
bha an taigh làn chun an dorais,
cha robh àite suidhe ann
ach geimhil chumhang air an staighre.

Dh' éisd mi ris an t-sailm: am fonn
a' falbh leinn air seòl mara
cho dìomhair ri Maol Dùn:
dh'éisd mi ris an ùrnaigh
seirm shaorsinneil, shruthach –
iuchair-dàin mo dhaoine.

An uair sin thàinig an searmon
– teintean ifrinn a th' anns an fhasan –
bagairt neimheil, fhuadan
a lìon an taigh le uamhann is coimeasg.

Is thàinig an cadal-deilgneach na mo chasan …

GOSPEL 1955

I was at the meeting last night;
the house was full, packed to the door,
there was no place for me to sit
but a cramped nook on the stairs.

I listened to the psalm: the tune
transporting us on a tide
as mysterious as Maol Duin's;   [A miraculous navigator in early Gaelic literature]
I listened to the prayer
a liberating, cascading melody –
my people's access to poetry.

Then we got the sermon
– the fires of hell are in fashion –
vicious, alien threats
that filled the house with confusion and terror.

And I got pins-and-needles in my feet ...

translated from the Gaelic by the author

FEIN-FHIREANTACHD

Chan iarr iad orm ach
gal aithreachais peacaidh
nach buin dhomh
's gu faigh mi saorsa
fhuadan nach tuig mi:

ludaradh ann an uisge
an déidh uisge tana, guinteach
am feallsanachd –

agus gun amharas chrochadh iad
an nigheadaireachd anns na nèamhan.

SELFRIGHTEOUSNESS

They ask of me only
to weep repentance for a sin
that does not concern me
and I shall get in return an alien
freedom I don't understand:

to be drubbed in one thin,
wounding water after another
of their philosophy –

and confidently they would hang
their washing in the heavens.

translated from the Gaelic by the author

KENNETH WHITE

1936 –

A HIGH BLUE DAY ON SCALPAY

This is the summit of contemplation, and
    no art can touch it
blue, so blue, the far-out archipelago
    and the sea shimmering, shimmering
no art can touch it, the mind can only
    try to become attuned to it
to become quiet, and space itself out, to
    become open and still, unworlded
knowing itself in the diamond country, in
    the ultimate unlettered light

A. C. JACOBS
1937–1994

SUPPLICATION

Lord, from this city I was born in
I cry unto you whom I do not believe in:
(Spinoza and Freud among others saw to that)
Show me in this place in which I started
Where I have gone wrong.

Descend neither in Kirk not synagogue
Nor university nor pub.

But on a handy summit like Ben Lomond
Make me a new Sinai, and please God
Can we have less of the thou-shalt-not?

ROBIN FULTON

1937 –

PERFECTIONISTS

Sparrows chip at their statue-in-progress,
the air. Shoals of leaf-shadows nudge and nudge.
Those baking stones will never become loaves.
Pines sweat resin, would like to walk but can't.

The dead, those doers of nothing – they're
perfectionists. I always have one or
another of them by me. The cool vast
calm they spread, like waters I can run on.

TOM LEONARD

1944 –

THE GOOD THIEF

heh jimmy
yawright ih
stull wayiz urryi
ih

heh jimmy
ma right insane yirra pape
ma right insane yirwanny us jimmy
see it nyir eyes
wanny uz

heh

heh jimmy
lookslik wirgonny miss thi gemm
gonny miss thi GEMM jimmy
nearly three a cloke thinoo

dork init
good jobe theyve gote thi lights

LIZ LOCHHEAD
1947 –

THE OFFERING

Never in a month of them
would you go back.
Sunday,
the late smell of bacon
then the hard small feeling
of the offering in the mitten.
Remember how the hat-elastic cut.
Oh the boredom,
and how a lick of spittle got purple dye or pink
from the hymn-book you worried.

Maybe your neighbour would
have technicoloured pictures of
Jesus curing lepers
between the frail tissue pages of her bible
or she'd stroke you with the velvet
of a pressed rosepetal
till someone sucking peppermint
and smelling of mothball
poked you and hissed that you weren't to fidget.
Remember the singing
(with words and actions)
and how you never quite
understood the one about Nic-
odemus Coming to the Lord by Night.

Sunday,
perhaps an auntie
would visit with a cousin. Every Sunday
everyone would eat ice cream
and your mothers would compare you,
they'd stand you by the doorstop
and measure you up.

Sunday, maybe later in the evening
There'd be a Brethren Meeting.
Plain women wearing hats to cover
uncut hair. And
singing, under lamp-posts, out in our street.
And the leader
shouted the odds on Armageddon, he
tried to sell Salvation.
Everybody turned their televisions up.

Never in a month of them
should you go back.
Fond hope.
You'll still find you do not measure up.
The evangelist still mouths behind glass unheard.
You'll still not understand
the singing, the action or the word.
Ice cream will cloy, too sweet, too bland.
And the offering
still hard and knotted in your hand.

CATRIONA NicGUMARAID/
CATRIONA MONTGOMERY
1947–

DAN

Teaghlach a' bristeadh,
m'acraichean air am fuadachadh le gaoith,
dachaigh m'òige a' siubhal dhan mhunadh,
ceò tinneis is aois a' dùmhlachadh mo shunnd,
sgleò uaigneach a' snàgail air mo chridhe,
drisean a' geurachadh mo bhèil
is mo spiorad-sa a' tuiteam
dhan t-sloc dhubh ro uaigneach gheur.

M'anam-sa a' siubhal thugad,
a' leum nan slugaidhean 's nam beann;
m'anam-sa a' dèanamh tàimh riut,
a' lorg sìth am measg an stoirm;
m'anam-sa a' dèanamh gaol riut
is an saoghal a' bristeadh sìos.

M'anam-sa a' dèanamh tàimh riut,
a' lorg sìth am measg an stoirm.

SONG

A family breaking up,
my anchors scattered by storms,
my childhood home retreating to the horizon,
the mist of old age and sickness darkening my joy,
a solitary vapour creeping over the heart,
the bitterness of thorns in my mouth
and my spirit falling
to the sharp lonely blackness of the pit.

My soul journeys towards you,
leaping over gulf and mountain:
my soul makes its home with you,
seeking peace amid the storm,
my soul makes love to you
as the world breaks down.

My soul makes its home with you,
seeking peace amid the storm.

translated from the Gaelic by the author

FEARGHAS MacFHIONNLAIGH
1948 –

LAOIDH NACH EIL DO LENIN

cailèideascop-Dhia
beò-dhathan dian-loisgeach

uile-ghlòrmhorachd
na chaoir-bhuidealaich

solas dreòsach neo-bhàsmhor
a' spreadhadh tro phriosm nan dùl

bogha-froise drilseach na shìneadh
o bhithbhuantachd gu bithbhuantachd

sàr-iomlanachd sheachdfhillte
sìorraidheachd shruthshoillseach

rinneadh na h-uile dhathan leat agus às
d' eugmhais cha d' rinneadh aon dath a rinneadh

leatsa dathan a' chosmais

na solais-bhliadhnaichean air fad mar
phlathadh-seòid do lùdaig-fhàinne

leatsa dathan na talmhainn

Niagara a' tàirneanach san oidhche
is tuil-sholais oirre

drùchdan drìthleannach sa mhadainn
a' crithinn air lìon damhain-allaidh

leatsa dathan an danns
fir-chlis is stròb-sholas

A HYMN WHICH IS NOT TO LENIN

kaleidoscope-God
conflagration of living colours

all-gloriousness
ablaze

incandescent immortal light
exploding through the elemental prism

effulgent rainbow spanning
from everlasting to everlasting

sevenfold absolute perfection
fluorescent infinitude

all colours were made by you
and without you was no colour made that was made

yours the colours of the cosmos

the sum-total of all light-years but
a jewel-gleam of your pinkie-ring

yours the colours of the earth

floodlit Niagara
thundering in the night

iridescent morning dewdrop
trembling on a web

yours the colours of dance
aurora borealis and strobe

leatsa dathan a' ghaoil
coinfèataidh air sìoda geal

leatsa dathan na gàire
cleasan-teine is sùilean cloinne

leatsa speictream na beatha
leatsa a-mhàin

's leinne an dubhaigeann
ma dhùnas Tu do rosgan

yours the colours of love
confetti on white silk

yours the colours of laughter
fireworks and children's eyes

yours the spectrum of life
only yours

and ours the abyss
should Your eyelids close

translated from the Gaelic by the author

ANDREW GREIG

1951–

A GOOD TALKING TO

When the din fades
and ghosts of the day disperse
into the wallpaper of an ordinary room
a voice speaks quietly
and I listen.

It has recently begun
to address the divine.
Do not be alarmed!
I am always polite
it says in an aside.

What does it say to the divine
this pertinent voice?
please sustain me thank you
Communications are simple
among the adept.

I would wish to be someone
who could address without blushing
a vast stadium
even if the multitudes
have picked up their coats and streamed home.

JOHN BURNSIDE
1955 –

CANTICLE

When it rains
and the garden is cool

and blackbirds return to the wet
borders of our land,

we think ourselves the tenants
of a borrowed house,

with nothing to protect, nothing to claim,
only the moment when singing is resumed

amongst the trees,
and evening fills the grey and green

reflections of the people we reveal
in darkened glass:

the people in a psalm,
firstborn and true,

arriving here by chance,
just passing through.

THE NOLI ME TANGERE INCIDENT

There was nothing to touch. The smell of daybreak tinted with frankincense; the feel of an empty sheet and something slipped away; a moment's unidentified blackness receding among shadows. She waited. After some time there were cries and threats, memorised wounds, the taking of depositions. They spoke of flesh, they gathered with the dead, but she remained in the cool garden, trying to place the voice that had gone before her to the still centre of the shade, fixing in her mind the sound like poured water and the black footprints rising through gravel; a hint, perhaps, or only a supposition; nothing you would mistake for resurrection.

CAROL ANN DUFFY

1955–

PLAINSONG

Stop. Along this path, in phrases of light,
trees sing their leaves. No Midas touch
has turned the wood to gold, late in the year
when you pass by, suddenly sad, straining
to remember something you're sure you knew.

Listening. The words you have for things die
in your heart, but grasses are plainsong,
patiently chanting the circles you cannot repeat
or understand. This is your homeland,
Lost One, Stranger who speaks with tears.

It is almost impossible to be here and yet
you kneel, no one's child, absolved by late sun
through the branches of a wood, distantly
the evening bell reminding you, *Home, Home,*
Home, and the stone in your palm telling the time.

from THREE PAINTINGS

2 THE VIRGIN PUNISHING THE INFANT

He spoke early. Not the *goo goo goo* of infancy,
but *I am God.* Joseph kept away, carving himself
a silent Pinocchio out in the workshed. He said
he was a simple man and hadn't dreamed of this.

She grew anxious in that second year, would stare
at stars saying *Gabriel? Gabriel?* Your guess.
The village gossiped in the sun. The child was solitary,
his wide and solemn eyes could fill your head.

After he walked, our normal children crawled. Our wives
were first resentful, then superior. Mary's child
would bring her sorrow . . . better far to have a son
who gurgled nonsense at your breast. *Googoo. Googoo.*

But I am God. We heard him through the window,
heard the smacks which made us peep. What we saw
was commonplace enough. But afterwards, we wondered
why the infant did not cry. And why the Mother did.

JACKIE KAY
1961–

BABY LAZARUS

When I got home
I went out into the garden –
the frost bit my old brown boots –
and dug a hole the size of my baby
and buried the clothes I'd bought anyway.
A week later I stood at my window
and saw the ground move and swell
the promise of a crop,
that's when she started crying.
I gave her a service then, sang
Ye banks and braes, planted
a bush of roses, read the Book of Job,
cursed myself digging a pit for my baby
sprinkling ash from the grate.
Late that same night
she came in by the window,
my baby Lazarus
and suckled at my breast.

W. N. HERBERT

1961–

THE MANUSCRIPT OF FEATHERS

Saint and hermit send
each other news by seagull.
They never meet.
They never speak.
They do not discuss
the date of Easter.

Cuthbert on Farne is tempted
by the fur of sea-otters: it is like
the detached pudenda of the mermaids.
The moon is like their breasts:
it presses coldly on the shut balls of his eyes,
it fills their sockets with softness.

Herebericht is safe within his lake,
islanded from demons, speaks
with the freshwater fish about
the scent of home, its wholeness
of moss and quartz.
After this they offer themselves
to the roasting tongue of his cooking stone.

Cuthbert is beset again by gold:
coins of it leap from the evening waters
and cover his raggedy blanket,
every inch chinking with
a drowned king's hoard.
Otters sit outside his hut
and toast him with sunken wine.

Herebericht has visions of apocalypse
in which the world is reduced to islands,
in which the sea is flame,

in which each human sits, naked, sweating, watching
the tide eat at their shorelines.
He sniffs at the pebbles.
They smell jaspery.
They smell of Heaven.

The gull they send between them
carries no messages
scrolled around its leg.
Instead it is itself illuminated:
every feather written on in script
which only they can read.

KATHLEEN JAMIE

1962 –

SKY-BURIAL

On the litter I tilt, sweat,
sail the day-blue
iris of sky; my eyes
flick open like a doll's.
Friends, am I heavy? You bear me
under larches in their first green,
pink nipply flowers
       droop, tease my lips.
Iris leaves rustle, babble of streams.
Your feet seek stones, slip
the water's glassy sheen.
Level me, *steady*, your murmurs
could be   turbanned merchants
in far-flung bazaars,
my arms lashed gently to my side.

Are we there? whispers a child, no,
      the stone trail twists
I out-stare the blind sky,
   twin hawks
spiral the stair of their airy tower,
king & queen calling
repulsed   bound.

A heather plateau;
travelling winds bring home on their backs
scented oils,
     rotting birds, bog-weeds.
Arenas of peat-lips
speak of forests, old wolves.
Dry lochans reveal
    deer-spoor
creamy long-bones of trees.

Now friends, women in a ring,
raise your arms
part the blue sky
to a dark pupil; intelligent eye,
        ice-black retina of stars

slip me in.

        And if the child asks,
as you dust your hands,
turn down toward home in the green glen

        where do they go, the dead?
            Someone at last
may crack a small joke,

one say she feels watched;
one tug soft arching branches
over the burn.

You may answer him:
        here,   here,

                                here.

Midsummer on the high moor
my eyes flick open:
                    bouquets
of purple iris, midnight
cathedrals of sky.

The wind unravels me
winter birds will arrive.

DON PATERSON
1963–

PROFESSION OF FAITH

God is not the sea, but of its nature:
He scatters like the moonlight on the water
or appears on the horizon like a sail.
The sea is where He wakes, or sinks to dreams.
He made the sea, and like the clouds and storms
is born of it, over and over. Thus the Creator
finds himself revived by his own creature:
he thrives on the same spirit he exhales.

I'll make you, Lord, as you made me, restore
the soul you gifted me; in time, uncover
your name in my own. Let that pure source
that pours its empty heart out to us pour
through my heart too; and let the turbid river
of every heartless faith dry up for ever.

after Antonio Machado

RODDY LUMSDEN

1966–

THE WORLD'S END

Supposing you were wrong and I was right,
I was lying through there thinking
of a place where we and the land must part,

of where a child swings on a wire fence
watching, and where might be found
a paperback whodunnit, blown brown,

where a river stalls and seeps into the grass,
where all the footprints lead one way
and no one, on a late shift, stamps your pass,

where a clisp of light in the willow-herb
is what was dropped from the swag
in the chase, or a shred of a Sixties hothouse;

a place some call a border, some an edge,
as if the many missing or a saviour
will rise in welcome when we step over.

ABOUT THE EDITORS

Meg Bateman lives on the Isle of Skye and works at Sabhal Mòr Ostaig (the Gaelic College). She is author of *Aotromachd agus dàin eile/Lightness and other poems* (Polygon, 1997).

Robert Crawford, originally from Glasgow, now lives in St Andrews, where he is Professor of Modern Scottish Literature at the University. His most recent collection of poems is *Spirit Machines* (Cape, 1999).

James McGonigal was born in Dumfries and is Head of Language and Literature in Glasgow University's Faculty of Education. His collection of poetry *Driven Home* (Mariscat Press) was published in 1999.

NOTES ON THE POETS

These notes follow the order of the poems in the anthology, and include some comments on anonymous works.

SAINT COLUMBA (c. 521–597) Born in Donegal, Columba studied in Ireland and founded the monastery at Derry before being exiled to Scotland for his part in the Battle of Cuildheimhne in 563. Landing on the island of Iona, he founded a monastery there which was, and is today, one of the great centres of Christianity in Scotland.

DALLÁN FORGAILL (fl. 600) 'The Little Blind One of Testimony'/Eochu mac Colla, was probably commissioned by St Columba's cousin, Áed, King of Cenel Conaill, to compose 'Amra Choluimb Chille' in the years immediately following Columba's death in 597. Dallán Forgaill was probably a professional poet based in Ireland who had experience of monastic life and was venerated as a saint himself. The poem was treated as a sacred text during the Middle Ages, and was believed to have salvific properties. Four of its ten principal sections are given here.

ANON (c. 700) 'The Dream of the Rood'. This is one of the greatest surviving Old English poems. The earliest known version forms some textual fragments carved on the Ruthwell Cross in what is now Dumfries-shire. The poem is written in a distinctively northern form of Old English, which would have been spoken in Northumbria when that kingdom extended on both sides of what is now the Scottish-English border.

SCHOOL OF COLUMBA (?eighth century), 'Noli Pater'. This hymn, which appears in the Irish *Liber Hymnorum*, is one of a number of hymns traditionally associated with Columba and Iona. It appears to be a lyrical amalgam of several elements.

MUGRÓN, ABBOT OF IONA (d. 981) was Abbot of Iona and head of the Columban family of monasteries in both Scotland and Ireland from 965. The poem here follows the form of the *lorica* (breastplace), a formulaic poem chanted to gain both the physical and spiritual protection of the Godhead, of a particular saint or divine object.

EARL ROGNVALD KALI (ST RONALD OF ORKNEY) (d. 1158) was nephew of St Magnus of Orkney, in whose honour he built Kirkwall Cathedral in the Viking style, after conquering the Northern Isles in 1136. A poet and friend of poets, he was murdered in Caithness in 1158.

MUIREADHACH ALBANACH (fl.1220) belonged to the Uí Dálaigh, the Irish family of hereditary poets. He escaped to Scotland in 1213 after killing his chief's steward, and returned to Ireland only after being pardoned in 1228. During this time he established what was to become the longest-serving family of hereditary poets in Scotland, the MacMhuirichs. The Book of the Dean of Lismore, compiled in Perthshire between 1512 and 1542, is the sole source for the poem included here which addresses the Virgin as the mighty Queen of Heaven. Other poems give evidence of his having been on pilgrimage in the Adriatic.

ANON, *from* the Incholm Antiphoner (14th century). This short piece comes from the Latin manuscript known as the Incholm Antiphoner, which takes its name from the island in the Firth of Forth on which a monastery dedicated to Columba was founded. In antiphonal singing verses are sung alternately as responses.

ROBERT HENRYSON (?1424–?1506) worked as a schoolteacher in Dunfermline, and may have studied at Glasgow University. Regarded as one of the greatest Scottish poets, he is best remembered for his Aesopian *Moral Fables* and for his *Testament of Cresseid*, which takes up the story of the heroine of Chaucer's *Troilus and Criseyde*.

WILLIAM DUNBAR (?1456–?1513) studied at the University of St Andrews and, from 1500, became court poet to King James IV, who perished with many of his nobility at the Battle of Flodden in 1513. Dunbar's work includes bawdily secular as well as religious poems and is remarkable for its energetic versatility. He delights in the elaborate language of 'aureate diction'.

GAVIN DOUGLAS (c.1474–1522) was born in Tantallon Castle, East Lothian, son of the fifth Earl of Angus. Educated at the University of St Andrews, in 1503 he became Provost of St Giles, and in 1515 Bishop of Dunkeld. With his *Eneados* (a Scots version of Virgil's *Aeneid*) he became the first person to translate an entire classical epic into a modern vernacular language. Exiled in the wake of Flodden, he died of plague in England.

GEORGE BUCHANAN (1506–1582) was born at Moss, near Killearn, in Stirlingshire, and educated at the universities of Paris and St Andrews. Exiled for a satirical attack on Cardinal Beaton, he taught at the university of Coimbra in Portugal, but was condemned as a heretic and imprisoned by the Inquisition. Despite Protestant sympathies, he became tutor to Mary, Queen of Scots, and later to King James VI. He was regarded as one of the finest European Latinists of his day, and became Moderator of the newly founded Church of Scotland in 1567.

ATHAIRNE MACEOGHAIN (fl. c.1558) belonged to the hereditary family of MacEwans, poets to the Campbells of Glenorchy. This poem and another by him, also on contempt of the world, survive in the 1631 Gaelic translation of Calvin's Catechism, *Adtimchioll an Chreidimh*.

JAMES, JOHN and ROBERT WEDDERBURN (d. 1553, 1556, 1557) were the sons of a Dundee merchant, educated at the University of St Andrews, and eventually banished from Scotland for their Protestant beliefs. Enthusiasts for reformation, they compiled the *Gude and Godlie Ballatis*, a collection of ballads and sacred as well as secular songs.

WILLIAM KETHE (c.1530–1594), a Scot, spent time in Frankfurt and Geneva, where he helped to translate the Bible into English and to compile a book of metrical psalms. 'All people that on earth do dwell' was originally published in Geneva in 1561, then in the first Scottish Psalter in 1564. In the Scottish Psalter Kethe's 'Him serve with fear' in line three became 'Him serve with mirth'. Kethe went on to become rector of Childe Okeford in Dorset.

MARY, QUEEN OF SCOTS (?1542–1587), daughter of King James V and Mary of Guise-Lorraine, came to Scotland in 1561, having succeeded to the Scottish throne when she was six days old. As a Catholic monarch at the time of the Scottish Reformation, she attempted a policy of religious reconciliation, but was overthrown in 1567 after her marriage to the Earl of Bothwell following the murder of her second husband, her cousin Darnley. She abdicated in favour of her son, James VI, but was eventually executed in England, accused of plotting against Queen Elizabeth I.

ALEXANDER HUME (c.1556–1609) was son of the fifth Lord Polwarth and studied at the University of St Andrews. After spending time at the court of King James VI, where he wrote his beautiful, clear poem about midsummer's day, 'Of the Day Estivall', he became a minister of the Church of Scotland.

ELIZABETH MELVILLE OF CULROSS, LADY CUMRIE (c.1574–c.1630) was daughter of James Melville of Halhill and married John Colville, son of Alexander, commendator of Culross. In her lifetime she was admired as a religious poet, though little of her work survives.

WILLIAM DRUMMOND OF HAWTHORNDEN (1585–1649) studied at the University of Edinburgh and inherited the family house of Hawthornden, near Edinburgh, on his father's death in 1610. He lived there in retirement, writing much verse in the Petrarchan tradition. Ben Jonson visited him in 1618, and wrote an account of their conversations. Drummond is distinguished for his mellifluous use of English.

SIR WILLIAM MURE OF ROWALLAN (1594–1657) was born at Rowallan, Ayrshire, the family estate. A good deal of the poetry of this 'pios & learned' man was written in support of the Covenanters. He became a Member of the Scottish Parliament in 1645, having fought in the Scottish army at the Battle of Marston Moor in the preceding year.

DONNCHADH MACRAOIRIDH (d. c.1630) was probably a trained poet and his verse utilises loose classical metres. Four of his poems survive in the Fernaig MS (late 17th-century), three of them religious works in which he demonstrates a complete acceptance of God's will.

JAMES GRAHAM, MARQUIS OF MONTROSE (1612–1650) was educated at the University of St Andrews, and signed the National Covenant against the Anglican policy of King Charles I, though he later fought on the King's side in the Civil War. Eventually, after exile in Europe, he was executed in Edinburgh for attempting to lead a Highland rebellion in favour of King Charles II.

A COMMITTEE OF THE GENERAL ASSEMBLY OF THE CHURCH OF SCOTLAND (1650) oversaw the adoption of psalm translations drawn up by the Westminster Assembly. These often incorporated earlier work by Scottish poets. The first line of the 23rd Psalm, for instance comes from a version by Zachary Boyd (1584–1654), while much of the rest draws on a 1639 version by Sir William Mure of Rowallan (see above). These metrical psalms came to be associated with Scotland because of their widespread use throughout the country.

ANON (?Seventeenth Century), Prayers and 'Smooring the Fire'. Though these pieces were transcribed on South Uist in the twentieth century by the American-born Scottish folklorist Margaret Fay Shaw, they are thought to be much earlier in origin, perhaps dating from as early as the late-sixteenth century.

SILEAS NA CEAPAICH/SILEAS MACDONALD (c.1660–c.1729) was daughter of Gilleasbuig, chief of the Catholic MacDonalds of Keppoch. On her marriage to Gordon of Camdell she moved east to Tomintoul. There is evidence that she did not start composing until she was about forty. Her verse is varied, encompassing traditional praise, Jacobite songs, and poems about her friends, family and faith. See Colm O Baoill, *Bardachd Shilis na Ceapaich* (Scottish Gaelic Texts Society, 1972).

ALLAN RAMSAY (1686–1758), born in Leadhills, Lanarkshire, became a wig-maker, then a bookseller, founding a circulating library in Edinburgh. A poet and anthologist, he was active in reviving interest in poetry in Scots collected in such anthologies as *The Ever Green* (1724). His pastoral verse-drama *The Gentle Shepherd* won much praise, and Burns admired his work.

ROB DONN/ROBERT MACKAY (1714–1778) is valued for his perceptive and witty poetry about the people, both noble and humble, in the Reay Country of Sutherland. He is markedly different from other eighteenth-century religious poets in that his approach is that of the social commentator rather than evangelist. The sermon-like structure of the poem here and its appeal to human dignity are typical of his work. See Ian Grimble, *The World of Rob Donn* (Edinburgh, 1979).

DUGHALL BOCHANAN/DUGALD BUCHANAN (1716–1768) was born in Strathyre, Perthshire. He underwent a dramatic conversion after narrowly escaping death three times, and worked as a catechist for the 'broken men of Rannoch'. His poetry makes an appeal to Highlanders to forsake their secular world, so recently torn apart by Jacobite and Hanoverian differences, and to look to another world order – that ordained by Christ. His poetry is highly imagistic and his collection of hymns is still found in most Presbyterian Gaelic households.

ROBERT FERGUSSON (1750–1774) was born in Edinburgh and educated at St Andrews University. He became a clerk in Edinburgh and a member of the town's Cape Club before falling ill with severe depression. He died insane at the age of twenty-four. Fergusson was a sophisticated writer in English and Scots. His memory was venerated by Burns, who paid for Fergusson's tombstone in Edinburgh's Canongate Kirkyard.

JOHN MORISON (1750–1798) was educated at King's College in Aberdeen where he took his MA in 1771. A distinguished Scottish divine and poet, he became minister at Canisbay in 1780 and was a notable contributor to the volume of *Translations and Paraphrases, in Verse, of Several Passages of Sacred Scripture* issued by the Church of Scotland in 1781.

ROBERT BURNS (1759–1796) was born near Alloway and worked on his father's farm at Mossgiel, near Mauchline, Ayrshire. He achieved fame with the publication of *Poems, Chiefly in the Scottish Dialect* in Kilmarnock in 1786; soon a volume of his verse was published in Edinburgh where he was received as a 'Heaven-taught ploughman.' A great song collector as well as an original poet, Burns wrote in English and in Scots. In later life he worked as an exciseman in Dumfries; rheumatic heart disease killed him.

JAMES GRAHAME (1765–1811) was educated at Glasgow University. Admitted an advocate in 1795, he was ordained in the Church of England in 1809, but died of encephalitis soon after. Politically a Whig, his liberalism is reflected in his attacks on tithing and the Church of Scotland, slavery, and Highland clearances. His *Poems in English, Scotch, and Latin* were published in Paisley in 1794, and *The Sabbath* in 1804.

A COMMITTEE OF THE GENERAL ASSEMBLY OF THE CHURCH OF SCOTLAND was appointed in 1741 to extend the available metrical psalmody. Their immediate suggestions were considered too evangelical by the Moderates in the General Assembly, but in 1781 there appeared *Translations and Paraphrases, in verse, of several Passages of Sacred Scripture*, later supplemented in the early nineteenth century and generally known as *The Paraphrases*.

CAROLINA OLIPHANT (1766–1845), daughter of a Perthshire Jacobite, became Lady Nairne after her marriage, and travelled extensively in Europe and Ireland. She published a number of popular, often Jacobite songs under her pseudonym Mrs Bogan of Bogan.

ANNA NIC EALAIR (fl. 1800) probably belonged to Argyll or Perthshire. This is her only surviving work. While much of her imagery clearly comes from the Song of Songs, her great joy in knowing Christ is typical of the Highland Evangelical Revivals of the late-eighteenth and nineteenth centuries. We should maybe look to secular women's song in Gaelic for the frank physical union with Christ which the poet imagines.

JAMES HOGG (1770–1832) was born on an Ettrick farm and spent years as a shepherd before coming to Edinburgh in 1810 and working as an editor and poet. A friend of Walter Scott, he had a rich knowledge of Border oral culture. His great novel *The Private Memoirs and Confessions of a Justified Sinner* (1824) examines extreme Calvinist belief.

WALTER SCOTT (1771–1832) studied at Edinburgh University and became Sheriff-Depute of Selkirkshire in 1799. He made his literary reputation as a ballad collector and as poet of such best-selling works as *The Lay of the Last Minstrel* (1805). Later he authored a series of globally successful historical novels, beginning with *Waverley* (1814). An Episcopalian, Scott's portrayal of Scotland was complex and massively influential.

ROBERT ALLAN (1774–1841) was a flax-dresser's son from Kilbarchan who became a muslin weaver. Many of his Scots songs were set to music and anthologized, but his own collection of poems was a commercial failure. Poor and unhappy, he emigrated to New York to join his youngest son, a portrait painter. He died six days after landing.

JOHN LEYDEN (1775–1811) was educated at Edinburgh University and tutored in St Andrews. A tenant farmer's son from Denholm, Roxburghshire, he taught himself thirty languages. In 1799 he published a book about European settlement in Africa. He helped Walter Scott collect Border Ballads, then emigrated to the Far East, dying in Java shortly after publishing a book on Burmese, Malay, and Thai languages.

WILLIAM TENNANT (1784–1848) was born in Anstruther and educated at St Andrews University, where he became Professor of Oriental Languages. As well as serious verse dramas, Tennant wrote several longer comic poems. 'Anster Fair' is a vivacious poem about his birthplace, and 'Papistry Storm'd' deals with the destruction of St Andrews Cathedral by the Reformers.

GEORGE GORDON, LORD BYRON (1788–1824) was born in London and educated in his mother's city, Aberdeen, then at Harrow and Cambridge. Byron was intimately acquainted with Calvinism from his childhood. The success of his longer narrative poems, finest of which is *Don Juan*, made him an international celebrity, scandalizing and delighting readers with his ironic accounts of erotic and other matters. He died at Missolonghi, supporting the Greek struggle against the Turks.

THOMAS CARLYLE (1795–1881) was born in Ecclefechan in Dumfriesshire and entered Edinburgh University at the age of 15. He became a teacher, then an essayist specialising in German literature and political history. His best known work is *Sartor Resartus* (1833–34). Among contemporaries, his ideas were deeply influential in their focus on the private virtues of work and duty and the public strengths of heroic leaders.

GOBHA NA HEARADH/THE BLACKSMITH OF HARRIS, JOHN MORISON (c. 1796–1852) was closely associated with the Evangelical religious revival in Lewis and Harris, working as a catechist from the 1820s onwards, latterly for the Free Church. His poetry explores some of the central religious conflicts of the age.

CHARLES, LORD NEAVES (1800–1876) was born into a legal family in Edinburgh and became a judge in the court of session in 1854. He contributed regularly to *Blackwood's Magazine*, and his *Songs and Verses, Social and Scientific* (4th edition, 1875) are lively expessions of his wide ranging interests.

HORATIUS BONAR (1808–1889) served as a minster in Kelso from 1837 to 1866, before joining the Free Church and becoming minister of Chalmers Memorial Church in Edinburgh. His hymns were collected in three volumes as *Hymns of Faith and Hope*.

NORMAN MACLEOD (1812–1872) was born in Campbeltown, the son of a minister, and studied at Glasgow University before serving in Dalkeith and at the Barony Church in Glasgow. He was founder of the Evangelical Alliance, wrote many books and edited the magazine *Good Words*.

WILLIAM EDMONDSTOUNE AYTOUN (1813–1865) was born and studied in Edinburgh, becoming Professor of Rhetoric and Belles Lettres at Edinburgh University. His poetical works include *Lays of the Scottish Cavaliers* (1849) and the spoof 'Spasmodic' poem, *Firmilian* (1854).

MARY MACDONALD (1817–c. 1890) came from Ardtun in Mull. She is best known as the author of the Gaelic carol printed here, 'Leanabh an àigh', and sung now throughout the world as 'Child in the Manger'.

JOHN R. MACDUFF (1818–1895) was born near Scone, Perthshire, educated at Edinburgh University, and became a Church of Scotland minister in Glasgow, Rome, and elsewhere. He corresponded with David Livingstone and published various books of hymns, verse, and prose, including *Ripples in the Starlight* (1889).

GEORGE MACDONALD (1824–1905) was a weaver's son and Congregationalist minister who became an original writer of such fairy tales as *The Princess and the Goblin* (1872) and *The Princess and Curdie* (1883), often coloured by Christian and mystical symbolism or shaped by powerful allegories of good and evil. His vividly imagined adult fiction influenced C. S. Lewis and J. R. R. Tolkien.

ANNE ROSS COUSIN (1824–1906) was the wife of a minister of the Free Church of Scotland. She wrote a number of popular nineteenth century hymns, and her poems were published as *Immanuel's Land and other poems* in 1897.

JAMES MACFARLAN (1832–1862) lived a short, strange and self-destructive life, mostly in poverty, in Glasgow. His poems caught the sense of alienation in the nineteenth century city, as well as the attention of Dickens (who published some in his journal *All the Year Round*) and Thackeray, who admired the poem printed here.

ALEXANDER CARMICHAEL (1832–1912) was born on Lismore and educated at Greenock Academy. He combined work as an excisemen in the Hebrides with field research on Gaelic culture and customs, contributing articles to various antiquarian publications and finally collecting, editing and sometimes sweetening the gathered invocations, blessings and incantations in *Carmina Gadelica* (1900).

JAMES THOMSON ('B. V.') (1834–1882) was born in Port Glasgow and educated at an army school in Chelsea, before becoming an army schoolmaster. Rationalist and aetheistic ideas attracted him. His isolation and alcoholism in London contributed to the dark themes of life's futility in 'The City of Dreadful Night' (1874), a powerful pessimistic vision of late Victorian urban existence.

GEORGE MATHESON (1842–1906) is remembered as a hymn writer. He was born in Glasgow, and, although blind from the age of 18, pursued a brilliant academic career at the University there. He became minister at Innellan, and then in Edinburgh, writing many works of devotion.

ROBERT LOUIS STEVENSON (1850–1894) wrote novels, essays, travel books, plays and children's fiction and poetry. Born in Edinburgh, he studied firstly engineering and then law before travelling for the sake of his health through Europe, the United States and ultimately the Pacific, where he became a powerful critic of European exploitation. His work has seen recent critical revaluation of its modernity.

JOHN DAVIDSON (1857–1909) was born in Barrhead, where his father was a minister of the Evangelical Union. He taught briefly in Scotland before working as a writer and journalist in London. His 'Fleet Street Eclogues' made new poetic use of the modern city scene, and the materialistic *Testaments*, proclaiming the need for social reform and a scientific outlook, influenced Hugh MacDiarmid.

JESSIE ANNIE ANDERSON was born in 1861 in Ellon, Aberdeenshire. After a childhood accident left her paralysed, she was educated at home by her mother. Some dozen collections of her lyric poems were published in the early years of the twentieth century, with a late resurgence in *This is Nonsense* (1926) and *A Singer's Year* (1928).

VIOLET JACOB (1863–1946) was born near Montrose into a landed family. She married an army officer and spent time in India, then returned to the North-East. She wrote short stories and novels but was primarily a poet, and her confident local voice was one of the earliest in the twentieth century revival of writing in Scots.

CHARLES MURRAY (1864–1941) was born in Alford, Aberdeenshire, and for most of his life worked as a civil engineer in South Africa. He retired to the North-East, where his collection *Hamewith* (1900) had already made him well-known through its supple and authentic use of Aberdeenshire Scots.

MARION ANGUS (1866–1946) grew up in Arbroath, where her father was a minister. On his death she moved to Aberdeen to care for her sister and invalid mother. Her poetic voice, late to develop, was a distinctive one in the Scots revival, often catching the terseness of the ballads which influenced her work.

ANDREW YOUNG (1885–1971) was born in Elgin and was ordained a Free Church minister, later becoming an Anglican priest and a canon of Chichester Cathedral. His remarkable nature lyrics are both intensely felt and accurately observed, while longer works in *Out of the World and Back* (1958) combine religious reflection with visionary narrative.

DOMHNALL RUADH CHORUNA/DONALD MACDONALD (1887–1967) was born in North Uist. His experience of the First World war is memorably caught in the early poetry, and his later work displays a quiet religious conviction in the posthumous *Domhnall Ruadh Choruna* (1969, and, with English translation, 1995).

EDWIN MUIR (1887–1959) was born in Deerness, Orkney. A traumatic early move to industrial Glasgow continued to shape the archetypal terrain of his poetry. He worked in London as a writer and critic, as well as in Rome and in Prague, where he and his wife, the novelist Willa Anderson, made notable translations of Franz Kafka. *The Labyrinth* (1949) is perhaps his best known collection.

HUGH MACDIARMID (1892–1978) was born in Langholm, Dumfriesshire, and its landscape and landscape shaped him as much as Orkney's did Muir. As journalist and polemicist for a variety of literary and political causes, as well as by his formidable poetic range, he made a major impact on twentieth-century Scottish literature. His *A Drunk Man Looks at the Thistle* (1926) combines metaphysical speculation with satirical or intimate reflections on Scottish life.

NAN SHEPHERD (1893–1981) was educated at Aberdeen University, and later worked as a lecturer in English at the college of education in that city. She wrote novels and criticism as well as poetry.

JOE CORRIE (1894–1968) worked as a miner in Fife before becoming a full-time writer, and is best known for his early plays, particularly *In Time o' Strife* (1926), which portrayed working-class life and language with a frankness and humour sometimes likened to those of Sean O'Casey's plays in Ireland.

NAOMI MITCHISON (1897–1997) published some 70 books in her long career, and is best known for her novels and stories which evoke the world of classical Greece and Rome, though her thematic range is wide and unorthodox. Her interest in mythology perhaps ran counter to the more scientific concerns of her family, the Haldanes.

WILLIAM SOUTAR (1898–1943) was born in Perth, and was educated at Edinburgh University. A progressive illness left him increasingly bedridden, yet he continued to record his vivid response to life in poems, journals and dreambooks. His nationalism led him to focus on bairn rhymes in Scots which would be accessible to children of subsequent generations.

AM PUILEAN/ANGUS CAMPBELL (1903–1982) was born on Lewis and moved to Bernara, where his father was a lay preacher. He wrote an autobiography recounting his experience as a prisoner of war, and also highly perceptive and witty poems of social comment on Gaelic community life, which exhibit verbal brilliance and great independence of mind.

KATHLEEN RAINE (1908–) is a poet and scholar whose contemplative and lyrical poetry has been influenced by the writings of William Blake, W. B. Yeats and Edwin Muir, in its focus on inner spiritual quest and the relationship between dream and reality, and between the human and natural worlds.

KIRKPATRICK DOBIE (1909–1998) was a retired grain merchant from Dumfries who began writing only late in life yet who produced a body of poetry at once lyrical and sinewy, its strength deriving from sharp observation and a confident use of rhyme. *Selected Poems* (1992) draws from his locally published pamphlets.

NORMAN MACCAIG (1910–1996) was a classicist by education, a primary headteacher (and latterly university lecturer) by profession, and a much loved poet and reader of his own poetry. He explored the natural world of his Gaelic ancestors, and the cityscape of his native Edinburgh, in lyrics which are sharp, surprising, wry, metaphysical and, sometimes, bleak.

SOMHAIRLE MACGILL-EAIN/SORLEY MACLEAN (1911–1996) brought the Gaelic poetic tradition into contact with modernity in politics and literature, most notably in *Dàin do Eimhir* (1943) where love lyrics and social responsibilities intersect. His influence and example are still profound. *From Wood to Ridge: Collected Poems in Gaelic and English* was published in 1989.

DOUGLAS YOUNG (1913–1973) was a linguist, translator and scholar. He was born in Tayport, Fife, and studied Classics at St Andrews and Oxford, later teaching the subject at universities in Scotland and North America. He was Chairman of the Scottish National Party from 1942 to 1945.

DEORSA MAC IAIN DEORSA/GEORGE CAMPBELL HAY (1915–1984) was born in Renfrewshire, grew up in Argyll, and studied at Oxford. He wrote poems in Gaelic (which he learned in his teens) and in Scots and English, and was influenced by medieval Gaelic metrics. His wartime experience in North Africa shocked him: 'Bisearta' from that period is one of his best known poems.

W. S. GRAHAM (1918–1986) was born in Greenock but lived most of his life in poverty in Cornwall. His poetry offers an oblique but powerful and often moving exploration of the mysteries of language and being, where oddness of syntax and imagery mirrors the complexities of communication itself.

MURIEL SPARK (1918–) is better known as a novelist and short story writer than as a poet, although she edited *Poetry Review* in the 1940s and published her *Collected Poems* in 1967. Educated in Edinburgh, an experience which provided material for *The Prime of Miss Jean Brodie* (1961), she worked in Africa from 1936–1944. From a Jewish family, she became a Catholic.

ELMA MITCHELL (1919–) was born in Airdrie. A librarian, she worked in broadcasting and in journalism in London before settling in Somerset. Her compassionate and energetic poetry was published as *The Human Cage* (1979).

EDWIN MORGAN (1920–) was born in Glasgow and has combined an academic career in English Literature (latterly as Professor at Glasgow University) with an energetic creative life involving translation, experimental sound and visual poetry, opera and verse drama, as well as many collections notable for their lyricism, sharp social observation and modernity. *Collected Poems* (1990) and *Collected Translations* (1996) reveal this remarkable range.

GEORGE MACKAY BROWN (1921–1996) came from Stromness in Orkney and, with the exception of studies with Edwin Muir at Newbattle Abbey College and then at Edinburgh University, he remained there all his life. His novels, short stories and poems (notably *Fishermen with Ploughs*, 1971) explore characters and places from Orkney's past and present within the perspective of his Catholic faith.

RUARAIDH MACTHOMAIS/DERICK THOMSON (1921–) was born on Lewis and became Professor of Celtic in the University of Glasgow. He was co-founder and editor of the literary journal *Gairm*, and has published many collections of poems exploring with subtlety and humour the ambivalences of the Gaelic experience in contemporary Scotland: see *Creachadh na Clarsaich/Plundering the Harp* (1982).

CATRIONA NICDHOMHNAILL/CATRIONA MACDONALD (1925–) was born and raised in Staffin, Skye, to which she returned to raise a family after working on the mainland as a domestic and nurse. A member of the Church of Scotland, she began writing hymns in her late forties, and over sixty of these are published as *Sgeul na Rèite* (1981) and *Na Bannan Gràidh* (1987).

ALASTAIR REID (1926–) was born in Whithorn, the son of a minister, and has spent much of his life abroad, working in Spain, the United States, Latin America and the Caribbean as a cultural journalist, translator and poet. *Whereabouts: Notes on Being a Foreigner* (1987) reflects on this experience.

IAIN CRICHTON SMITH (1928–1998) was born on Lewis and was educated there and at Aberdeen University. A schoolteacher for many years, he became in 1977 a full-time writer, in Gaelic and English, of prose and poetry which is intensely imagined and of great tonal range. His *Collected Poems* (1992) explore the tensions and contradictions within Gaelic history and personal life.

DOMHNALL MACAMHLAIGH/DONALD MACAULAY (1930–) was born on Bernara, Lewis, and taught in the Universities of Aberdeen and Glasgow, where he was Professor of Celtic. His poetry balances fine intellectual control, a sceptical outlook, and metrical experimentation in a rhythmically subtle free verse: see *Seobhrach as a' Claich* (1967).

KENNETH WHITE (1936–) was born in Glasgow and studied there and at the Universities of Munich and Paris, where he became professor of twentieth-century poetics at the Sorbonne in 1983. Travel and real or imagined pilgrimage are his characteristic themes, as in *Travels in the Drifting Dawn* and *The Bird Path: Collected Longer Poems* (both 1989).

A. C. JACOBS (1937–1994) was born in Glasgow where he grew up in a traditional Jewish family, which moved to London in 1951. He later lived in Israel, Scotland, London, Italy and Spain, where he died. He once wrote 'My real language is probably Scots-Yiddish', and he became a translator of Hebrew poetry. His *Collected Poems and Selected Translations* were published in 1996.

ROBIN FULTON (1937–) was born in Arran (where his father was a minister) and educated at Edinburgh University. Since 1973 he has lived in Norway, where he is a distinguished translator of Scandinavian poetry. His collections of poetry include *Tree Lines* (1974) and *Collected Poems* (1987).

TOM LEONARD (1944–) is an influential Glasgow poet and critic whose experimentation with the rhythms and tones of colloquial language combines humour with a committed sense of social justice for the disenfranchised. His anthology *Radical Renfrew* (1990) reveals the richness of working-class writing in 19th-century newspapers and journals.

LIZ LOCHHEAD (1947–) was born near Motherwell, studied at the Glasgow School of Art and worked as a teacher before becoming a full-time writer. She is now probably better known as a dramatist but a confident use of voice, character and sharp social observation was evident from her earliest poems.

CATRIONA NICGUMARAID/CATRIONA MONTGOMERY (1947–) was born in Roag, Skye. Educated in Glasgow, she has worked as a writer-in-residence, teacher, script-writer and actor. Her poetry, concerned with love, the dissolving Gaelic world of her youth and a hard-won spiritual peace is published in *A' Choille Chiar* (1974) and *Rè na h-Oidhche/The Length of the Night* (1994).

FEARGHAS MACFHIONNLAIGH (1948–) was born in the Vale of Leven and spent the early years of his life in Canada before returning to Scotland. A committed

Calvinist, nationalist and poetic innovator, he published two long poems, *A' Mheanbhchuileag* (1981) and *Bogha-frois san Oidhche* (1997).

ANDREW GREIG (1951–) was born in Bannockburn and studied philosophy at Edinburgh University. A former university writer in residence and a Himalayan climber, he has written novels as well as several acclaimed collections of poetry, including *Men on Ice*, *The Order of the Day* and *Western Swing*.

JOHN BURNSIDE (1955–) was born in Dunfermline, and brought up there and in Northamptonshire. In several remarkable collections (including *Common Knowledge*, *Feast Days*, *The Myth of the Twin*) he has explored nature, the numinous and their intersections, and while declining to be categorised as a religious poet, he remains intensely interested in ideas of the soul, incarnation and resurrection.

CAROL ANN DUFFY (1955–) was born in Glasgow but has worked mainly in England where she was brought up. Her poetry (including such collections as *Selling Manhattan* and *The World's Wife*) has made a powerful impact in its confidence and range, and she was widely considered a potential and radical choice for Poet Laureate on the death of Ted Hughes.

JACKIE KAY (1961–) was brought up in Glasgow, the black child of white adoptive parents, and has written movingly about that experience in *The Adoption Papers* (1991) which won many prizes. She has also explored gay experience in drama and verse, and written poetry for children, including *Two's Company*.

W. N. HERBERT (1961–) was born in Dundee and educated there and at Oxford University, where he researched the poetry of Hugh MacDiarmid. As editor of literary journals and as writer in residence in Scotland and England, he has been a radical poetic voice both in English and in Dundonian Scots: *Forked Tongue* (1994) epitomises the edgy energy of his work.

KATHLEEN JAMIE (1962–) was born in Renfrewshire, studied philosophy at Edinburgh University and now lives in Fife. The strength and independence of her poetic voice was recognised early, in *Black Spiders* (1982) and *The Way We Live* (1987). A climber, she has written prose and poetry about her travels in Pakistan, and her restless spirit is evoked in the title poem of *The Queen of Sheba* (1994).

DON PATERSON (1963–) is from Dundee, and has worked as a jazz musician, a writer in residence and a poetry editor. The combination of jaunty nihilism, street-wise energy and lyrical sophistication in his collections *Nil Nil* (1993) and *God's Gift to Women* (1997) won many admirers, though the tone of *The Eyes* (1999) is notably more sombre.

RODDY LUMSDEN (1966–) was born in St Andrews and educated at Edinburgh University. His first collection *Yeah, Yeah, Yeah* (1997) explores the chaotic nature of contemporary Scottish urban life in a style which blends aplomb with formal elegance.

ACKNOWLEDGEMENTS

MUIREADHACH ALBANACH: from 'Eistidh riomsa, a Mhuire mhór'/'O great Mary, listen to me' (newly translated for this volume by Meg Bateman), © Meg Bateman, reprinted by permission of the translator; MARION ANGUS: 'The Tree' from *Sun and Candlelight* (Porpoise Press, 1927), reprinted by permission of Faber & Faber Ltd; ANONYMOUS: 'The Dream of the Rood' (newly translated for this volume by Robert Crawford), © Robert Crawford, reprinted by permission of the translator; 'Os mutorum'/'Memorial of St Columba', translated by Gilbert Márkus, from *The Triumph Trees: Scotland's Earliest Poetry AD 550–1350*, edited by T. O. Clancy (Canongate, 1998), reprinted by permission of the publisher; 'Urnaigh'/'Prayer' (two prayers) and 'Smaladh an Teine'/'Smooring the Fire', translated by Margaret Fay Shaw, from *Folksongs and Folklore of South Uist* (1955; repr. Oxford University Press, 1977), reprinted by permission of the translator; GEORGE MACKAY BROWN: 'Healer' from *Selected Poems 1954–1992* (John Murray, 1996), and 'They Came to an Inn' from *The Wreck of the Archangel* (John Murray, 1989), reprinted by permission of the publisher; DUGALD BUCHANAN: from 'An Gaisgeach'/'The Hero' (newly translated for this volume by Meg Bateman), © Meg Bateman, reprinted by permission of the translator; from 'La a'Bhreitheanais'/'The Day of Judgement' from *Gaelic Poetry in the Eighteenth Century: A Bilingual Anthology*, edited and translated by Derick Thomson (Association for Scottish Literary Studies, 1993), reprinted by permission of the translator; GEORGE BUCHANAN: 'Ioannis Calvini Epicedium'/'Elegy for John Calvin' (newly translated for this volume by Edwin Morgan), © Edwin Morgan, reprinted by permission of the translator; 'Hymnus in Christi Ascensionem'/'For Christ's Ascension' (newly translated for this volume by James McGonigal), © James McGonigal, reprinted by permission of the translator; 'In Iulium Pontificem'/'Oan Paip J 2' (newly translated for this volume by Robert Crawford), © Robert Crawford, reprinted by permission of the translator; JOHN BURNSIDE: 'Canticle' and 'The Noli Me Tangere Incident' from *Feast Days* (Secker & Warburg, 1992), reprinted by permission of The Random House Archive & Library; ANGUS CAMPBELL: from 'Am Fear Nach Ainmich Mi'/'The One I Shall Not Name', translated by Derick Thomson, from *An Introduction to Gaelic Poetry* by Derick Thomson (Gollancz, 1977), reprinted by permission of the translator; KIRKPATRICK DOBIE: 'Round About Christmas' from *Against the Tide* (Dumfries: privately printed, 1985), reprinted by permission of Ann Karkalas; ROB DONN: 'Marbhrann do chloinn Fhir Taigh Ruspainn'/'The Rispond Misers', translated by Derick Thomson, from *Gaelic Poetry in the Eighteenth Century: A Bilingual Anthology*, edited by Derick Thomson (Association for Scottish Literary Studies, 1993), reprinted by permission of the translator; CAROL ANN DUFFY: 'Plainsong' and 'Three Paintings: 2, The Virgin Punishing the Infant' from *Selling Manhattan* (Anvil Press Poetry, 1987), reprinted by permission of the publisher; DALLAN FORGAILL: from 'Amra Choluimb Cille'/'Elegy of Columba', translated by T. O. Clancy, from *Iona: The Earliest Poetry of a Celtic Monastery*, edited by T. O. Clancy and Gilbert Márkus (Edinburgh Univeristy Press, 1995), reprinted by permission of the publisher; ROBIN FULTON: 'Perfectionists' from *Lines Review*, No. 114 (September 1990), reprinted by permission of the author; W. S. GRAHAM: 'A Note to the Difficult One' from *Collected Poems 1942–1977* (Faber & Faber, 1979), © The Estate of W. S. Graham, reprinted by permission of Margaret Snow, literary administrator for the estate of W. S. Graham; ANDREW GREIG: 'A Good Talking To' from *The Order of the Day* (Bloodaxe Books, 1990), reprinted by permission of the publisher; GEORGE CAMPBELL HAY: 'Priosan da Fhein an Duine?'/'Locked in the Human Cage?' (newly translated for this volume by James McGonigal), reprinted by permission of the translator; W. H. HERBERT: 'The Manuscript of Feathers' from *The Laurelude* (Bloodaxe Books, 1998), reprinted by permission of the publisher; A. C. JACOBS: 'Supplication' from *Collected Poems and Selected Translations*, edited by John Rety and Anthony Rudolf (The Menard Press/Hearing Eye, 1996), © Estate of A. C. Jacobs c/o Menard Press, reprinted by permission of the publisher; KATHLEEN JAMIE: 'Sky-burial' from *The Queen of Sheba* (Bloodaxe Books, 1994), reprinted by permission of the publisher; EARL ROGNVALD KALI: 'Mockery of Irish monks on a windswept island' (newly translated for this volume by Paul Bibire), reprinted by permission of the translator; JACKIE KAY: 'Baby Lazarus' from *The Adoption Papers* (Bloodaxe Books, 1991), reprinted by permission of the publisher; TOM LEONARD: 'The Good Thief' from *Intimate Voices: Selected Works, 1965–1983* (Galloping Dog Press, 1984; Vintage, 1985), reprinted by permission of the author; LIZ LOCHHEAD: 'The Offering' from *Dreaming Frankenstein & Collected Poems* (Polygon, 1984), reprinted by permission of the publisher; RODDY LUMSDEN: 'The World's End' from *Yeah Yeah Yeah* (Bloodaxe Books, 1997), reprinted by permission of the publisher; DONALD MACAULAY: 'Soisgeul 1955'/'Gospel 1955' and 'Fèin-fhìreantachd'/'Self-righteousness' from *Nua-Bhardachd Ghaidlig* (Southside, 1976), reprinted by permission of Canongate Books; NORMAN MACCAIG: 'In a Level Light' and 'July Evening' from *Collected Poems* (Chatto & Windus, 1990), reprinted by permission of The Random House Archive & Library; HUGH MACDIARMID: 'O Jesu Parvule' and 'The Innumerable Christ' from *Complete Poems, 1920–1976* (Martin Brian & O'Keefe, 1978), reprinted by permission of Carcanet Press; DONALD MACDONALD OF CHORUNA: 'Chuala mi'n Damh Donn'/'I Heard the Brown Stag', translated by Fred Macaulay, from *Orain is Dain le Domhnall Domhnallach a Uibhist a Tuath: Songs and Poems by Donald MacDonald from North Uist* (Comann Eachdraidh Uibhist a Tuath, 1995), © 1995 Comann Eachdraidh Uibhist a Tuath, reprinted by permission of the publisher; SORLEY MACLEAN: 'Ban-Ghàidheal'/'A Highland Woman', 'Calbharaigh'/'My Een are Nae on Calvary' (with Scots translation by Douglas Young) and 'Tiodhlacadh sa Chlachan'/'Funeral in Clachan' from *From Wood to Ridge: Collected Poems* (Carcanet, 1989), reprinted by permission of the publisher; ELMA MITCHELL: 'Comparative Religion' from *The Human Cage* (Peterloo Poets, 1979), reprinted by permission of the publisher; NAOMI MITCHISON: 'The House of the Hare' from *An Anthology of Scottish Women Poets*, edited by C. Kerrigan (Edinburgh University Press, 1991), reprinted by permission of David Higham Associates; CATRIONA MONTGOMERY: 'Dan'/'Song' from *Re na H-Oidhche/The Length of the Night* (Canongate, 1994) reprinted by permission of the publisher; EDWIN MORGAN: 'Message Clear', 'Columba's Song' and 'The Fifth Gospel' from *Collected Poems* (Carcanet, 1990), reprinted by permission of the publisher; MUGRON: 'Cros Chríst', translated by T. O. Clancy, from *The Triumph Tree: Scotland's Earliest Poetry, AD 550–1350* (Canongate, 1998), reprinted by permission of the publisher; EDWIN MUIR: 'The Way', 'Scotland 1941', 'The Child Dying' and 'One Foot in Eden' from *The Complete Poems of Edwin Muir*, edited by P. H. Butter (ASLS, 1991), reprinted by permission of Faber & Faber; CHARLES MURRAY: 'Gin I Was God' from *Hamewith and Other Poems* (Constable, 1927), reprinted by permission of Colin Milton on behalf of the Charles Murray Memorial Fund; CATRIONA NICDHOMHNAILL: 'Mo Chalman' from *Sgeul na Reite* (Stornaway Religious Bookshop, 1981), reprinted by permission of the author (newly translated for this volume by Meg Bateman, and reprinted by permission); DON PATERSON: 'Profession of Faith' from *The Eyes* (Faber & Faber, 1999), reprinted by permission of the publisher; KATHLEEN RAINE: 'Heirloom' from *Collected Poems 1935–1980* (Allen & Unwin, 1981), reprinted by permission of the author; ALASTAIR REID: 'Scotland' from *Weathering: Poems and Translations* (Canongate, 1978), reprinted by permission of the author; 'O, Licht Amo' the Hills' from *In the Cairngorms* (The Moray Press, 1934), reprinted by permission of John Clouston; IAIN CRICHTON SMITH: 'When They Reached the New Land' from *The Exiles* (Carcanet Press, 1984), reprinted by permission of the publisher; WILLIAM SOUTAR: 'Faith' and 'Franciscan Episode' from *Poems in Scots and English* (Scottish Academic Press, 1975), reprinted by permission of the publisher; MURIEL SPARK: 'Like Africa' from *Collected Poems* (Macmillan, 1967), reprinted by permission of David Higham Associates; ST COLUMBA: 'Altus Prosator'/'The Maker on High' from *Collected Translations* by Edwin Morgan (Carcanet Press, 1996), reprinted by permission of the publisher; DERICK THOMSON: 'An Ceistear'/'The Catechist' and 'Leodhas as t-Samhradh'/'Lewis in Summer' and 'Srath Nabhair'/'Strathnaver' from *Plundering the Harp: Collected Poems 1940–1980* (Macdonald, 1982), reprinted by permission of the author; KENNETH WHITE: 'A high blue day on Scalpay' from *Handbook for the Diamond Country: Collected Shorter Poems, 1960–1990* (Mainstream Publishing, 1990), reprinted by permission of the publisher; ANDREW YOUNG: 'Here and There' from *Selected Poems*, edited by Edward Lowbury and Alison Young (Carcanet Press, 1998), reprinted by permission of the publisher; DOUGLAS YOUNG: 'The Shepherd's Dochter' and 'The Twenty-Third Psalm o King Dauvit' from *A Clear Voice: Douglas Young, Poet and Polymath* (Macdonald, 1976), © Clara Young, reprinted by permission of Clara Young.

Every effort has been made to trace or contact all copyright holders. The Publishers would be pleased to rectify any omissions brought to their notice at the earliest opportunity.

INDEX OF POETS